Displacement, Elimination and Replacement of Indigenous People:
Putting into Perspective Land Ownership and Ancestry in Decolonising Contemporary Zimbabwe

Edited by
Jairos Kangira, Artwell Nhemachena & Nelson Mlambo

Langaa Research & Publishing CIG
Mankon, Bamenda

Publisher:
Langaa RPCIG
Langaa Research & Publishing Common Initiative Group
P.O. Box 902 Mankon
Bamenda
North West Region
Cameroon
Langaagrp@gmail.com
www.langaa-rpcig.net

Distributed in and outside N. America by African Books Collective
orders@africanbookscollective.com
www.africanbookscollective.com

ISBN-10: 9956-550-31-0

ISBN-13: 978-9956-550-31-9

About the Contributors

Professor Jairos Kangira earned his PhD in Rhetoric Studies from the University of Cape Town, South Africa. He is an international scholar of rhetoric, particularly presidential rhetoric. Prof Kangira has travelled the length and breadth of the world delivering conference papers, guest-lecturing and conducting workshops in universities - the latest workshop being the International Rhetoric Workshop that was held at Uppsala University, Sweden. The workshop was attended by 50 PhD students in rhetoric from across the world. He has published extensively in the field of rhetoric and language. He is the Dean of the Faculty of Humanities and Social Sciences at the University of Namibia (UNAM). Previously, he was the Head of the Department of Language and Literature Studies at UNAM. He was the Deputy Dean of the Faculty of Arts at the University of Zimbabwe before he relocated to Namibia in 2006, joining the then Polytechnic of Namibia (now Namibia University of Science and Technology). Having great interest in research and publication, Prof Kangira successfully established two international journals in Namibia, *Nawa Journal of Language and Communication* at NUST in 2007, and the *Journal for Studies in Humanities and Social Sciences* at UNAM in 2012, and became the founding editor of both publications. He is also the founding board member of the UNAM Press where he has played a leading role in the publication of many academic books. Prof Kangira's other qualifications are: a Master of Philosophy in Linguistics, a Special Honours in Linguistics degree and a Certificate in Education from the University of Zimbabwe; a Bachelor of Arts from the University of South Africa; and a Postgraduate Certificate in Tertiary Education Management and a Master of Tertiary Education Management from the University of Melbourne, Australia. Prof Kangira has made a great impact in the development of the English language in Namibia.

Dr Artwell Nhemachena holds a PhD in Social Anthropology; MSc in Sociology and Social Anthropology, BSc Honours Degree in Sociology. In addition to having a good mix of social science and law courses in his undergraduate studies, he also has a Certificate in Law.

He has lectured in Zimbabwe before pursuing his PhD studies in South Africa. His current areas of research interest are Knowledge Studies; Development Studies; Environment; Resilience; Food Security and Food Sovereignty; Industrial Sociology; Agnotology, Sociology and Social Anthropology of Conflict and Peace; Transformation; Sociology and Social Anthropology of Science and Technology Studies, Democracy and Governance; Relational Ontologies; Decoloniality and Anthropological/Sociological Jurisprudence. He has published over 80 book chapters and journal articles in accredited and peer-reviewed platforms. He has also published over twelve books in accredited and peer reviewed platforms.

Dr Nelson Mlambo holds degrees from the University of Zimbabwe, University of Namibia and Stellenbosch University. He is currently a Lecturer in the Department of Language and Literature Studies at the University of Namibia. An author of three books and more than twenty refereed journal articles, Dr Mlambo has also supervised more than fifteen masters and PhD students. Dr Mlambo's research interests are in the area of literary studies, particularly focusing of recent theorisations which are of relevance to Africa's present challenges. Of late Dr Mlambo has been researching on the value of health communication in multilingual societies as well as the significance of postcolonial ecocriticism in genocidal literature, with a specific focus on the Herero/Germany fiction about the genocide.

Professor Ruby Magosvongwe who holds a Doctor of Philosophy from the University of Cape Town, is Associate Professor in the Department of English at the University of Zimbabwe, where she is the current Chairperson. Since April 2017, Prof Magosvongwe has been the Acting Editor-in-Chief of *Zambezia*, University of Zimbabwe's Humanities Journal. Prof Magosvongwe is also currently an Academic Researcher with the Department of English Studies, UNISA. She has also been influential in growing and nurturing talent in the Arts through the National Arts Council of Zimbabwe where she is currently a Board member. In addition, she has been involved with the Cover-to-Cover National Writing

Competitions that seek to unearth and grow the creativity of young Zimbabweans before their University studies. Furthermore, Prof Magosvongwe has been a member of the Zimbabwe International Book Fair Association Executive Board between 2009 and 2013 at which point she took over as Deputy and Chairperson of the Zimbabwe International Book Fair Association General Council to date. Ruby Magosvongwe was also Acting Director: Information and Public Relations in the Vice Chancellor's Office at the University of Zimbabwe between November 2008 and April 2010. In addition to being a published writer, Prof Magosvongwe has published academic articles and book chapters in peer-reviewed journals and peer-reviewed books respectively. She compiled and co-edited *Africa's Intangible Heritage and Land: Emerging Perspectives* (2016) and *Dialoguing Land and Indigenisation in Zimbabwe and Other Developing Countries: Emerging perspectives* (2015), both published by University of Zimbabwe Publications. She also co-edited *Re-discoursing Africana Womanism* (2012); *African Womanhood in Zimbabwean Literature: New Critical Perspectives on Women's Literature in African Languages* (2006). Refusing to be pigeonholed, her research interests are inter- and transdisciplinary with her primary focus on Literature and Land, Literature and Gender, English Literature, African Literature, Cultural Studies and Comparative Literature.

Professor Enna Sukutai Gudhlanga holds a D Phil from UNISA, BA and MA from the University of Zimbabwe. She is an Associate Professor in African Languages and Literature and is the Chairperson of the Department of Languages and Literature at Zimbabwe Open University. Enna holds certificates in Gender Mainstreaming from OSSREA, CODESRIA and UNIDEP. Enna is interested in the study of Africa and the development of its literatures, cultures and world outlooks. Her main concern is the ultimate self-definition and complete mastery of the African people's own life. Her publications include: *Gender, Politics and Land Use in Zimbabwe, 1980-2012* (Dakar: CODESRIA, 2015). She has presented papers on gender issues at many international conferences and been awarded research grants by several organisations to research on gender issues in Zimbabwe. Enna is also interested in socio-linguistic issues like democracy, language rights, planning and policy.

Professor Charles Pfukwa is a war veteran of the Zimbabwe liberation struggle. Upon his return from the liberation war, Pfukwa studied for his BA and MA degrees at the University of Zimbabwe. He obtained his PhD in Applied Linguistics from the University of South Africa. He has published widely in Zimbabwean onomastics, Zimbabwean cultural studies and the Zimbabwean liberation war. His research interests include onomastics cultural studies, popular music in Zimbabwe, and narratives of Zimbabwean liberation's war. He is an Associate Professor and the Executive Dean of the Faculty of Social Sciences and Humanities at Bindura University of Science Education. He is the Editor of *Dande*, a Faculty journal at the University. He is also a Research Associate in the Unit of Language Empowerment at the University of Free State.

Angeline Mavis Madongonda holds a Master of Arts in English and is a senior lecturer in the Department of Languages and Literature at the Zimbabwe Open University. She is currently a doctoral candidate with the same institution. She has authored a number of journal articles which include "Nurturing Mother Nature: Exploring the Zimbabwean woman's role in environmental conservation through storytelling." (2017) in *African Journal of Children's Literature Vol. 1 No. 2* and book chapters such as "The language of pain: (Re)interpreting nature as metaphor in Yvonne Vera's *Under the tongue*" in *Emerging Perspectives on Yvonne Vera* Eds. Pauline Dodgson-Katiyo and Helen Cousins (2012). She has co-edited the book *The Art of Survival: Depictions of Zimbabwe and the Zimbabwean in Crisis* (2015) with Anna Chitando and Joseph Chikowero. Her research interests include subaltern voices in Zimbabwean and African literature. Her current research focus is on gender issues in both traditional and contemporary writings in Zimbabwe.

Dr Blessing Makunike is a holder of BSc Honours Degree in Politics and Administration and a Masters Degree in Public Administration from the University of Zimbabwe. He received his PhD in African Studies from the University of the Free State (South Africa). He is a past recipient of the Eric Abraham Academic Fellowship (University of Cape Town, South Africa). His research interests are in land and agrarian reform, poverty alleviation, indigenous knowledge systems, and rural development.

Coletta M. Kandemiri is currently a PhD candidate at the University of Namibia in the Faculty of Humanities and Social Sciences. Her PhD thesis is on the literary representations of the Herero-Nama 1904-1908 genocide. She completed her Master of Arts in English Studies degree and her main interest is in literature that relates to social life. She obtained her first degree at the University of Zimbabwe after which she joined the University of Namibia for a Master of Arts in English Studies degree. Kandemiri's passion for literature is driven by the fact that literature is all about "creatures" called human beings. She sees literature as a point from which all other life affairs stem from.

Dr Shuvai Chingwe holds a PhD in Development Studies, Master of Science Degree in Public Administration and a Bachelor of Science Degree Honours in Politics and Administration. Her PhD thesis was an exploration of self-determined development practices as a panacea for poverty reduction. She is currently lecturing at International University of Management (Namibia) in the School of Postgraduate Studies. Her current research interests are in Indigenous communities, indigenous livelihoods, indigenous knowledge systems, research methodology and public policy. She has published on the use of indigenous research methodologies in Indigenous communities.

Dr Collen Sabao is a Senior Lecturer of Linguistics and Communication in the Languages and Literature Department at University of Namibia. He is also an American Council of Learned Societies Fellow and African Humanities Fellow. His research interests are in Phonetics and Phonology, Political Discourse, Media Discourse, Appraisal Theory and Rhetoric. He has published extensively in these areas.

Table of Contents

Chapter One

Theorising Displacement, Elimination and Replacement: An Introduction to Decolonising Land Issues

Artwell Nhemachena, Jairos Kangira & Nelson Mlambo

Introduction

The concepts of *terra nullius* (empty land) and *res nullius* (without owners) which were employed to dispossess Africans and other colonised peoples foreshadowed the displacement and elimination, including the genocide of colonial victims (Nhemachena, Warikandwa & Mtapuri 2017). Paradoxically, even as White farmers, who are descendants of colonialists, in southern Africa – including Zimbabwe – resist repossession of land by Blacks who were robbed of their resources during the enslavement and colonial era, transnational corporations, foreign states, foreign institutions and individuals are currently engaged in grabbing African land wherein the peasants are receiving no compensation for displacements and they also rarely receive notice ahead of the dispossession and displacement (Warikandwa, Nhemachena & Mtapuri 2017; Warikandwa, Nhemachena, Mpofu & Chitimira 2019). Foreign transnational corporations and individuals are disguised as foreign investors when they come to the continent of Africa to dispossess and displace Black African famers in the ongoing twenty-first century new scramble for Africa. Naturally, to assume that precolonial land was empty is, by extension, to erroneously imply that the colonialists were not displacing or dispossessing anyone. The sad presupposition is that if Africa, and the rest of the colonised continents, comprised "emptiness", then logically colonialist were not displacing emptiness – for emptiness cannot be displaced – it can only be settled, occupied, civilised and developed, all in scare quotes. Similarly, colonial assumptions, backed by some psychological theories, that African

1

minds were blank slates presuppose emptiness of African minds that supposedly had to be civilised, developed, and educated by the colonisers, again all in scare quotes. These colonial discourses on the emptiness of Africa and the emptiness of African minds were meant to legitimise colonial plunder, robbery, looting and exploitation. These discourses also arrogantly presuppose that with their alleged emptiness, Africans could not even give names to themselves, and to their countries and continent – enslaved Africans had to assume the names of their slave masters, colonial Africans had to assume the names of the colonisers and even postcolonial Africans rely on colonial categories and ideologies precisely because African ideas have long been displaced and eliminated. In short, Africa was alleged to be all emptiness even as the colonialists displaced the Africans, eliminated African taxa, including African names and institutions. To cover up for the dispossession, displacement and theft of African resources, colonialists had to apply the presuppositions of emptiness on Africans and Africa. Displaced Africans, who took refuge in the forests, were simply addressed as "bushmen"; displaced Africans that took refuge in the mountains and forests were simply addressed as indistinct from animals living in the bushes and forests; displaced Africans were addressed as underdeveloped, backward, savages, barbarians and beastly particularly when they resisted the colonial displacement and dispossession. The Africans that were dispossessed of their land and livestock and then displaced to marginal lands, and without draught power, were simply addressed as unable to farm productively. The displaced, dispossessed and resisting Africans were simply addressed as savages and devilish, and thus they were further displaced from the Godly realm, often, just because they resisted colonial dispossession and displacement.

The uphost of the foregoing is that emptiness by extension meant that Africa was empty of Godliness, in spite of paradoxical Eurocentric theological assumptions of omnipresence of God. In this respect, it is ironic to assume the omnipresence of God in the world while at the same time presupposing that God was absent from Africa. Africa was portrayed as empty and without God but full of demons that justified missionary salvific expeditions to the continent.

In other words, the missionaries considered themselves to be on missions to displace and eliminate demons on the African continent and in this regard, Africans were themselves assumed to be descendants or sons and daughters of the Devil – residing in the soil or underground rather than in Heaven, which was considered to be due for displacement and elimination. In all this, the missionaries did not cognise that they were in fact bringing the colonial Devil that would dispossess, displace, steal, rob and exploit Africans generation after generation. Thus, instead of seeing the Devil in the colonial dispossession, displacement, theft and robbery that impoverished Africans, missionaries would ironically portray resisting African spirit mediums, and leading precolonial African prophets as the Devil that was resisting colonial, supposedly Godly, robbery dispossession and displacement of Africans (Nhemachena 2016). Instead of applying the labels "demons of poverty, theft, robbery and dispossession" to colonialists, missionaries ironically applied the terms to resisting spirit mediums and African victims of colonial dispossession, displacement, elimination, genocide and robbery (Nhemachena 2016). Similarly, in the contemporary era, neo-colonial transnational corporations, that are currently dispossessing Africans in massive transnational land grabs of the 21st century, are not necessarily blamed or demonised for impoverishing, robbing and dispossessing Africans – instead it is Africans and their states that are widely demonised for poverty and want on the continent. In all this, it is conveniently forgotten that the African continent is a massive international crime scene, wherein Africans and their states are not the only players (Warikandwa & Nhemachena 2017). Colonial and neo-colonial institutions continue to displace, devolve and offload their blameworthiness, ironically, to African victims of centuries old and resilient colonial dispossession and displacement. Put in other words, Africans have become beasts for carrying neoimperial blameworthiness which is conveniently and surreptitiously displaced from imperial centres and then emplaced on harpless peoples of the continent.

When colonialists came to Africa to colonise, including dispossessing, eliminating and displacing Africans, they were in fact outsourcing their own imperial problems generated by the enclosure systems and population growth and impoverishment back in Europe. Colonialists did not dispossess and displace Africans so that they could use the land productively for the benefit of Africans – rather they colonised Africans because they were outsourcing their own problems back in the metropolitan centres: they were keen to resolve their own problems back in the metropolitan centres and not African ones. Africans are even in the contemporary era regarded as mere incidentals, if not accidentals, in the world. In this sense, colonialists were not necessarily wrong when they argued that colonisation would bring about civilisation, development, progress, peace and so on – the problem is that out of gargantuan gullibility, Africans have not asked the question civilisation where?, development in whose realm, progress in whose domain and peace for who? Because colonisation and imperialism effectively outsourced metropolitan or European problems to Africans, it is possible to see that colonisation brought peace in Europe where its citizens would have fought destructive civil wars if problems arising from impoverishment and enclosure systems had not been resolved by colonising Africans and stealing African land. If Europe had not colonised Africans, there would not have been peace – because poverty and want would have produced violent conflicts. If Europe had not colonised Africa, it would not have developed or made progress, without exploiting the Africans and their resources. Thus, to outsource metropolitan problems is in effect to displace, deflect and devolve the problems to Africans. Since the enslavement and colonial eras, Africans have not necessarily been carrying their own problems or burdens, rather they have been carrying the problems or burdens of the Euro-American metropolitan centres that have for centuries been engaged in outsourcing their troubles to citizens of the peripheralised continents and nations. Today, although global peace institutes, organisations and movements would appear to be the funders of global peace projects, we argue herein that it is Africans who inordinately bear the burden of world peace – world peace is achievable because Africans are denied restitution, restoration and reparations for enslavement and colonial wrongs yet this expense that Africans bear is not recognised in scholarly publications on the sources of funding for global peace projects. The point here is that the ultimate sources of funding for global peace projects are not the Euro-American peace institutions, movements, civil society organisations and Nongovernmental Organisations or the transnational corporations – the Africans who have to bear with unresolved dispossession, enslavement, neocolonial robbery, theft and exploitation are the ultimate sponsors of global peace projects. Africans have simply been displaced from the podia for acclamations – Africans, in this regard, remain global demons supposedly not worth any global acclamations even as they are being sacrificed for the sake of peace at a global level.

Underscored in the foregoing is the fact that colonisation, including the dispossession, elimination and displacement of Africans can be understood as forms of global ritual sacrifices in the interest of Euro-American metropolitan centres that continuously outsource their problems and troubles to the African continent and peoples. In this regard, the aim of the colonialists and the so-called Euro-modernists was not to bring about modernisation including rationality and an end to rituals of sacrifice in Africa – what colonialists and neoimperialists simply did was to transpose and appropriate the ancient rituals of sacrifice which neocolonialists have applied for centuries in Africa since the enslavement era. The productivity that colonialists and their descendants claim to have on farms in Africa is in effect achieved by sacrificing African men, women and children, who are paid next to nothing and who have endured the absence of restitution and restoration of their land after independence. A focus on discourses on productivity, of colonially acquired farms, alone neglects the crucial dimension of sacrifice that makes [irrational] neocolonial production possible in the first place. The neo-colonial and neoimperial economies including agroeconomies are not necessarily rational if looked at from the point of view of the dispossessed, displaced, eliminated and exploited Africans – they are global economies of sacrifice that are worse than the small-scale traditional rituals of sacrifice. There has not been any march of progress, modernisation, civilisation and development in the context of globalised ritual economic sacrifices including

5

displacement and dispossession of land – the march of linear time is a myth that is already being debunked in quantum and complexity theories (Rajan *et al* 2018; Vaccaro 2018; Camaren *et al* 2014; Burnes 2007).

Africans were colonially ritually displaced from their fertile land and they were moved to marginal land with neither fertility nor rainfall – in many cases they were moved to areas infested with mosquitos, tsetse flies and wild animals. Similarly, to assume that the land was *res nullius* or without owners erroneously implies that the colonialists did not steal the land from Africans. The colonial assumptions of *res nullius* ignore the ways in which colonial notions of ownership displaced African notions of ownership and possession. In other words, Africans were not only physically displaced but displaced, also, were their epistemologies including proprietary rights in their tangible and intangible heritages. At the core of the assumptions of *terra nullius* and *res nullius* is the question of the humanity of the colonised peoples. This is so because in assuming that Africa was empty, the colonialists implied that it did not have human presence - they did not mean to suggest that it was without animals, flies, trees, rivers and so on. In fact, the idea was to conflate African people with animals – Africans were, in the eyes of the colonialists, indistinct from the animals of the wild that roamed the forests on the continent. Contrary to some scholarly assumptions that Euro-Americans brought humanism and human rights to Africa, in fact colonialists portrayed and treated Africans as animals. In this sense, assumptions of *terra nullius* were deployed to displace Africans from their planes of humanity to the planes of animality; they were also meant to displace Africans from their fertile lands to marginal lands and in so far as colonisation was accompanied by genocide, some Africans were displaced from the realms of the living to the realms of the dead – in other words, they were eliminated. Those that remained alive were subjected to processes of assimilation (Van Den Berghe 1963; Idowu 1969) which effectively displaced their indigenous cognitive schema – in short, they were cognitively, spiritually and ideologically displaced such that, in Frantz Fanon's (1967) terms, they became 'black skins white masks'.

The foregoing underscores the fact that displacement is multifaceted and multidimensional. In a global context where there is overwhelming emphasis on biopolitics and corporeality, it is not surprising that scholarly attention has largely been on physical displacement of human beings affected by colonisation, conflict and violence, natural disasters and so on. In this regard, huge resources have been utilised, for instance, in the United Nations High Commission for Refugees and other organisations, to assist displaced human beings. International and national laws have been enacted to carter for displaced people - international and national laws have been made to proscribe the elimination, including through genocide, of other people (Vungsiriphisal *et al* 2013). However, given the increasing emphasis on zoepolitics, rather than the traditional biopolitics, it is necessary to consider how displacement plays out in the emergent global zoepolitics where emphasis on the body is being displaced and replaced with vitalism and spirituality. The emergent displacement of human consciousness which is being shifted and implanted into technological substrates (Nhemachena 2016) and the scholarly emphasis on travelling spirits (Lambek 2009) underscore the emergent global zoepolitics and the attendant need to examine ways in which spirits are displaced.

Spirit Possessed but Materially Dispossessed? The Colonial Legitimation of the Displacement of Africans

There is a paradox in the colonial portrayals of Africans as, on the one hand, possessed by supposedly demonic and animistic spiritual forces while at the same time the colonialists were actually busy dispossessing the same Africans at a material level. The spiritual noncorporeal possession, which was emphasised by colonialists, was meant to mollify Africans that were actually suffering colonial material dispossession even as they were addressed as [spiritually] possessed. The colonial emphasis on spiritual possession was meant to displace Africans from the plane of colonial material dispossession in the same way colonial ideological possession was meant to divert African attention away from ongoing material dispossession at

7

another level. In the contemporary era, there is sadly Eurocentric resuscitation of colonial ideologies of animism including animistic possession. The emphasis on spiritual possession also underlines the colonial antipathy for the corporeal bodies of Africans that become suffused with spiritual forces which were meant to take them to another level where there is absence of distinction between the human and the animal, the human and nature. In fact the colonial scholars' emphasis on African spirit possession was meant to caricature Africans who were being materially dispossessed by the colonialists. Colonialists needed to divert attention away from ongoing material dispossession of Africans by overemphasising spirit possession, including animistic ideologies on the continent of Africa. It baffles the mind how, on one hand, colonialists portrayed Africans as incapable of possessing and owning land on the continent while on the other hand they portrayed the Africans as possessed and possessing spirits including foreign spirits (*mashave*). Thus, whereas, in Shona language spirit mediums are not necessarily possessed but they experience *kusvikirwa* (literally to be reached/arrived at/connected to) by the spirit – on the other hand colonial scholars portrayed them as possessed, which term has different valency to *kusvikirwa*.

Although some scholars have argued that traditional global politics emphasised biopolitics and materialities as contrasted with the contemporary era that is noted as emphasising zoepolitics – including vitalism (Van Paaschen 2015; Schinkel 2010), we contend that colonial politics emphasised spirituality and Spiritism including spirit possession for Africans while it also focused, in the case of colonialists, on materialities including the theft of African resources. We argue herein that the focus on vitalism including travelling spirits, would negate the historical explanations of African resistance to displacements in terms of ancestral graves and *rukuvhute* (umbilical cord) – these would require reinterpretation. If spirits travel, it follows that human beings cannot resist displacement on the premise that they will be leaving behind their ancestors. The traditional explanation that Africans facing displacement would not leave their ancestors behind presupposed that African ancestors were not mobile; it assumed that the ancestors were tied to place. In other words, the assumption was that African ancestors were interchangeable with the graves into which the bodies were buried – it erroneously presumed that African ancestors became graves and that the graves became the ancestors. The point here is that African ancestors were, at least potentially, mobile but to perform rituals to render them mobile required material and epistemological resources which colonised and dispossessed Africans did not have. In this regard, it was not the fear of leaving ancestors behind that generated resistance to colonial displacement, rather it was the absence of material and epistemological resources necessary to render ancestors mobile. The mobility of African ancestors has always been facilitated by rituals which needed resources of various kinds (Nhemachena 2017). Thus, much as the mobility of human individuals requires the performance of various rituals (whether secular or sacred) including the securing of and production of passports, the mobility of African ancestors also required the performance of rituals in their honour. The problem has been that neo-colonial authorities and institutions forced dispossessed Africans to move even as they no longer had the resources to perform rituals for their ancestors. Colonialists simply demonised African ancestry and urged Africans to desert the ancestors who - due to colonial dispossession of land, livestock and other resources - no longer had rituals performed in their honour. We argue here that having been dispossessed of their land, cattle, goats, sheep and other livestock which constituted resources for rituals, Africans could no longer ritually render their ancestors mobile – the ancestors were thus colonially immobilised and rendered static.

If African ancestors were ordinarily ritually rendered mobile, it follows that they did not necessarily belong to the past or to the traditional as portrayed by colonial Eurocentric scholars. With precolonial mobility, African ancestors were not necessarily imprisoned in particular places. Africans were not merely about pastness or traditions but with mobile ancestors, Africans also had futures from which they were colonially displaced and then erroneously misplaced in pastness and traditions. The point here is that displacements have to be read together with misplacements –

colonialism was not merely about displacement of Africans but it was also about the misplacement of Africans who were thereby imprisoned in the crevices of time – that is, the temporal past. To be cast in the crevices of the past is in effect to be imprisoned at a temporal level, yet for Africans to be futuristic without restitution and reparations for the past wrongs amounts to imprisonment in utopia and futuristic mythologism. With colonialism, Africans lost both their temporal and spatial comfort zones – they were spatially and temporally imprisoned in sterile colonial crevices. Africans were deprived of their proper temporal and spatial placements on their continent. Recovery requires attention to and the reconfiguration of both space and time in ways that are suitable to African renaissance as a desideratum. In their efforts to get restitution, restoration and reparations, Africans do not only feel the pressure of the walls of spatial imprisonment but they also feel the pressure of the walls of temporality – time has been colonially crafted in ways that imprison Africans, ironically even as Eurocentric scholars and thinkers portray their temporalized discourses on progress and modernisation as freeing or liberating Africans. In fact the time for colonial "civilisation", "progress" and "modernisation", as depicted in Eurocentric colonial discourses, was also the time when Africans suffered colonial dispossession, displacement, robbery, theft and exploitation by the colonialists. Colonial time is not necessarily liberating – it displaces African temporalities. To use the term displacement alone for colonial wrongs would understate the effects for Africans – Africans were displaced and misplaced during the colonial era. They were displaced from their spaces and temporalities and then emplaced in colonial and imperial places and spaces which were not suitable for African human habitation. Africans were uprooted from their real places and forced to go and live in places which where non-places to them. In other words, colonial penal institutions were not limited to conventional prisons and jails – colonial spaces and temporalities were more broadly also experienced by Africans as imprisonation in so far as they defined, emplaced and confined Africans within colonially set spatial and temporal boundaries.

Via Eurocentric education systems, the colonialists cognitively, linguistically, socially, materially, culturally, economically, politically, spiritually and morally displaced Africans from their cultures, spirituality, ideas, materialities, morals and ethics and legal systems. Africans were then misplaced in Eurocentric epistemic, spiritual, legal and cultural spaces marked by subservience. In this way, processes of assimilation are effectively processes of displacement and misplacement, disorientation, misorientation and reorientation in the ways of the colonialists. Africans have been displaced from their indigenous languages that are now facing the threats of extinction, they are displaced from their material resources which are being looted and externalised by transnational corporations trawling the continent (Nhemachena, Warikandwa & Mtapuri 2017). Africans are also displaced and disoriented from their indigenous knowledge systems which are being exploited by global pharmaceutical corporations securing patents for themselves using African indigenous pharmaceutical knowledge (Nhemachena, Mlambo & Kaundjua 2016). Africans are displaced and disoriented from their indigenous institutions including the family, marriage, genealogies, histories, cultures, religions, economies, polities and so on. To make displacement, misplacement and disorientation tasty, colonialists have adroitly deployed the concepts of change, transition, transformation, progress, development and modernisation. But such change, transformation, progress, development and modernisation have largely entailed the further displacement and misplacement of Africans who are now being replaced by colonialists - some descendants of colonialists are now claiming indigeneity in Africa and other places where they have, for centuries, made efforts to empty the original indigenous people (Harris *et al* 2013; Kowal *et al* 2017; Tsosie 2005; Zack 2017; Tuck *et al* 2013). African spirit mediums have been displaced and replaced with climate and weather engineers who manipulate the atmosphere to try and make rain. African chiefs and kings have been displaced and replaced with colonial administrators some of whom are even addressed formally as "chiefs". African miners and blacksmiths were displaced and replaced with transnational corporations that are mining and smelting

11

ore on the continent. Precolonial African schools and universities have been displaced and replaced with colonial academies that now span the breadth and width of the continent (Nhemachena, Warikandwa & Amoo 2018; Nhemachena & Warikandwa 2017). African talking drums have been displaced and replaced with colonial media that are now considered to be conventional forms of disseminating information. More fundamentally, African ancestors were deposed, displaced and replaced with the gods and goddesses of the colonialists. African ancestors were deposed and displaced from the land on which they had been guardians and owners since time immemorial. They were displaced and then misplaced as demons. While they portrayed heaven as the ultimate destination for the Euro-American dead, colonialists ironically brought their own gods and goddesses to Africa. Naming months and weekdays after their gods and goddesses, colonialists, thus, commissioned their own spirituality on Africa. Days such as Tuesday (god Tiw's day), Thursday (god Thor's day), Wednesday (god Woden's day); Friday (goddess Frig's day) were named after European gods and goddesses of warfare, thunder, love and eloquence that were brought to Africa to depose, displace and replace African ancestors (Nhemachena 2016; 2017). Equally, months of the year such as January (god janus/Ianuarius), February (god Februum), March (god Martius), April (god Aprilis) May (god Maius) June (god Iunius), July (god Julius) and August (god Augustus) were named after European gods and goddesses that displaced and replaced African ancestors. In this sense, it is not only African people that have been displaced from their land, but also their ancestors have been deposed and displaced from their land. Portrayed as demons, African ancestors have been targeted for "condemnation" and "cleansing" from their land and continent more broadly. In the same vein, living Africans have been stirred to despise their ancestry such that the ancestors have been displaced from their progeny as much as from their land. Intriguing in this are the ways in which the displaced Africans and their ancestors have been labelled as "demons" to be dispossessed, deposed, exploited, imprisoned, condemned and displaced. The deposition and displacement of ancestors presuppose the erasure of

12

ancestral sources of knowledge including [but not conflatable with] place-based knowledge. In fact, the notion of place-based knowledge runs the danger of portraying African indigenous knowledge as simply emanating from place or from nature (which Eurocentric epistemologies would call Mother Earth, which ironically they do not hesitate to penetrate) – this would legitimise the ongoing piracy of African knowledge systems that are being transnationally exploited without regard to African ownership rights. To uncritically portray such indigenous knowledge systems as place-based would make it appear as if the knowledge does not belong to Africans but to places or to nature – it erroneously anthropomorphises nature and legitimises the Eurocentric colonial discourses about the existence of animism in Africa (Nhemachena 2016; 2017). In other words, it helps to further depose and displace African human beings from the plane of humanity – human beings need not be rendered indistinct from nature, including animals.

Underscored in the foregoing are the dangers of anthropomophisation of nature and the attendant conflation of African human beings with nature, including animals. Discourses about "*mwana wevhu*" (son/daughter of the soil) are being exploited to legitimise the anthropomorphisation of nature (Nhemachena 2017; Nhemachena, Kangira & Mlambo 2018). These discourses insidiously displace humanity onto the same place with nature – instead of privileging human mothers and fathers, addressing the soil as a mother/father displaces the human parents and replaces them with soil/nature, which is considered to be a parent. Thus, discourses about Mother Earth simply replicate the colonial displacement of African human beings into the same realm with nature/animals. Such discourses do not decolonise but, in so far as they repeat colonial discourses, they facilitate recolonisation of Africans. In the contemporary era, such discourses are addressed in terms of animism, anthropomorphism, biocentrism, ecocentrism, ecopsychology, ecosophy, ecophilosophy, ecocriticism and so on (Nhemachena, Kangira & Mlambo 2018)– the foundational idea is to decentre and displace the human [African] beings in the guise of privileging nature including environmentalism. Necessary to note is the fact that colonialists privileged African nature/environments as well while they ironically treated African human beings with disdain. Colonialists have always preferred nature/environments rather than African human beings. Africans were colonially deposed and deemed to be at the same level with nature, including animals. In this sense, contemporary discourses that seek to popularise flat ontologies, onticology and heterarchy (Bryant 2011; Dekker *et al* 2017), in place of hierarchy, merely replicate colonial discourses wherein African human beings were considered to be at the same level with nature/animals (Nhemachena 2016; 2017).

Discourses about "sons/daughters of the soil" or "*Mwana wevhu*" are being popularised in Eurocentric discourses about animism and posthumanism within a context where the remains of Cecil John Rhodes – the arch-imperialist who spearheaded the colonisation of Zimbabwe, Zambia, South Africa, Malawi and many other countries – have been interred in the Matopo Hills. Rhodes' remains were interred, according to his wish, at the Matopo Hills and specifically at Malindidzimu where indigenous people heard the voices of God and their ancestors (Ranger 1989; Charumbira 2015). The question here is whether the burial of Cecil John Rhodes, and other colonialists, at the Matobo Hills would qualify them and their kin as sons and daughters of the Zimbabwean soil? As Charumbira (2015) notes:

> Rhodes's choice of Matobo Hills as his burial space and as a future "national" burial ground of all (settler white) Rhodesians, who would have served their country with honour, was a final act of inscribing new ancestors onto a long – inhabited landscape as though it had been an empty space all along...More importantly, his burial in the Matobo Hills meant the obscuring of the landscape as a sacred African space and royal burial ground, with the most recent royal person buried there being the Ndebele Kingdom/nation founder, Mzilikazi...Rhodes's choice of the Matobo Hills as his burial site and the absurd idea that solid granite be carved for his remains by cheap African labour...

Obviously, Rhodes's kin and descendants would want to claim that they are also sons and daughters of the soil and that they have connections or relations with the Zimbabwean soil and land - much as in broader discourses about umbilical cords and connections to the land/soil. Clearly, in displacing African ancestors from the Matobo Hills, Rhodes intended to disrupt and displace African genealogies and claims to guardianship and ownership of the land and other natural resources in Zimbabwe. One question that arises is whether postcolonial and decolonial exorcism of foreign colonising spirits and ideologies would constitute displacement or re-placement at a metaphysical or ideational level? The point here is that displacement should be understood in relation to decolonisation. If displacement is construed without regard to the exigencies of decolonisation, it will function as an apology for the status quo, preventing decolonisation. In other words, decolonisation necessitates the displacement and exorcism of the colonial ideologies and spirits some of which explain queer practices and identities among Africans (Nhemachena, Warikandwa and Amoo 2018). What Rhodes forgot in his quest to replace African ancestors was that in African cosmologies, one had to possess rectitude in order to become an ancestor – ancestry was about morality, ethics and observance of laws in the land (Nhemachena 2017; Nhemachena, Warikandwa & Amoo 2018). Witches, sorcerers, thieves and murderers would not have rituals of bringing the spirit back home (Nhemachena 2017). Such rituals were not performed for the wayward, criminals, witches and sorcerers. In any case, it is cause for wonder why colonialists like Cecil John Rhodes and his ilk demonised Mbuya Nehanda, Sekuru Kaguvi, Mukwati and others as witchdoctors and evil when it was the colonialists that were perpetrating criminality, evil and demonic actions including violence, theft, robbery, rape, dispossession, displacement and exploitation of African people. Colonialists should have seen evil and criminality in their own deeds: they should have seen the demons in themselves. It is possible to argue that Africans were sons and daughters of Nehanda, Kaguvi, Mukwati and others but because these guardian and divine figures were demonised by colonialists, the Africans had to address themselves as sons and

15

daughters of the soil instead. The point was that colonialists could not easily and logically demonise the soil that explained their colonial motivations – however, they could safely demonise Nehanda, Kaguvi, Mukwati and others. The point here is that the phrase *"mwana wevhu"*/son/daughter of the soil need to be interpreted within the colonial context in which it emerged.

Writing about Euro-American spirits that destabilise African nation states by afflicting and using Africans as mediums, Behrend *et al* (1999: 13) writes thus:

> The disenchantment of the modern world and the disappearance of spirits, as foretold by Westerners, has not taken place, either at home or in other parts of the world. In Africa as well as in Europe, many spirits and their mediums are part of local as well as global or transglobal cultures. Thus, we find Christian spirits named Hitler and Mussolini or King Bruce after Bruce Lee, the kung-fu actor, in a pantheon of new Christian holy spirits in Northern Uganda, who are waging war against the government...

Indeed Cecil John Rhodes's ghost could be sitting, at the Matobo Hills, in Zimbabwe and preventing the full decolonisation and liberation, including restitution and restoration of the land to the Black Zimbabweans. Like any other spirit, it would obviously require and, if subconsciously, possess and use African human mediums. Occurring at both metaphysical and physical levels, corporeal and noncorporeal levels, displacement needs to be understood in ways that factor in its complexity. Displacement needs not be narrowly conceived in terms of political violence because there are also ideational, metaphysical and spiritual forms of displacement that occur due to spiritual forms of violence. As noted above colonialists did not only physically displace Africans but they also displaced African ancestors and ideas at metaphysical and ideational levels. There are also epistemological, linguistic and cognitive forms of displacement that occur due to the violence of Eurocentric epistemologies being foistered on Africans. Whereas colonialist perpetrated various kinds of displacement of Africans, the contemporary policies on displacement narrowly focus on physical and bodily forms of displacement that constitute policy documents and legislative enactments at various levels of society and the world. Africans have been and are being displaced in manifold ways that remain invisible in national and international policy making and implementation.

Displacements from Nation States to Virtual Spaces and Eliminating Ownership Rights over National Resources

As hinted above, colonialists displaced Africans from their humanness including from their Ubuntu. Africans have been displaced from their precolonial civilisations. They have been displaced from their humanness and then portrayed in terms of animism, as indistinct from animals. The sale and transportation of Africans into slavery was undergirded by the displacement of Africans from their humanness – the slave drivers had to assume that Africans were animals to be bought and sold, driven away and forced to work (Nhemachena 2016). Enslaved Africans were also assumed to be indistinct from machines or pieces of technology – deprived of humanness. Contemporary discourses on posthumanism and transhumanism (see Nhemachena, Warikandwa & Amoo 2018) also presuppose absence of distinction between African human beings and pieces of technology – Africans are once again displaced from their humanness. In this regard, the figures of the posthuman and transhuman decentre and displace human beings from the plane of humanness and humanity – the processes of displacing human beings from the human plane are basically about eliminating humanity and humanness – they are processes of genocide insidiously performed by another means. Posthumanism and transhumanism constitute processes of erasure or elimination of humanity and humanness in the same way animistic enslavement and colonial discourses legitimised erasure and elimination of African humanity and humanness premised on Ubuntu.

Significantly, Africans are being displaced from their territories onto cyberspaces. The transnational capitalist order is creating

17

cyberspaces onto which Africans are being frontloaded in a context where they are being deprived of their territorial places and spaces. Cyberspaces have become alternative spaces onto which Africans are being emplaced as they are ironically being replaced on their territorial and national spaces. Africans are being displaced from their embattled nations, states, indigenous spaces and places which, particularly in the context of the ongoing transnational land grabs, are being seized by transnational corporations and foreigner states (Nhemachena, Warikandwa & Mtapuri 2017). Cyberspaces destabilise notions of indigeneity, nationality, nativism, statehood and territoriality – displaced Africans have been provided with cyberspaces within which to fight their own states, cultures and societies and take refuge. Put in other words, assimilationistic cyberspaces facilitate the elimination of indigenous people, nationhood, statehood, nativism and territoriality. They facilitate the deterritorialisation of Africans in a world that is increasingly celebrating flows, fluidity, becomings, circulation and networks – flows, fluidity and circulation are terms that undergird displacement and elimination rather than placeness and emplacement (Nhemachena, Hlabangane & Kaundjua 2019). In this regard, the celebration of global circulations, flows and fluidity is in essence the celebration of displacements and the attendant dislocations and disruptions. Notions of flows, circulations and fluidity all underscore the absence of secure mooring in territorial and spatial terms – they underline displacement and elimination because to flow and to circulate presuppose displacement. But the concepts of flows and circulation do not necessarily imply freedom or liberation because even the enslaved and colonised Africans were put into circulation across the world, across spaces and places where they laboured for the benefit of the slave masters and colonialists. In other words, circulations and flows occur at the instance of masters that benefit from displacing and eliminating others – the fluidity, circulation and flows of cyberspaces are not necessarily liberating but they like every other form of displacement are processes of erasure and elimination of indigenousness. Instead of valourising territorial and nation state indigeneity, there is increasingly celebration of digital nativism

(Georgakopoulou *et al* 2015) which is often used to destabilise territorial and nation state spaces. We argue that the idea in destabilising nation states and territories is to insidiously depose, displace and eliminate nationalist liberation movements that are premised on territories and nation states. In this sense, the idea is to replicate colonial displacements in a world that is increasingly characterised by the new scramble for Africa (Nhemachena, Warikandwa & Mtapuri 2017; Southall *et al* 2009).

In the light of the foregoing, it is possible to notice that some forms of displacements are erroneously addressed as and celebrated in terms of flows, fluidity and circulation – this effectively prevents policy makers from including them in relevant policies on displacements. In other words, if displacing other people is proscribed, the question is why displacing other people's resources is not addressed in terms of displacements but global flows, circulations, fluidity and so on. While there are international, national and regional policies proscribing the displacement and even migration of Africans to other countries particularly to the Euro-American world, there are no similar policies to proscribe the movement of African resources that are [in the guise of circulation, flows and fluidity] displaced and moved from the continent. Transnational corporations are busy moving African resources from the continent in a global context where Africans are ironically not free to move to the Euro-American world. Conversely, descendants of colonialist are busy digging in and claiming indigeneity in Africa in an ironic world where Euro-America is building walls to prevent the migration of Africans into their realms. The key question here is why allow the global circulation and flows of African resources in a context where Africans themselves remain prisoners of neocolonised spaces and temporalities.

Chapter Outlines

Ruby Magosvongwe's chapter two argues that apart from fictionalised and historicised land injustices, evidence shows that disruptions and dislocations of displacements and dispossessions is abundant and prolific. Thus, demanding that the 'genuine' family of humankind transforms attitudes so that genuine renewal, sustainable peace, secure livelihoods for all and efforts towards re-building Zimbabwe from the ashes of colonial occupation and the armed liberation struggle, could become a reality. The chapter advances the hope that the tragedy with human nature that is selfishly selective in our seeing, our knowing, our reading, our hearing and our thinking, do not impede genuine land renewal in Zimbabwe. For too long, the elite, propertied White settlers and the international community have continuously delayed efforts at dealing a permanent blow to the carnage of land injustices glaring in the faces of an erstwhile insensitive and pretentious lot singing their voices hoarse for observance and safeguarding of human rights in the debt-ridden and 'developing' countries such as Zimbabwe. The historical fictional narratives selected in this chapter decry the duplicity and cannibalistic trend authored at Effective Occupation's indigenous land dispossessions and recurrent displacements that remain the worst enemy towards genuine renewal and transformation of livelihoods across the racial divide. Settler colonialism, especially barbaric and exclusionary settler minority land-hold to the peril of indigenous populations, cannot be postponed to perpetuity with lives and livelihoods of the marginalised Black majority continuously plunging into further mayhem. Without sinking into the abyss of historical amnesia, people-centred development must first deal with the inequities created at Effective Occupation whose ripple effects continuously foment and nurture crises for the Black majority who have no other country, no other home, no alternative haven, and no other land.

In chapter three, Collen Sabao argues that the role played by spiritual legends and spirit mediums in the construction of the Zimbabwe land disputes metanarrative can never be downplayed. There is within the Shona spiritual/religious cosmos, an intrinsic link between man and his land, as well as between ancestry and land. The constant allusion to the spiritual realm, especially the legends of Nehanda, Chaminuka and Kaguvi during and after the Zimbabwe liberation wars demonstrates the unfettered belief that the Shona people have over the influence and power of the spiritual realm. The ancestors, whose remains are interred in the land are guardians and owners of the land on which we live at their pleasure. As such, the liberation wars and the post-liberation discourses on land ownership in Zimbabwe evince both physical and spiritual dimensions. The deep seated belief in ancestry and *Mwari* (God) evinces itself in the manners in which during the liberation war (the second Chimurenga to be precise), allusions to ancestry and spirit mediums were used for morale and as a propagandistic tool to recruit new soldiers. The manners in which freedom fighters constantly consulted spirit mediums for both guidance and war strategy speaks to the nature of religious/spiritual convictions that the Shona freedom fighters had towards the words and actions of the spiritual world. It also resonates with the general belief systems within most African cultures that there is a an inexorable link between the dead and the living – in other words death is a mere graduation into the afterlife and thus the 'dead' still live amongst and within us, influencing and controlling our existence and fates.

In chapter four Charles Pfukwa argues that Simon Chimbetu, through his songs, directly and indirectly championed the cause of the displaced Black people in Zimbabwe and called for redressing the situation through land reform and restitution programmes. Chimbetu's songs reveal that there are limitless possibilities of telling the Zimbabwean story through an artistic medium that is often underrated. In other words, through Sungura music and other musical genres, we get multiple interpretations and images of Zimbabwean pasts, their triumphs and tragedies. This discussion shows that there are many ways to document, narrate and celebrate the histories, cultures, literatures and all forms of cultural heritage of a people.

Angeline Mavis Madongonda and Enna Sukutai Gudhlanga's chapter five demonstrates that through his poetry anthology *Rukuvhute*, Chirikure Chirikure has managed to bring to the fore the significant role of women in fostering identity and linkage to the land among the people of African descent. He has further demonstrated that in Shona cosmology women are not second class citizens but are in concert with their men through complimentary roles in identity formation. Chirikure Chirikure successfully integrates the umbilical cord, language and the mother figure to delineate the connections within Shona oral culture and cosmology. The umbilical cord motif clearly demonstrates the ties between the mother, the land and identity as well as the connections between life and death. He managed to tap from the rich repertoire of Shona folklore and mythology showing how the woman is held in very high esteem. The umbilical cord motif was also successfully used to denote the Shona people's identity, their connection to and ownership of their land. Chirikure's use of the indigenous Shona language concretises the identity question and also directly connects one to his place of origin.

In chapter six, Colleta Kandemiri and Nelson Mlambo analyse two novels *The Grass is Singing* and *Waiting for the Rain* and they underscore the impact of displacement on both the displacer and the displaced in the process of displacement. They argue that *The Grass is Singing* shows how the displacers ravaged the land they had dispossessed of Black people through the character Slatter, while *Waiting for the Rain* presents how displacement contributed to land degradation through the Manyene Tribal Trust Land resettlement area. Furthermore, as a result of colonial displacement, other pertinent issues such as loss of cultural footing, segregation, stereotyping, subjugation and humiliation of Black people, Black invisibility, the creation of dystopia, violence, environmental concerns, to name but a few radiated thereafter as consequences. It may therefore be concluded that the displacement that took place during colonial times resulted in the development of some of the contemporary struggles faced by some Zimbabweans even after close to four decades of political independence. The displacement resulted in loss of cultural footing, loss of livelihoods, African economic disorientation and loss of identity, landlessness and environmental degradation.

Angeline Mavis Madongonda's chapter seven argues that Musayemura Zimunya's recreation of home appears to be where his heart belongs in the rural Eastern Highlands where he grew up. For him, the city is repulsive and unaccommodating; it is meant to destroy the Black man and woman. However, Zimunya's sympathy lies with the Black man and he appears to attribute his suffering to the activities of the woman, yet the woman is worse off with colonial laws that bar her from areas of industry and commerce. The woman claims the city space in her own way, exposing the various ways the city has impinged on her freedom and that of her male counterpart. Through his anthology *Country Dawns and City Lights*, Zimunya unravels not just the racial segregation of the city, but also the spatial marginalisation of the city. His anthology also demonstrates the gendered dimension of both his poetry as well as the spatial relationships in the city. His exclusion from this poetry collection of political events and struggles of his day, however, may have afforded Zimunya the opportunity to focus on other aspects of the socio-economic experiences of the Black man in colonial Rhodesia.

Chapter eight, which is authored by Shuvai Chingwe looks at the effects of land dispossession on the livelihoods of the San people of southern Africa and more specifically the Tshwa people of Zimbabwe. This chapter acknowledges the San people as the original inhabitants of southern Africa. The dispossession of ancestral lands has negatively affected their livelihoods and put them in marginal positions economically, socially and politically. The dispossession of ancestral lands has put their hunting and gathering culture at the verge of extinction. This chapter concludes that there is dearth in research and documentation of the Tshwa indigenous people of Zimbabwe's culture and more importantly in the recognition of them as indigenous people. Hence, they are regarded like any other Zimbabwean, without recognition of the importance of their culture and how their painful history of land dispossession and cultural disregard has contributed to their present marginalised position.

In chapter nine, Blessing Makunike argues that land restitution encompasses redistribution of land to the Black poor, who either possess little or no land. This is important because for the poor, land is the primary means of generating a livelihood and a main vehicle for investing, accumulating wealth, and transferring it between generations. While historical grievances over land theft are a given, these should be looked at together with the more generalised demand for the redistribution of land for productive uses. The key objective of the land restitution policy in Zimbabwe should also be to establish a more efficient and rational structure of land and natural resource utilization. Such a structure should not protect the interests of minority elite groups at the expense of optimal land utilisation, increased productivity, employment growth, improved income distribution, and environmentally sustainable use of resources. This is what the research also tried to assess through an examination of land restitution policies of the Government of Zimbabwe. With regards to the case study, it appears that the level of awareness concerning the land reform programme was quite high in Mashonaland East province. However, it seems that not everyone was convinced by the reasons given for embarking on the land restitution exercise. There were mixed feelings on whether it was a "vote winning strategy" or a "desire to revive the economy". While many people were aware of the programme and some benefited from it, Government still has to convince people of the programme's good intentions.

Enna Sukutai Gudhlanga's chapter ten demonstrates how Patrick Chakaipa and Thomson Kumbirai Tsodzo portray the gendered dispossession of land in colonial Rhodesia. *Dzasukwa-Mwana-Asina-Hembe* and *Pafunge* were published during the colonial period and could not safely discuss land dispossession in colonial Rhodesia. Taking such a stance would have resulted in the novels being regarded as subversive literature and would have never been published. Discussing land issues was considered political by the then government. Thus the authors had to use their literary prowess to conceal land issues in excessive beer drinking and religious satire to capture the theft of land from Black men and women, and to present the different gender roles in relationship to land in a colonial set up. Through the use of metaphors, symbols and literary images the selected authors were able to expose the colonial pieces of legislation which resulted in the colonial dispossession of land belonging to Black people.

In chapter eleven Nelson Mlambo & Jairos Kangira explore the literary presentations on resistance to land repossession in

Zimbabwe. The chapter also looks at the political economy of displacements and ways in which to build a better Zimbabwe. The chapter explores how short, imaginative narratives mirror the desirability of peace, the innovative ways to prevent violence and the democratisation processes that are hoped for in everyday life. The cyclical nature of violence around land is clarified and the goal is to show that for the nation to sail past the land crisis, this issue has to be addressed and if handled well enough, the socio-economic crisis may be contained.

References

Behrend, H. *et al.* (1999) *Spirit Possession: Modernity & Power in Africa.* Madison: The University of Wisconsin Press.

Bryant, L. R. (2011) *The Democracy of Objects.* Open University Press.

Burnes, B. (2007) Kurt Lewin and Complexity Theories: Back to the Future? In *Journal of Change Management* vol 4 (4): 309 – 325.

Camaren, P. *et al.* (2014) Linking Complexity and Sustainability Theories: Implications for Modelling Sustainability Transitions in *Sustainability* vol 6: 1594 – 1622.

Charumbira, R. (2015) *Imagining a Nation: History and Memory in Making Zimbabwe.* University of Virginia Press.

Dekker, E. *et al.* (2017) Heterarchy. In Marciano, A. *et al.* (eds) *Encyclopedia of Law and Economics.* New York. Springer.

Fanon, F. (1967) *Black Skin, White Masks.* Grove Press, Inc.

Goergakopoulou, A. *et al.* (2015) *The Routledge Handbook of Language and Digital Communication.* Routledge.

Harris, M. *et al.* (2013) *The Politics of Identity: Emerging Indigeneity.* Broadway NSW: UTSePress.

Idowu, H. O. (1969) Assimilation in 19th Century Senegal, in *Cahiers d'Etudes Africaines* vol 34: 194 – 218.

Kowal, E. *et al.* (2017) Indigeneity and the Refusal of Whiteness, in *Postcolonial Studies* vol 20 (1): 101 – 117.

Lambek, M. (2009) Traveling Spirits: Unconcealment and Undisplacement, in Huwelmeier, G. *et al.* (eds) *Traveling Spirits: Migrants, Markets and Mobilities*. New York: Routledge.

Nhemachena, A. & Warikandwa, T. V. (2017) On the Challenges of African Mining and Environments in the New World Order: An Introduction, in Nhemachena, A. & Warikandwa T. V. (eds) *Mining Africa: Law, Environment, Society and Politics in Historical and Multidisciplinary Perspectives*. Bamenda: Langaa RPCIG.

Nhemachena, A. (2016) Animism, Coloniality and Humanism: Reversing the Empire's Framing of Africa, in Mawere, M. & Nhemachena, A. (eds), *Theory, Knowledge, Development and Politics: What Role for the Academy in the Sustainability of Africa?* Bamenda: Langaa RPCIG.

Nhemachena, A. (2016) Double-Trouble: Reflections on the Violence of Absence and the 'Culpability' of the Present in Africa, in Mawere, M. *et al.* (eds) *Violence, Politics and Conflict Management in Africa: Envisioning Transformation, Peace and Unity in the Twenty-First Century*. Bamenda: Langaa RPCIG.

Nhemachena, A. (2016) Hearing the Footfalls of Humanoid Robots: Technoscience, (Un-)employment and the Future of Development in Twenty-First Century Africa, in Mawere, M. (ed) *Underdevelopment, Development and the Future of Africa*. Bamenda: Langaa RPCIG.

Nhemachena, A. (2017) *Relationality and Resilience in a Not So Relational World? Knowledge, Chivanhu and (De-)coloniality in 21st Century Conflict-Torn Zimbabwe*. Bamenda: Langaa RPCIG.

Nhemachena, A., Mlambo, N. & Kangira, J. (2018) Materialities and the Resilient Global Frontierisation of Africa: An Introduction, in Nhemachena, A., Kangira, J. & Mlambo, N. (eds) *Decolonisation of Materialities or Materialisation of (Re-)Colonisation? Symbolisms, Languages, Ecocriticism and (Non)Representationalism in 21st Century Africa*. Bamenda: Langaa RPCIG.

Nhemachena, A., Mlambo, N. & Kaundjua, M. (2016) The Notion of the "Field" and the Practices of Researching and Writing Africa: Towards Decolonial Praxis, in *Africology: The Journal of Pan African Studies* vol 9 (7): 15 -36.

Nhemachena, A., Warikandwa, T. V. & Amoo S. K. (2018) Identity, Originality and Hybridity in Jurisprudence and Social Theory: An Introduction, in Nhemachena, A., Warikandwa, T. V. & Amoo, S. K. (eds) *Social and Legal Theory in the Age of Decoloniality: (Re-)Envisioning Pan – African Jurisprudence in the 21st Century*. Bamenda: Langaa RPCIG.

Nhemachena, A., Warikandwa, T. V. & Mtapuri, O. (2017) Transnational Corporations' Land Grabs and the On-going Second Mad Scramble for Africa: An Introduction, in Warikandwa, T. V., Nhemachena, A. & Mtapuri, O. (eds) *Transnational Land Grabs and Restitution in an Age of the (De-)Militarised New Scramble for Africa: A Pan African Socio-Legal Perspective*. Bamenda: Langaa RPCIG.

Nhemachena, A., Hlabangane, N. & Kaundjua, M. (2018) Human Bodies Becoming Mines? The Coloniality of Networks, Internet of Things, Big Data and Data Mining in Researching Africa, Paper presented at the University of South Africa College of Human Sciences on 21 September 2018: to be published in Africology: The Journal of Pan African Studies in 2019.

Rajan, D. *et al.* (2018) Quantum Blockchain Using Entanglement in Time, in *Quantum Physics* https://arxiv.org/abs/1804.05979.

Ranger, T. (1989) Whose Heritage? The Case of the Matopo National Park, in *Journal of Southern African Studies* vol 15 (2): 217-249

Schinkel, W. (2010) From Zoepolitics to Biopolitics: Citizenship and the Construction of 'Society', in *European Journal of Social Theory* vol 13 (2): 155 – 172.

Southall, R. *et al.* (2009) A New Scramble for Africa, in Southall, R. *et al.* (eds) *A New Scramble for Africa? Imperialism, Investment and Development*. University of KwaZulu Natal Press.

Tsosie, R. (2005) The New Challenge to Native Identity: An Essay on 'Indigeneity" and "Whiteness" in *Washington University Journal of Law & Policy* vol 18 (1)

Tuck, E. *et al.* (2013) Decolonization is Not a Metaphor, in *Decolonization, Indigeneity, Education and Society* vol 1 (1): 1-40.

Vaccaro, J. A. (2018) The Quantum Theory of Time, the Block Universe, and Human Experience in *Philos Trans A Math Phys Eng Sci* vol 376 (2123)

Van Den Berghe, P. L. (1963) Racialism and Assimilation in Africa and the Americas, in *Southwestern Journal of Anthropology* vol 19 (4): 424 – 432.

Van Paaschen, C. (2015) *Biopolitics and Zoepolitics in a Post – Political Era: Hegemonic Struggles in the Swedish Debate on Foreign Terrorist Fighters.* Lund University

Vungsiriphisal, P. *et al.* (eds) (2013) *Humanitarian Assistance for Displaced Persons from Myanmar: Roal Thai Government Policy and Donor, INGO, NGO and UN Agency Delivery.* Springer Science & Business Media.

Warikandwa, T. V., Nhemachena, A. & Mtapuri, O. (2017) *Transnational Land Grabs and Restitution in an Age of the (De-)Militarised New Scramble for Africa: A Pan- African Socio-Legal Perspective.* Bamenda: Langaa RPCIG.

Warikandwa, T. V., Nhemachena, A., Mpofu, N. & Chitimira, H. (ed) (2019) *Grid-Locked African Economic Sovereignty: Decolonising the NeoImperial Socio-Economic and Legal Force-Fields in the 21ˢᵗ Century.* Bamenda: Langaa RPCIG.

Zack, N. (ed) (2017) Indigeneity and U.S. Settler Colonialism, in Oxford Handbooks Online
http://www.oxfordhandbooks.com/view/10.1093/oxfordhb/9780190236955.001.0001/oxfordhb - 9780190236953 - e- 51

Chapter Two

Land Dispossession and the Genesis of Crises in Zimbabwe: Implications for Sustainable Livelihoods and People-centred Development as Depicted in Selected Zimbabwean Fictional Narratives

Ruby Magosvongwe

Introduction

Zimbabwean literary creations have taken a critical role in influencing attitudes and perceptions on how land in Zimbabwe continues to shape development thrusts that have till now been racially-oriented and elitist-driven. The inviolable existing historic legal instruments undergird apartheid development across the racial divide. Nevertheless, the present chapter interrogates the extent to which land dispossession has/not been the Genesis to the myriad crises dogging Zimbabwe's post-independence efforts towards sustainable livelihoods and people-centred development. Questions like: "Which people have legitimacy to land and why?"; "People-centred development using which and whose lenses and to what end?"; "Are sustainable livelihoods premised on differential human worth?"; "What is the measure for sustainable development and sustainable livelihoods?" The intricacies and labyrinthine links of land and its fundamental influences with the myriad crises in post-2000 Zimbabwe will be discussed using Benjamin Sibanda's *Whose Land is it Anyway* (2016); NoViolet Bulawayo's *We Need New Names* (2013); Eric Harrison's *Jambanja* (2006); Valerie Tagwira's *The Uncertainty of Hope* (2006), Brian Chikwava's *Harare North* (2009) and Charles Samupindi's *Death Throes* (1992), cross-referencing with Yvonne Vera's *Nehanda* (1993) as the primary texts.

Ideological contestations, claims of belongingness, entitlement, human rights and strife have become daily bread, a common feature characterising the Land Issue in Zimbabwe from the times of

29

Effective Occupation to date. From pre-colonial, colonial through to post-independence, and contemporary Zimbabwean politics and sustainable economic development discourses, land, identity and sustainable people-centred development are indelibly labyrinthine. In simpler terms, I am arguing that the real crises in Zimbabwe commenced with Effective Occupation in 1890, and not with land redistribution and land occupations/repossessions from 1998 as others would like to argue, believe and think. Occupations, distortions of identities and geophysical ethnic boundaries, including mechanically orchestrated pauperisation in the newly forced settlements/reserves, all of them crimes against humanity, began with colonial settler invaders dispossessing and displacing the indigenous land-owners using the currency of conquest and imposed foreign legalism. Cumulatively, the latter spell the watershed of all subsequent crises. Ironically, post-colonial discourses on crises in Zimbabwe continue focusing on the symptoms, a smokescreen approach, rather than interrogating the underlying causes that must be overhauled if sanity, human rights sustenance and social justice are to prevail in earnest.

Suffice to say that in the Zimbabwean context, everyone lives off the land in/directly, and therefore everyone has vested interests that must be safeguarded, making the subject multipronged, multi-disciplinary, multiple-layered and therefore highly contentious. The following picture partly sheds light on the genesis of the land question, spelling the real crisis in Zimbabwe that is still to be resolved, lest we forget:

This is how land was acquired in Zimbabwe.
This is a photo of British colonialists hanging
Africans in 1890s Bulawayo, Zimbabwe.
The photo was so prized by a British officer in
'Rhodesia' Robert Baden-Powell, founder of the
'Boy Scouts' and 'Girl Guides', that he kept it
in a scrapbook entitling it 'The Christmas Tree'.

My prognosis proceeds on the premise established thus, Effective Occupation spells permanent unquantifiable disaster, unless every one of our readers has the misfortune of historical amnesia. The latter partly amplifies the ethnographic approach that most nationalists and indigenous authors adopt when narrating/writing on issues to do with the Zimbabwean zillion dollar land conundrum: massive dispossession of the indigenous population, removals, displacements, disenfranchisement and perpetual squatter status and impoverishment through compulsory culling of cattle herds in view of the severely limited and corruptly distributed land. Cumulatively, without overhauling the horrendous racially-exclusive system at independence and beyond, the latter aspects continue compounding precarious livelihoods, poor sustenance, insecurities in their myriad forms, and general racial vulnerability, making the land issue racial and therefore political.

Labyrinthine link between Literary Depictions and Theoretical Frameworks-Grounding vis-à-vis deeply-held Land Perceptions/Prejudices

The most critical principle that helps to unravel the zillion dollar land conundrum pushes critical readers and thinkers to unmasking the Genesis of the same conundrum as is the thrust in the present discussion. How literary depictions of land explore the seemingly interminable maze concerning perceptions of being, dignity and the right to life as embedded in perceptions about access to and ownership of land cannot be ignored or left to chance. How and why is it that Africans are confined to overgrazed and overcrowded Tribal Trust Lands where people come to die (Mungoshi 1975) and overcrowded poorly developed townships teeming with poverty and crime while the Caucasian races are inviolably confined to the plush and pollution-free low density and middle suburbs, game ranches, conservancies, estates, commercial farms, highly rain-fed holiday resorts and exclusive clubs even in the politically independent nation state and country? The answer lies in the history of land as both a policy and political issue that remains unresolved since the indigenous populations' dispossessions and removals of the 1890s to date. While critics like Tunde Adeleke (2015) may fault such an approach as a backward-looking paradigm, which understanding is unfortunately monolithic and therefore sadly myopic, Chivaura (2016) rightly defends the position that the present chapter adopts:

The African worldview sees history as a living force which, like other arts, as p'Bitek (1986: 46) says, is an integral part of culture carried, not in books, but inside the head, to enliven the entire body of

32

the individual and society, in their everyday economic, social, political, religious and scientific endeavours, just to mention a few.

Rightly so, Chivaura's position that the view of history as "the past" as taught in schools and universities throughout Africa and the world, is not African, speaks to the realities of destinies and identities that colonially-engineered exclusivist land dispossessions inscribed across the racial divide, tragic especially for the Africans. "Armed with the knowledge of our past [that informs the heroic present], we can with confidence chart a course for our future".

Effects of policies and systems engineered to perpetually impoverish the inferior 'natives' live with the majority of the peoples till today, a crisis that still needs urgent attention, not foreign investment, infrastructure development and industrialisation alone. The question at hand is who the primary and principle beneficiaries of these land policies are. Why does the land question in Zimbabwe attract such controversy and hostile international relations? As long as that question is glossed over and avoided, the conundrum and acrimony continues seething underground unabated like a dormant volcano. History is therefore a current affair, shaping our present and future with its attendant in/securities. These are the stubborn facts that Zimbabwe's land crisis invite to be addressed in a sober manner with unflinching clear-mindedness. Even if this perspective sounds like an old overplayed tune, realities and simmering tensions on the ground beckon for a well-considered response, long term gains and losses notwithstanding.

From an Afrocentric perspective, the foregoing brain-teasers/crackers are the issues that the writers-cum-artists must be grappling with as their works shape communities' mis/fortunes for generations. "The writer cannot expect to be excused from the task of re-education and regeneration that must be done" (Achebe 1990: 45), while at the same time acknowledging the indigenous peoples' sins, foibles and blasphemies that have continued to undermine efforts towards self-regeneration. Afrocentricity is not all about glorification of African agency and achievements, but is cognisant of the need for critical self-examination and intelligent borrowing while

33

building on one's lived experiences/realities and solid cultural foundations. Malcolm X (1970: 55) rightly argues: "A man does not know how to act until he realises what he is acting against. And you don't realise what you are acting against until you know what they did to you".

Our writers across the racial divide address the post-2000 acrimony, intense political polarisation and crises beginning with the Fast Track Land Reform Programme, drawing international attention and Economic sanctions by Britain and her allies within the European Union and the United States of America that imposed the Zimbabwe Economic Recovery and Democracy Act (ZDERA) in 2001 under the George W Bush Administration. The writings subtly interrogate and introspect on why the land reform, an internal policy issue, has attracted such a stingingly harsh backlash. Chikwava (2009) and Bulawayo (2013) make a unique clinical survey of the land problem that some scholars and critics could mistake for a Government-funded propaganda project, yet that is not the case.

Most writers, Bulawayo and Chikwava included, write as a result of the struggles they have with their identities or the irony of their personal circumstances as individuals, or as a people. The result is that the writer surrenders the unravelling of those problematic experiences to the agency of his/her characters, which imaginative creativity partly rides on. For example, how can a critical writer/reader debunk the nexus between the "politically explosive topics of race and colonial history" (Barclays 2010: 152) over land? The evidence of pauperisation of one race and enrichment of the other at the expense of the displaced populations as a result of colonial machinations, then and now, are too glaring to miss or ignore. It increasingly becomes indefensible to deny that the 1890 British Effective Occupation currency and its apartheid policies of development and Manichean existence authored against the indigenous African majority was globally sanctioned, as was the case with the parcelling out of Africa at the notorious 1884-5 Berlin Conference that left Africa a decimated and dis-membered continent. This is the major crisis and nexus that must be overhauled in order for sustainable livelihoods and sustainable development for the majority to take root. "The stories after the whites took the land were [/are] only of grief, loss and longing" (Mukonori 2017: 264). Mugabe rightly observes:

> Land comes first before all else... This is the one asset that not only defines the Zimbabwean personality and demarcates sovereignty, but also an asset that has a direct bearing on the fortunes of the poor and prospects for their immediate empowerment and sustainable development... So, Blair, keep your England and let me keep my Zimbabwe (Barclays, 2010: 153, citing Mugabe's speech at the 2002 UN's Earth Summit hosted by South Africa under President Thabo Mbeki, held in Johannesburg in September 2002).

In the Zimbabwean context, history has proven beyond reasonable doubt that whoever holds the land holds the principle livelihood resource —the hen that lays the golden egg (Lessing 1950)—and the key to sustainable development since land carries all the resources critical for sustainable and secure livelihoods. Apart from the ruthless sanctions embedded in ZDERA, Harrison's *Jambanja* (2006) testifies to the myth that defends Whites' exclusionary entitlement to land. In my understanding, such historical facts testify to a dichotomous logic of human rights. While other peoples have a right to international protection by alien rule of law, ironically others belonging to the same family of humankind are relegated to perpetual silencing, decimation and exploitation of their land and resources for the benefit of their oppressors. What are human rights from the perspectives of dispossessed, impoverished, vulnerable and suffering masses? Which DEMOCRACY and whose economic recovery does ZDERA advance and seek to achieve?

"Denied restitution, restoration and compensation, African people are paradoxically encouraged to remain "peaceful" even as they are being (neo)-imperially cannibalised. Put in other words, in spite of absence of redress for (neo)-imperial plunder and exploitation, African people are consistently urged that peaceful coexistence (Vorster 2018) is all that matters even as they are being cannibalised by defiant (neo)-imperial forces" (Nhemachena,

Warikandwa & Mpofu 2018). To this end, "[a] people's worldview determines what constitutes a problem for them and how they solve [the same] problem" (Mazama 2001). Using the western wolf cannibalism theory garnished as civilisation and philanthropy, Chigwedere (2001) bemoans the unprecedented betrayal that indigenous Zimbabweans suffered at the hands of the White colonialists who grabbed their land culminating in starvation and forced labour on the same land they had been forcibly removed from and dispossessed of.

The issue of land and subsistence takes us back the riddle of the hen and the egg, arguing on which comes first and why. 'Whose story, which lenses and whose voice, why and to what end' (Magosvongwe 2003), becomes fundamental in our examination of the land debates in/on Zimbabwe as depicted in fiction narratives, the granary of a people's memory (Ngugi wa Thiongo 2009). To assume and believe that narratives/fiction is innocent and ideologically bankrupt is therefore the highest form of self-delusion. Encapsulations and sensitivity to people's survival needs, the writers' own survival interests and efforts towards sustainable livelihoods across class, gender, ethnic, religious and racial divides in the locally-generated literary depictions, especially those of the post-2000 phase, speak to the Waterloo that Zimbabwe faces today.

Ideological contestations embedded in literary creativity and memorialisation of experiences are therefore not divorced from survival interests, an aspect that the selected literary texts variously explore. Some of these narratives are too complex and sophisticated to have simplistic monolithic readings as they subtly spin and ricochet in their double-edged depictions, forcing readers to critically self-introspect. The latter explains why it is important to place Africans "within their own historical framework" (Mgbeadichie 2015: 9) and actors too, not necessarily indolent spectators waiting for history to happen to them. Power shifts do not necessarily trivialise the fundamental right to accessing primary natural resources, such as land, in order to guarantee sustainable livelihoods across society's broad spectrum. Land was the foremost galvanising principle for the armed liberation struggle (Mutasa 1985) and remains critical in shaping identities, securities, sustainable livelihoods and the country's economy. Mukonori (2017: 264) acknowledges in his memoir:

> When our people lost the war, which was brief and brutal, they were uprooted and forcibly relocated, pushed into the harsh country that their ancestors had long known was not suitable for life. Most were only able to keep some token belongings…Even the rich and powerful natives lost their land and cattle until they were as poor as all the rest.

The displacements and dispossessions inscribe not only precarious livelihoods, poverty and environmental insecurities, but also conjure interminable psychological damage and crippled mind-sets, evidenced by self-hate and determination to flee home to perceived safe havens elsewhere to affirm their dignity and humanity—"tatters of our country left behind, barely held together by American dollars, by monies from other countries" (Bulawayo 2013: 242). Yet, the same 'redemptive' flight to the Diaspora further dehumanised most incumbents:

> We would never be the things we wanted to be: doctors, lawyers, teachers, engineers…We dropped our heads in shame because we were no longer people; we were now illegals…
>
> And because we were illegal and afraid to be discovered we mostly kept to ourselves…We did not want their wrath…We did not meet stares and we avoided gazes. We hid our real names, gave false ones when asked. We built mountains between us and them, we dug rivers, we planted thorns… and flocked to unwanted jobs…
>
> We swallowed every pain like a bitter pill, drank every fear like a love potion, and we worked and worked.
>
> [in a] country that would never be ours (Bulawayo 2013: 241-245).

The image of the 'wretched of the earth' cannot be more graphic. Nameless. Defenceless. Homeless. Precariously insecure. The scum of the earth. Stateless even at that point. Illegals to be forcibly ejected if discovered. And we talk about sustainable livelihoods under such inhuman conditions. And we even unashamedly label those enduring such a lot indolent, unimaginative, uncivilised, ungrateful "hoodlums" (Harrison 2006). And, home beckons in its horrid state. Such are the horrors of differential human rights engendered by British 1890 Effective Occupation of Zimbabwe that an amnesiac historical memory erases from the real problem that the globe has swept under the rug. To people who have never been colonised, dispossessed, displaced, uprooted and flung to the wilderness, pauperised and continue to be a continual migrant at home and elsewhere, it would be difficult to fathom the unquantifiable injury and pain. The horrors are yet to be explored and quantified.

How our writers package our land stories therefore makes us or breaks us permanently. Raftopoulos (2009: 165) observes that the land reform inspired "white writing that inscribed a new sense of victimhood on white identities" which overtly and subtly translates to reinvention, re-inscription and buttressing of white right to land possession, ownership, 'inviolable' belonging as the victimhood milks global sympathy. Nevertheless, the "pernicious assumption that artistic creations can only be defined from the point of view of the classes of Europe" (Vambe 2002: 15) spells nothing but doom for the disenfranchised African. Similarly, such assumptions buttress systematic intellectual and cultural extermination of the indigenous populations that are continuously pushed to the margins by anti-human and anti-African frameworks and narratives.

The context and genesis of victimhood embedded in the White-authored narratives necessarily attracts examination from an objective and critical reader. Therefore, both Zimbabwean Literature in English and the geo-physical space from which it derives its name remain "contested terrain" (Moyo *et al.* 2008). Because of the central role that literary creativity-cum-memorialisation of experiences occupies in education and curricula across the ages in general, literary depictions and discourses about land and sustainable livelihoods across the racial divide deserve serious attention. This is especially critical in the sense that while other communities have archived information in print making it indelible, others have largely depended on oral transmission. Yet, the griots, story-bearers or repositories of such narratives are but finite beings.

The interface of literary depictions and fictionalisation of experiences as is the case with the post-2000 land redistribution efforts and processes is thus invaluable. Moyana (2000) rightly argues that with the continual passing on of the liberation war fighters, generations of those directly pauperised by initial colonial dispossessions as well as the founding African nationalists, erasure and alteration of indigenous land narratives become a real threat that must be addressed. Thus, the role that writers' depictions play in influencing and shaping perceptions of human dignity/identities/destinies/selfhood/right to being and belongingness, as well as eventual policy, intra- and international relations deserve critical attention. This is how societies have intrinsically reformed and renewed themselves across the ages, justifying the African-centred approach that the present analysis adopts in its appreciation of the selected texts set in and defining the psychological, geophysical and intellectual settings of land experiences in the identified texts. In any case, due recognition must be given to the events that make both theorisations undergirding texts and their appreciation plausible.

Gomo (2010: v) surmises of *A Fine Madness*: "It is refusal to have my experience interpreted for me by [aliens] whose kith and kin dispossessed my ancestors. The man on the spot must tell his story in order to prevent the tragedy from being repeated". Refusal to be named, described, defined, codified, circumscribed, pigeonholed, dissected, analysed and explained using alien frameworks/philosophies thereby subtly imbibing and given an agenda in contradistinction to one's survival interests, anchors the present discussion. Poisoning the source is rooted in poisoning the mind's perceptions first and foremost. Ours is not just a political-economic struggle, but a psycho-intellectual warfare that need not be underestimated. It is therefore erroneous and heinous that "Africans must always judge themselves using [alien] European standard, model or norm" (Hoskins 1992: 250). The value systems that we put at the centre of our literary analyses and appreciation undeniably speak and testify to the worldviews and interests that the literature envisages to safeguard. Yet, people cannot remain "happy slaves in [their] own land" (Maathai 2010: 161).

The acrimony characterising the land conundrum in Zimbabwe has its genesis in continual efforts to perpetually inferiorise and trivialise the local people's perceptions of and solutions to the all-time land injustice that global players deliberately ignore. Suffice to argue that differential human worth is recipe for disastrous socio-economic relationships locally and internationally. In short, as long as Africans' cultural heritage and perceptions of and right to land are not infused and recognised in the envisaged solution to the land issue in Zimbabwe, as much as their humanity and dignity, the acrimony and contestations remain perennial. It is an unforgivable and misleading falsehood that value of the human being and his/her dignity in the indigenous Zimbabwean worldview is predicated only on accumulated dollars and cents. Securities trans-generationally are largely derived from affinity with the land. In the indigenous Zimbabwean perceptions of dignity, identity, self-worth and unities across the ages (Magosvongwe 2014), technological innovation and material accumulation on their own are deficient in securing sustainable livelihoods.

For most indigenous peoples of Zimbabwe, though economic woes ejected them to the Diaspora, anchorage spiritually, materially, economically, socio-culturally, morally and relationally still remains in their homeland. Bulawayo's child narrator Darling in *We need new names* and Chikwava's nameless narrator in *Harare North,* protractedly dwell on these land and identity issues at the heart of their struggles, for a good reason. Psycho-intellectually and socio-culturally, a sense of un/belongingness haunts them. They remain outsiders as economic nomads in alien lands. It is therefore critical that literary creativity and criticism help interrogate the stumps impeding that anchoring, an essential step towards self-discovery, self-affirmation and self-drive, an aspect that the present chapter partly grapples with.

Ngugi wa Thiongo (1987: 7), resonating with Shona philosophy of intrinsic self-examination, rightly argues: "Happy is the traveller who is able to see the tree stumps in his way, for he can pull them up or walk around them so that they do not make him stumble". The anchoring philosophy as encapsulated in their maxims, thus, explains and justifies how social rights have been engendered, safeguarded and fossilised among many African communities across the ages, the indigenous Zimbabwean Shona communities included. So are the land narratives that generations have and continue to interact with for self-pride across the ages. Agreeing to alteration and or mutilation of the land narratives by some fictional narratives is metonymic of complicit in genocidal mutilation of minds and destinies of the concerned communities. Far removed from both time and place, these literary narratives authenticate land discourses' interface with social, political, economic, intellectual and fundamental human rights debates (Magosvongwe and Nyamende 2014), hence the critical African-centred navigation that the present article calls for. Achebe rightly avers unapologetically:

> African Literature is unashamedly, unembarrassingly...social. It is political, it is economic. The total life of man is reflected in his art. Our Literature is based on morality. Perhaps this sounds old-fashioned to you, but it is not to us.

That Zimbabwe is historically referred to as a country of four names (Mashiri 2005) in itself calls for the writers' interrogation. For example, why should the land between the Zambezi and the Limpopo rivers be called Rhodesia, Southern Rhodesia, a privately-owned possession by a British adventurer as if the land was 'an empty wilderness' in the first place? The then empire expansion currency still gives legitimacy to White supremacy in economic terms till today? Why? The 'empty' country then changes name to Zimbabwe-Rhodesia, carrying a surname as part of a White identity, and finally Zimbabwe after the great Zimbabwe Monument. Some sarcastic critics today refer to the same country as 'Zimbabwe, after the ruins'. The shifts in naming meant continual displacements and disruptions to development for the 'objectified' indigenous inhabitants. Bulawayo's trans-generational gaps in perceptions of home succinctly summarise these disastrous displacements that mean deeper loss and fragmentation with the continual uprooting of the 'squatters' on their ancestral lands.

Bulawayo's narrator Darling summarises the horrid effects of Black displacements and their disruptions to building sustainable livelihoods that the rest of the chapter dwells on. Home harbours memories of brokenness and fragility, fragile like a bottle that once broken can never be put back together to assume its original form and therefore permanently precarious. People live permanently at the crossroads as a result: "Stina said a country is a Coca Cola bottle that can smash on the floor and disappoint you. When a bottle smashes, you cannot put it back together" (Bulawayo 2013: 160). The image of the country symbolised by a Coca Cola bottle that could disappoint depicts Tagwira's "uncertainty of hope"— promises that could be elusive. The uncertainty and fluidity of such an environment is what pushes the people to leave their country in droves. Movement, migration and constant shifting of places also spell shifting fortunes or misfortunes that come with removal, displacement and resettlement, a condition that ironically characterises almost all Black indigenous and Black alien citizens' experiences with the land. Worse still, in more than one way, the experiences are more shattering when it comes to leaving one's country of origin. Subtly through the voice of the child narrator the tragedy slowly builds up: "Stina said leaving your country is like dying" (Bulawayo 2013: 160). And 'dying' takes myriad forms, including culturally, spiritually, socially, economically and psycho-intellectually, depending on people's dispositions and visions about their destinies and identities.

Bulawayo succinctly summarises conceptions of the indigenous broken lives across generations, broken identities, broken histories, broken and blighted futures even, using symbolism of land displacements that are perpetually disruptive:

> *There are two homes inside my head*: home before Paradise (shanty tin dwellings after forcible ejections and demolitions of 2005 Operation Restore Order Demolitions), and home in Paradise; home one and two. Home one was best. A real house. Father and Mother having good jobs… and then home two—Paradise, with its tin, tin, tin.

42

There are three homes in Mother's and Aunt Fostalina's heads: home before independence, before I was born, when black people and white people were fighting over the country. And then the home of things falling apart, which made Aunt Fostalina leave and come here. Home one, home two, and home three. *There are four homes inside Mother of Bones's head: home before the white people came to steal the country, and a king ruled; home when the white people came to steal the country and then there was war; home when black people got our stolen country back after independence; and then the home of now. Home one, home two, home three, home four.* When somebody talks about home, you have to listen carefully so you know exactly which one the person is referring to (Bulawayo 2013: 191-192).

Each generation's 'home' is a synecdoche of the incumbents' displacement and increasing disenfranchisement. Home displacements and dispossessions encapsulate the shifting country's history and elusive fortunes for the Blacks deciphered in the constantly shifting socio-political, spiritual, psychological and shattered material environments dogging each respective generation. The fossilisation of sedimentary experiences is ironically trashed when analyses of sustainable economies and livelihoods are conducted. Such is what our academia and policy-makers have earned for their country and posterity, contrary to the projections and depictions of the ideologically sensitive artists/writers. The tragedy is further heightened by marginalisation of our own languages. Our memories are kept in other peoples' granaries. Our children cannot even speak our own languages, they do not sound like us, further dismembered from their true African identities, 'sealing' the dismembering, uprooting and erasure of intangible cultural heritage as well. The latter, however, is a subject for another day.

The Post-2000 Land Conundrum and Crisis in Selected Narratives: Appreciation of Crises, Acrimony and Sustainable Development

Several disputations continue to be put forward concerning the post-2000 crises in Zimbabwe, among which include bad governance, bad economic principles and practices, poor planning, mismanagement, racism, political polarisation, corruption, violence, misrule, and general abuse of human rights and purported gross violations of property rights as evidenced by the land repossessions/ occupations/grabs and *jambanja* of 2000 and beyond. In my view the forgoing nomenclature of rampant land resettlements are symptomatic of a bigger problem that the holders of the land and economy have been reluctant to address for personal self-aggrandisement as well as for international political and economic expediency. But the question that remains to be broached and brokered is when exactly crisis begins politically, economically, socially, spiritually, environmentally and culturally from the perspective of the majority of the indigenous population. Samupindi's *Death Throes: The Trial of Nehanda*, though not widely acknowledged and acclaimed, proffers the genesis and oasis of the conundrum, supported by Ranger's *Revolt in Southern Rhodesia, 1896-97* (1967), Palmer's *Land and race in Rhodesia* (1977), later corroborated by Vera's *Nehanda* (1990), Thomas' *Rhodes: The race for Africa* (1996) and Hanlon, Manjengwa and Smart's *Zimbabwe Takes Back its Land* (2013), among others. The terms "theft by dispossession" and "primitive stealing" (Uadiale and Awala-Le 2018: 198) aptly summarise Whites' incessant abuse of legalism to have an exclusive land-hold in Zimbabwe and Africa in general. *Nehanda* projects a cultural and spiritual sacrilege embedded in Whites' avarice and arrogance. Mukonori's *A Memoir: Man in the Middle* (2017) similarly bemoans the violent grabs legitimised by laws and subsequent dispossessions, forced removals and resettlements and oppression. A visitor/White settlers comes in to settle at the rich pinnacle of the land contrary to all cultural traditional practices and expectations. Yet, "The land is our right. The land shall belong to us...the children of the soil" (Mukonori 2017: 267), the single slogan that has united the indigenous majority across the ages.

The foregoing explains why, from a White land-owner's perspective, and also historically from colonial capitalism, the political leader who raises the people to resist and fight subjugation and right to land and self-rule is condemned a 'witch', the fate that the legendary Nehanda suffered and murdered by hanging for her invidious role. In the English tradition as shown in Shakespeare's *Macbeth*, witches are wanton deceivers working with the powers of darkness to wreak havoc on a legitimate peaceful dynasty. Impliedly in the English tradition, witches are agents of violence, darkness, deception, intrigue and destruction. In the history of Southern Africa, Nehanda 'the witch' is the first and only recorded female who was hung and executed for fighting for her people's right to subsistence, land ownership and sovereignty. In an apparent intrigue, it appears that as far as the Zimbabwean situation is concerned, there are no human rights abuses according to the larger international community, calling upon the need to revisit what it means to be human and who the human beings are from the goings-on that flourish without much censure in the colonial period and its aftermath. One reads in-between the lines colonial justification of the extermination and subjugation of a 'primitive native people' and seizure of their lands with impunity. This is how identities of superiority and inferiority are buttressed, but urgently requiring redress and undoing in the post-2000 period if national togetherness, sustainable development and property rights are to be salvaged and achieved in a fragile peace. Both Blacks and Whites need re-education (Chigara 2012 a & b; Sacco 2008) on what it means to access land and to respect human right to subsistence.

From my indigenous and ethnological Shona upbringing I argue that creativity bereft of values does not take humanity forward, hence the reader/critic's mandate to interrogate the values underpinning a work of art. Materialistic ideologies alone plunge humanity into the quagmire of interminable conflicts premised on falsifications and veneer of differential human worth/dignity. Further, human dignity is not an issue of charity, explaining why indigenous people like Nehanda have not turned away, but fought and tenaciously waged armed liberation struggles to reclaim their land of ancestral heritage and trampled dignity. Samupindi's *Death Throes: The Trial of Mbuya Nehanda* (1992) and the protagonist's all time mantra offer an irrefutable example:

I told my people to stand their ground against these foreigners who were snatching away their land, cattle and heritage-plundering and routing in the process. They have decimated us as they did the Ndebele. Now the land is the playground for vultures. Bones and decaying carrion are the verdure in the valleys. But I warn you! I warn you oppressor that these bones will rise and wage a thunderous war to reclaim their heritage (Samupindi 1992: 39).

There were no extenuating circumstances for Nehanda's reprieve according to British colonial 'justice'. Like Baden Powell's infamous Christmas tree above displaying dangling bodies of some indigenous fighters/rebels, Nehanda's life was sealed by the colonial hangman's noose. Namibian genocide literature corroborates similar heinous extermination of the Herero and Namaqua in Namibia by German colonists around 1904 driven by avaricious grab of the indigenous peoples' land and resources. Hanging, the music of the day, in pursuance of the 32nd section of Her Majesty the Queen of England's 18th July 1894 Order-in-Council in the case "The Queen against Nehanda, in custody under sentence of death for murder, for which on the 20th April 1898 Watermeyer granted and signed the Warrant of Execution. The Obituary 27th April 1898 reads: "I certify that I have examined the body of Nehanda, upon whom sentence of death has been executed, and that life is extinct" (Samupindi 1992: 42). The public executions were designed to induce fear and therefore nurture surrender from would-be rebels and contenders.

Samupindi's depictions derived from National Archives records of Nehanda's trial and eventual execution exemplify that it is taboo and criminal for the indigenous colonised peoples to challenge alien White rule. According to Kahari (2009) the land dispossessions, displacements and violent removals were a crime against humanity. Schreiner (1897) similarly depicts the Shonas being smoked and blasted out of mountain caves and valleys by Cecil John Rhodes' Pioneer Column for wont of vast tracts of 'empty' land and ounces of gold, facts corroborated by Phyllis Johnson and David Martin (1985). Yet, the same colonial administration expected payment of taxes from the dispossessed, displaced and disenfranchised indigenous population to develop White areas. Their land and cattle—their material and economic security (Ramose 2005; Mungoshi, 1975)— grabbed at inception of colonial rule for the next eight decades, spelt genocidal proportions that make Mungoshi's Lucifer hate the anti-heroes of Manyene Communal Lands that reeks with death, barrenness, brokenness, emptiness, family disintegration and self-hatred.

The latter explains why Gomo's *A Fine Madness* advocates memorialising and immortalising the African experiences from the transcendental perspective of the African survivors and fighters who are re-building their communities relegated to fringes of 'civilisation' from the ashes of an armed liberation struggle. Genuine reconstruction and regeneration begins with repossessing the wrenched heritage of land and its symbolic material and cultural value systems. It is ironic and deafening that the United Nations excludes land expropriation, dispossession and displacement in its definition of violations of human rights. Thus, the human right to land and subsistence and principal crisis that the international community continues to ignore despite the celebrated and western shrill calls for respect for human rights as enshrined in the United Nations Human Rights Charter. When do human rights begin and end? Ironically, even the 2007 SADC Human Rights Tribunal "was intended to serve a similar function to the European Court of Human Rights" (Barclay 2010: 148). Nonetheless, the conundrum continuously gets complicated in that "[t]he colonists became locals…born on the land their parents had taken and therefore naturally only knew one home" (Mukonori 2017: 265). The land question no longer restricts itself to race in this regard.

The question is who is human deserving human rights and their safeguarding? Though two wrongs cannot make a right and if human rights are universally applicable, how defensible is the violence with which land was colonially acquired? How could Zimbabwe's land repossession programme rid itself of a racial discriminatory principle in targeting White-owned farms alone, in itself an illegal practice, if land-ownership itself had been historically racially-defined? Even then, 'land invaders' themselves are legally 'squatters' (Barclays 2010:

47

149) deserving the wrath of the law. The conundrum haunts generations across the racial divide. Moore (2003) explores the protracted efforts by the Tangwena people of Zimbabwe's Eastern Highlands towards retaining both selfhood and land against White invasion, a fact that Samupindi's *Death Throes: The Trial of Nehanda* has similarly inscribed. Harrison's *Jambanja* (2006) and Catherine Buckle's *African Tears* (2001) similarly describe the brutalities inflicted upon White commercial farmers at ejection from 'their' land. The question that remains: 'Can development and human rights be safeguarded and sustained using the principle of might alone as is the case in the Zimbabwean context'? In reconstructing and pursuing social justice, the interface between literature and history thus remains invaluable and poignant.

Further, can sustainable development and livelihoods be achieved among the indigenous African communities such as those in Zimbabwe, if the international community is selective in its application, observance and safeguarding of human rights? Which cultural centre and whose values anchor the United Nations definition of human rights and why? The veiled agenda that is unacknowledged nor publicly spelt out is the West's insistence for capitalist control and exploitation of natural resources, primary of which is land and its subsoil resources, for the benefit of European metropolis. There is hardly any departure from the 1884/5 Berlin Conference disastrous initiative. Tragically, land-ownership becomes colour-coded. Whites are internationally acclaimed farm-owners while Blacks are labourers who sacrifice themselves for a frugal existence and 'homes/shelter' at the farms (Barclays, 2010: 150). Nhemachena (2018: 148) equates the unequal relations to cannibalism whereby "imperial cannibalisation of Africa was hidden in discourses of 'civilisation' and 'development' of Africans". He rightly observes:

> Superficial discourses of human rights, democracy and good governance are simply apparatuses for imperial mimesis and seduction that are meant to subtly generate wide African consent to be cannibalised and devoured.

The build-up of the acrimony over land in Zimbabwe is what Chikwava's *Harare North* takes up, sarcastically and playfully recapturing in an Shona-English idiolect, the whole issue of selective dignity, differential human worth, property rights and exclusivist relational terms embedded in global capital accumulation, economic and human rights discourses that are amnesiac to history. Pilossof (2012) explores the dangers of Whites' relational approaches to land in Zimbabwe, sparking seething bitterness and turmoil engendered by colonial occupation, subjugation and exploitation highlighted above. Thus, conflicts and tensions about land displacements and recurrent dispossessions causing punitive economic sanctions against the country are thus cyclic history playing itself out. "Nations and peoples are largely the stories they feed themselves. If they tell themselves stories that are lies, they will suffer the future consequences of those lies. If they tell themselves stories that face their own truths, they will free their stories from future flowerings" (Ben Okri, *Birds of Heaven*).

Chikwava reconstructs the living history of the intensifying unresolved war over land as the genesis of the post-2000 land grabs and subsequent socio-political crises, including the ripple economic implosion that scatters peoples to the Diaspora. This nexus cannot be ignored. According to Shire (2003) the land explosion in post-2000 Zimbabwe are chickens coming home to roost. In this regard, Chikwava's nameless narrator's diagnosis of the real cause of the intensifying war over land in post-2000 Zimbabwe is worth noting, a narrative that is neither peculiar to nor confined to Zimbabwe alone:

> This opposition party supporter, he have been arrest on account of he is one of them people that attack party's supporters who have invade white man's farm…we only ask him why they attack the sons and daughters of the soil, but the traitor say the soil belong to the white man and that our brothers and sisters is invaders. Me I give him one small lesson in history of Zimbabwe – how in the 1890s them British fat stomachs grab our land, pegging farms by riding horse until it drop dead; that just mark only one side of the farm boundary and that's where the corner peg go. But even after this, the traitor, who have been

farm labour supervisor all his life...is still saying that the farmer buy the land. How do you say you buy land that was never sold by no one in the first place unless you like buying things that have been thief from someone? 'What kind of style is that?' me I ask him... (Chikwava 2010: 19).

In no uncertain terms, Chikwava's narrator demonstrates the factual scenario of colonial land- grabs representing "theft by dispossession" (Uadiale and Awala-Ale 2018: 198), thereby undermining indigenous sustainable development. Ironically, the same violently dispossessed Blacks are the ones now blamed for "land-grabs", "land-invasions" and "illegal land-occupations". Such is the tragedy of selective memory on issues to do with social injustice and impoverishment of the locals that are highly dramatised in the criminalisation of the land reform, however its form. Sacco (2008) and Bantekas (2012) query the human right logic of such an approach to land appropriation and how sustainable it can be. Magosvongwe (2014) and Abrahams (2000: 275) affirm that for Africans, land is the beginning and end of their lives. Chikwava's narrator contrasts the lived experiences with the "bookish falsehoods" (Chikwava 2010: 20) that education and tertiary institutions feed the unsuspecting world on using alien centres for critical theory. The invariable result remains continual psychological onslaught.

Chikwava's giving a fleeting dip into the colonial history of violent land-dispossession and expropriation, mischievously reminds readers of foundational facts that must be born in mind when crafting ways and means of dealing with the crises. Choosing to dwell on the protagonist's worries about the cultural ritual of Umbuyiso[1] for his departed Mother also ties up the narrator's concerns about the intertwined nexus between land and trans-generational identities that the indigenous peoples valorise. In the novel, 'Mother' carries dual significance — biological mother as well as home country that carries and nourishes livelihoods. Disconnection from the land

---

[1] Where is the reference?

symbolically means death, materially, spiritually, intellectually, culturally and relationally among other negatives.

By dwelling on Umbuyiso and Mother, Chikwava's nameless narrator prioritises the endeared socio-spiritual and socio-cultural rituals that seal identities, common heritage, belonging and bonding among the indigenous African families trans-generationally. That Umbuyiso drives him to the diaspora in search of material resources to fulfil the ritual symbolically signifies the nexus between local impoverishment and the British metropolis that must be obliged to pay reparations for the initial brutal colonial displacements and dispossessions. These are the factors that amnesiac 'tourist' readings into Zimbabwean land history refuse to appreciate and embrace: "How do you say you buy land that was never sold by no one in the first place unless you like buying things that have been thief from someone? 'What kind of style is that?'" (Chikwava 2010: 19)

By nature, land itself is exclusionary in terms of traditions, philosophy, spirituality and materiality, making studies limited to land and the economy alone far too myopic. This is why 1890 British Effective Occupation and the repression of the indigenous owners of land in 1896-7 First Chimurenga (Ranger 1967; 1985) the real genesis of the crises dogging the Zimbabwean communities across the ages, heightened by the post-2000 land grabs and repossessions. From the fictionalised history in *Harare North* and other literary creations, it is thus anomalous that the violence and trauma of the land occupations be studied outside the lived experiences and historical genesis of the rift and tensions. Misinformation, mis-education, misrepresentation and racially skewed depictions that are ahistorical and removed from the context of place and times often lead to anomalous analyses that prescribe and offer anomalous solutions to the real problems at hand, including "mistranslation of African modes of thought and ecological engagements" (Nhemachena, Kangira and Mlambo 2018: xiii). The explosive nature of the land issue can therefore not be separated from the impoverishing effects of displacement and dispossessions among the indigenous peoples, a case that requires careful thought and navigation as a result.

Tragically, alien-driven studies of land in Zimbabwe have torpedoed local knowledge, and impoverishment has till now been limited mainly to materiality alone. Land is too big to be circumscribed and confined thus. Like the Biblical King Ahab's covetous usurpation of Naboth's vineyard in 1 Kings 21, the ancestral and spiritual heritage of their land gives the Shona moral high ground to keep contesting for their right to land and life. They have no other land to call their own. They have no other country where they can get free right to perpetual habitation, a right that saw the Europeans joining forces fighting off Hitler's Nazi Germany's invasions in the Second World War.

For the indigenous Zimbabweans as shown through Chikwava's nameless narrator's endeavours, securities are differently rooted in the cultural significance of land as the sole abode, assurance, carrier and signifier of life in its totality and wholeness, a subject for another chapter. The post-2000 and crises and the ripple effects must therefore be appreciated contextually. For example, it is very easy to misread, misinterpret and misunderstand the land depictions and economic implosion that Chikwava's narrative gives:

> To the right of station entrance one newspaper vendor stand beside pile of copies of *Evening Standard*. On front page of every one of them papers President Robert Mugabe's face is folded in two. I can still identify His Excellency. The paper say that Zimbabwe has run out of toilet paper Chikwava, 2010: 1 "Prologue").

Ironically, the *Evening Standard* draws international attention to the shortage of toilet paper in Zimbabwe — the cheapest and most basic commodity —, lampooning and satirising the economic failure of the Mugabe regime. The source or root of the dire shortages and an implosive economy is never hinted at. As a fourth estate, media influences perceptions in a very real way. The economic failure is sarcastically linked with the land repossession that Chikwava's narrative brings up to explain the unfortunate economic implosion. Zimbabwe's economy is mainly agro-based, hence the ripple effects of migration, spiralling unemployment and poverty that Chikwava's nameless narrator interrogates. Thus, what meets the eye in the sarcastic *Evening Standard* leading story hardly tells the whole story about the crises. The undergirding quagmire that the Mugabe regime must contend with is never sniffed out. Instead, the paper appears to celebrate the so-called "self-inflicted penury" (Saunders 2006) arising from indigenous Africans' contesting and repossessing their ancestral land from White commercial farmers. The African reading of the unfolding misfortunes brings into focus the penury of colonial dispossession that must be addressed and reparations 'paid' through the repossessions. Chikwava exposes the *Evening Standard*, like other Western-sponsored NGO reports, as an unflinching tool that western imperialists manipulate to summarily castigate and demonise the Zimbabwean government for cannibalising its own peoples, yet the reverse is the fact.

Paradoxically, the colonial exclusionary access to the principal resources using legal instruments such as the 1930 Land Apportionment Act, 1951 Land Husbandry Act, and the 1969 Land Tenure Act, have since hitherto remained sacred despite the continued apartheid development transposed wholesale onto the post-independence state, to the peril of the Africans (Muzondidya 2009). The land issue in Zimbabwe is a matter of the logic of human rights abuses against the local population that the international community has never entertained for reasons they best understand. Chikwava's narrative therefore spins and ricochets in the face of the critic of Zimbabwe's/Mugabe's mismanagement of the economy in the post-independence era. The crises that Chikwava and other writers explore and expose are just indicators and symptoms of a deeper long-standing problem that the international community and other anti-African critics desire to be permanently forgotten. But human beings have a memory, such as Chikwava's narrator highlights above. Further, arguments for compensating dispossessed White farmers exclude their labourers whose loses are even more life-rending, having been subjected to lives of marginalisation and recurrent migration from farm to farm in search of better wages (Harrison 2006). Locally and internationally, the landless and 'propertyless' African majority have no human rights, "reducing

53

[them] to scavenging animals" (Nhemachena 2018: 141), to every right-thinking person's chagrin, that is if human rights are indeed universal. Chikwava's depictions invite re-thinking over who the real perpetrators of violence are in terms the vicissitudes regarding land, the economy and power in post-2000 Zimbabwe. The depictions show the original colonial project's contradictions and its "unparalleled ability to manipulate and exploit crises for its benefit" (Uadiale and Awala-Ale 2018: 199).

Chikwava's satirical depiction of the contradictions and horrors of land dispossession in colonial and post-colonial Zimbabwe takes the discussion to Bulawayo's *We need new names* (2013) that encapsulates the tragedies and vagaries of land displacements from colonial land dispossessions to the post-2000 land repossessions and Operation Restore Order aka Murambatsvina, a history spanning over four generations. The child narrator's misgivings with Murambatsvina's shanty Paradise set up at the margins of Bulawayo city after the 2005 Operation Restore Order in the 'kaka' country is similarly thought-provoking and glaringly telling over the yet to be resolved land inequities and differential human rights in Zimbabwe. "The operation further heightened land seizures in Zimbabwe, as individuals were desperate for land" (Chiduza 2018: 354). The tsunami symbol (Bulawayo 2013: 66-67), a synecdoche of terror, poverty, hunger, trauma, destruction, dispossession and violence succinctly encapsulates lives of turmoil characteristic of the poor landless property-less majority that populate most communities on the margins that are ironically again racially circumscribed and defined. There are no whites in the shanty township, neither are their young subjected to such indescribable violence. The juxtaposition of shanty Paradise —all tin and stretches…the shacks (Bulawayo 2013: 34)—to opulent and serene Budapest, symbolically captures the lived experiences of pauperisation and precarious existence of the Black majority sacrificed for the comforts of the minority alien propertied elites, at the time. Sadly, for survival, the dispossessed and disempowered "abandon the tatters that were our country… not think[ing] about mending the tatters, all [they] thought was: *Leave, abandon, flee, run—anything. Escape*" (Bulawayo 2013: 245). They succumb to further humiliation and disenfranchisement as they flee home for the Diaspora that further cannibalises them:

> And the jobs we worked…Backbreaking jobs. Jobs that gnawed at the bones of our dignity, devoured the meat, tongued the marrow. We took scalding irons and ironed our pride flat" (Bulawayo 2013: 244).

The selected literary narratives therefore memorialise gruesome images that tell a people's present pauperisation inscribed in a past that the international community would rather have us forget. Instead, Western media propaganda and White-authored land narratives would have critics shift blame to the victims of decades of dispossession and disenfranchisement. African poverty is ironically heaped and blamed on self-induced indolence (Harrison 2006) and corruption alone. The genesis of scarce resources, primary of which is differential human worth justifying inequities in accessing land as the key material resource continues to be disqualified as critical determinant of Black poverty in the 21st century. Corruption is intricately interwoven with limited access to principal resources that is fertile ground for a myriad human rights abuses and stagnation of development for the marginalised majority. Benjamin Sibanda's *Whose land is it anyway* further explores and contextualises injuries of such displacement marginalisation in post-land redistribution Zimbabwe.

Nevertheless, discourses of chaotic land reform in a corruption-rife and cronyism environment, making Black-led land redistribution unsustainable, plays to the gallery of land redistribution critics who would rather have a minority own and enjoy the wealth of the land while everyone else survives on crumbs from their tables. Harrison's *Jambanja* is unapologetic about White superiority and Africa sinking back into the dark abyss of savagery at the departure of Whites who are supposedly intellectually, materially, psychologically and economically astute managers of the land. *Jambanja* itself, a term depicting violence, chaos and 'madness', is used to satirise and mock Black efforts at re-organising land distribution and access. Narratives by Sibanda (2016) and Harrison (2006) have corroboration from

Hanlon *et al* (2013; 2015) on the need for State support and markets—local and international— for agriculture to be rewarding and lucrative for those settling on and taking charge of the land.

From the foregoing historical fictional narratives' analyses, land remains the constant denominator and determinant of either poverty or affluence, the major motivation for people's allegiances to political parties' ideologies. Its accessibility, ownership and use are the bedrock of sustainable livelihoods, cordial socio-cultural relationships, environmental and spiritual security, and stable communities generally. Land is everything that the indigenous need because of the multiple securities that it offers/embraces. Historically, Zimbabwean lived experiences also corroborate land is an indisputable game-changer. Barclays (2010), Lazarus (2008), Sadomba (2011), Scoones *et al.* (2011), Hanlon *et al.* (2013) and Sibanda (2016) variously show how land has remained a galvanising/mobilising factor and the mainstay to the "politically explosive topics of race and colonial history" (Barclays 2010: 152). The disruptions and impoverishment traceable to the uprooting, displacements, resettlements and dispossessions authored by the 1890 British Effective Occupation, further buttressed by land settlements of World War 1 and 2 White war veterans, separating the alien land-grabbers from the now destitute "niggers and kaffirs" (Barclays 2010: 150), remain the constant factor demanding practicable remedies. "The people of Zimbabwe, orphans of a cruel colonial agenda, live now with a severe amnesia of their own past and heritage" (Mukonori 2017: 264).

It also remains ironic that the international community respects exclusionary alien-crafted laws drawn up to legalise illegal White occupations, vandalism and immoral land-grabs against a militarily and economically weaker people. Efforts to redress the same laws that authored unscrupulous inequities, transposed onto the politically independent nation and country, continue to be criminalised as retrogressive. Sadly, in such an unequal environment, flagrant abuses of indigenous peoples' right to subsistence continue with impunity in an age whereby human rights advocacy by the international community seems to be at its peak ever. There is no worse duplicity in the history of victims of colonial capitalism and displacements. Zimbabwean politics and historical fiction expose land as the real remedy to frugal living conditions, corruption, political instability, racial hostility and violence characterising most Black peoples' lives in pre- and post-independence Zimbabwe. Because of its central place in peoples' conceptions of destinies, securities, identities and dignity, land remains the major medium of patronage in Zimbabwean politics. Sibanda's *Whose Land is it anyway* (2016) that we cannot afford space in the present chapter for want of brevity, succinctly summarises the constant shifts in land displacements before and after land-occupations, dwelling intricately on the plight of the colonially dispossessed landless Black majority, but more specifically on the plight and horrid experiences of the 'man in the middle's relentless efforts towards achieving sustainable livelihoods. The category of the 'man in the middle' includes the coloureds, farm labourers, domestic workers, women, landless youths and peasant women, the 'jilted' ex-combatants continually exploited for their patriotism, and even church priests at times, cumulatively deserving a separate examination.

In the post-land evictions period, land-owners across the racial divide adopt dirty frustrating strategies to muster control of labour and kill off productivity on farms repossessed by the indigenous peoples—another irking point regarding self-importance and expendability of those considered lesser human. Harrison (2006) admits to White vandalism and disposal of machinery and farm equipment, as well as buying labourers' loyalty/trust using trinkets and inducing fear of losing 'homes', at the onset of Black farm occupations. The labourers' fears of losing the only 'homes' they have known is real (Barclays 2010:150-152; Sibanda 2016). People who worked for White commercial farmers could not stay after the take-overs because in view of the new Black farm-owners, they were "contaminated by the White man's ways" (Sibanda 2016: 259) and feared to be "colluding with the White man" (Ibid: 258), yet, "the farmer's property had to be destroyed" (Ibid: 119) for ironically simple-minded people genuinely believe that "[w]hatever symbolises the privilege that our erstwhile rulers enjoyed must be destroyed thoroughly. [They]/We need a fresh start" (Sibanda 2016: 284). Occupations on their own do not spell the resolution to land displacements and un/sustainable livelihoods engendered by colonial land dispossession. Rather, fresh terror is unleashed on the unsuspecting would-be land beneficiaries, engendering further mayhem induced by opportunist politicians and bureaucrats' avarice, instigating viciousness of police brutality against 'unofficially resettled' land invaders, who are subjected to further forced removals despite their having pioneered recovery of the lost lands. Themba Ndlovu, who pioneers and engineers such resettlements and occupations in the Macheke Hwedza areas, and labelled terror to all White farmers in the area, also hailing from Nhowe Communal Lands in Macheke is ironically denied ownership of land on invaded farms in the area. Paul Kamera, a land officer from the Ministry of Lands in Harare, displaces Themba Ndlovu on grounds of an Ndebele-sounding name, a presumed Ndebele ancestry and therefore deemed an alien in the area, coupled with the fact that Themba had not applied for resettlement on the occupied farms. From indications of the shifting goal posts, including legalism to orderly resettlements using contradictory discriminating factors, the land revolution remains to be yet amicably resolved.

From the depictions in Sibanda's *Whose land is it anyway*, there arises a fresh conundrum on how to deal with the repossessed land intra-racially, in itself thorny, very tricky and potentially explosive because of ethnic identities, class differences, cronyism, corruption, abuse of power/office, police brutality-induced displacements, avarice and drive for self-aggrandisement among the opportunistic politicians vis-à-vis the genuinely disempowered peasants and farm workers. It thus goes without saying that post-2000 farm-occupations and farm-invaders' eventual fate demand separate examination in the debacle of displacements and quest for sustainable livelihoods. The goings-on on the resettled farms show the landless peasants, land-hungry and homeless former farm labourers, marginalised and vulnerable masses, particularly 'unsettled' liberation struggle ex-combatants who are perpetually prone to continual displacement, pawns in the hands of politicians and the ruling elite. They are kept running and hoping.

Conclusion

A close reading of our writers' memorialisation of Blacks' lived historical experiences partly helps unravelling the answer to the real problem of land in/accessibility that cannot be perpetually ignored, not only in Zimbabwe, but in Southern Africa and other former colonies. Re-reading, re-visiting, re-thinking and re-constructing history through historical fictional narratives is envisaged to proffer practicable holism to the land problems as legalism alone cannot offer sustainable solutions to the ravages of displacements that mostly the majority landless have suffered for generations, in an ancestral country 'divinely' their own. *Death Throes: The Trial of Nehanda, Harare North, Jambanja, We need new names* and *Whose land is it anyway*, are just but a few of the numerous narratives that repeat the same narrative of land injustices and precarious existence that one racial grouping has endured for generations at the pleasure of a minority White settler race that continues milking and enjoying the sympathy of the broad international White community. "No amount of ideological ritual chanting of "justice", "equality", "freedom", "democracy", "transparency" "accountability", or "rule of law" has helped to undo historical effects of material dispossession, enslavement, disinheritance and impoverishment in Africa" (Nhemachena *et al.* 2018: 2).

Apart from fictionalised and historicised land injustices, evidence shows that disruptions and dislocations of displacements and dispossessions is abundant and prolific. Thus, demanding that the 'genuine' family of humankind transforms attitudes so that genuine renewal, sustainable peace, secure livelihoods for all and efforts towards re-building Zimbabwe from the ashes of colonial occupation and the armed liberation struggle, could become a reality. It is my firm hope that the tragedy with human nature that is selfishly selective in our seeing, our knowing, our reading, our hearing and our thinking, do not impede genuine land renewal in Zimbabwe. For too long, the elite, propertied White settlers and the international community have continuously delayed efforts at dealing a permanent blow to the carnage of land injustices glaring in the faces of an erstwhile insensitive and pretentious lot singing their voices hoarse for observance and safeguarding of human rights in the debt-ridden and 'developing' countries such as Zimbabwe. The historical fictional narratives selected in this chapter decry the duplicity and cannibalistic trend authored at Effective Occupation's indigenous land dispossessions and recurrent displacements that remain the worst enemy towards genuine renewal and transformation of livelihoods across the racial divide. Settler colonialism, especially barbaric and exclusionary settler minority land-hold to the peril of indigenous populations, cannot be postponed to perpetuity with lives and livelihoods of the marginalised Black majority continuously plunging into further mayhem. Without sinking into the abyss of historical amnesia, people-centred development must first deal with the inequities created at Effective Occupation whose ripple effects continuously foment and nurture crises for the Black majority who have no other country, no other home, no alternative haven, and no other land.

References

Achebe, C. (1990) *Hopes and Impediments*. New York: Doubleday.

Adeleke, T. (2015) "Africa and Afrocentric Historicism: A Critique". Retrieved from Scires. http://www. Scrip.org/journal/aaaahshttp://dx.doi.org/10.4236/ahs.2015.4 3016.

Buckle, C. (2001) *African tears: The Zimbabwe land invasions*. Johannesburg: Covos-Day Books.

Barclay, P. (2010) *Zimbabwe: Years of Hope and Despair*. London. Berlin. New York. Sydney: Bloomsbury.

Bulawayo, N. (2013) *We need new names*. New York/Boston/London: Reagan Arthur Books.

Chiduza, L. (2018) The Jurisprudence of the Zimbabwean Judiciary on the Protection of the Right to Property with Specific Reference to the Fast Track Land Reform Programme and Operation *Murambatsvina*. In Nhemachena, A., Warikandwa, T. V. and Amoo, S. K. (Eds.) (2018) *Social and Legal Theory in the Age of Decoloniality: (Re-)Envisioning Pan-African Jurisprudence in the 21st Century*. Mankon, Bamenda, Cameroon: Langaa Research & Publishing CIG. 327-365.

Chikwava, B. (2009) *Harare North*. Harare: Weaver Press.

Chivaura, V. G. (2016) African History: An Intangible Living Force. In Magosvongwe, R., Mlambo, O. B. and Ndlovu, E. (Eds.) (2016) *Africa's Intangible Heritage and Land: Emerging Perspectives*. Harare: University of Zimbabwe Publications.1-5.

Gomo, M. (2010) *A Fine Madness*. London: Ayebia Clarke

Harrison, E. (2006) *Jambanja*. Harare: Maioio Publishers.

Hoskins, J. A. (1992) "Eurocentrism vs Afrocentricism: A Geopolitical linkage Analysis". Retrieved from http://www.jstor.org/stable/278453323.

Magosvongwe, R. (2003) African Literature: Whose Story, Which Lenses and Whose Voice? Unpublished paper presented at the Zimbabwe International Book Fair Indaba, Monomotapa Crowne Plaza, Harare, 29th July, 2003.

Magosvongwe, R. (2014) Land and Identity in Zimbabwean Fiction Writings in English from 2000 to 2010: a Critical Analysis. University of Cape Town, Unpublished DPhil thesis.

Magosvongwe, R. and Nyamende, A. (2014) This is our Land: Land and Identity in Selected Zimbabwean black- and white-authored fictional narratives in English published between 2000 and 2010. *South African Journal of African Languages (SAJAL) 35* (2): 237-248.

Manjengwa, J., Hanlon, J. and Smart, T. (2015) Zimbabwe Takes Back its Land: Is this the 'Best Use' of the Land". In Makwavarara, Z., Magosvongwe, R. and Mlambo, O. B. (Eds.) (2015) *Dialoguing Land and Indigenisation in Zimbabwe and other Developing Countries: Emerging Perspectives*. Harare: University of Zimbabwe Publications.

Mazama, A. (2001) The Afrocentric Paradigm: Contours and Definitions. *Journal of Black Studies 3* (4):387-405.

Mgbeadichie, C. (2015) Critical Concept of Afrocentrism in Nigerian Literature. University of Exeter, Unpublished PhD thesis.

Moyana, R. (2000) An Historical study of a Selection of the white Rhodesian Novel in English, 1890-1994: Content and Character. Harare: University of Zimbabwe, Unpublished PhD Thesis.

Moyo, S., Helliker, K & Murisa, T. (ed.) (2008) *Contested Terrain: Land Reform and Civil Society in Contemporary Zimbabwe.* Pietermaritzburg: S & S Publishers.

Mukonori S. J. Father F. (2017) Man in the Middle: A Memoir. Harare: The House of Books (Pvt) Ltd.

Mungoshi, C. (1975) *Waiting for the rain.* Salisbury: Salisbury Publishing House.

Mutasa, G. (1985). *The Contact.* Gweru: Mambo Press.

Muzondidya, J. (2009) From Buoyancy to Crisis, 1980-1997. In Raftopoulos, B and Mlambo, A. (Ed.) (2009) *Becoming Zimbabwe* Harare: Weaver Press. 167-200.

Nhemachena, A. and Kaundjua, M. (2018) Incorporated or Cannibalised by Posthuman Others? Sanctions and Witchcraft in Contemporary Zimbabwe. In Nyamnjoh, F. B. (Ed.) (2018) *Eating and Being Eaten: Cannibalism as Food for Thought.* Mankon, Bamenda, Cameroon: Langaa Research & Publishing CIG.127-155.

Nhemachena, A., Mlambo, N. and Kangira, J. (2018) "Materialities and the Resilient Global Frontierisation of Africa: An Introduction". In Nhemachena, A., Kangira, J. and Mlambo, N. (Eds.) (2018) *Decolonisation of Materialities or Materialisation of (Re-)Colonisation? Symbolisms, Languages, Ecocriticism and (Non)Representation in 21st Century Africa.* Mankon, Bamenda, Cameroon: Langaa Research & Publishing CIG. 1-53.

————————————————— (2018) "Foreword". In Nhemachena, A., Kangira, J. and Mlambo, N. (Eds.). (2018) *Decolonisation of Materialities or Materialisation of (Re-)Colonisation? Symbolisms, Languages, Ecocriticism and (Non)Representation in 21st*

Century Africa. Mankon, Bamenda, Cameroon: Langaa Research & Publishing CIG. p.xiii-xv.

Nhemachena, A., Warikandwa, T. V. and Mpofu, N. (2018) "Transitology as Cannibalism/Cannibalism as Transitology: An Examination of (Neo)Imperial Processes of Consuming African people". *Africology: Journal of Pan African Studies, Vol 2.* No.6: 45ff.

Raftopoulos, B. (2009) "The Crisis in Zimbabwe, 1998-2008". In Raftopoulos, B. and Malmbo, A. (Eds.) (2009) *Becoming Zimbabwe.* Harare: Weaver Press. 201-232.

Ramose, M. B. (2005) *African Philosophy through Ubuntu.* Harare: Mond Book Publishers.

Samupindi, C. (1990) *Death Throes: The Trial of Nehanda.* Gweru: Mambo Press.

Scoones, I. Marongwe, N., Mavedzenge, B., Mahenehene, J. and Murime, F. (2010) *Zimbabwe's Land Reform: Myths and Realities.* Woodbridge: James Currey.

Shire, G. (2003) "The Case for Robert Mugabe: Sinner or Sinned Against". *The Black Scholar 37* (1): 32-35.

Sibanda, B. S. (2016) *Whose land is it anyway.* Harare: Self-publishing.

Tagwira, V. (2006) *The Uncertainty of Hope.* Harare: Weaver Press.

Uadiale, M. and Awala-Ale, A. (2018) Gendered Experiences: Land Grabs and the De-Feminization of Africa's Agrarian Futures. In Nhemachena, A., Kangira, J. and Mlambo, N. (Eds.) (2018) *Decolonisation of Materialities or Materialisation of (Re-)Colonisation? Symbolisms, Languages, Ecocriticism and (Non)Representation in 21ˢᵗ Century Africa.* 195-218.

Vera, Y. (1993) *Nehanda.* Harare: Baobab Books.

wa Thiongo, Ngugi. (1987) *Devil on the cross.* Oxford: Heinemann Educational Publishers.

wa Thiongo, Ngugi. (2009) Recovering Our Memory: South Africa in the Black Imagination. In *The Steve Biko Memorial Lectures 2000-2008.* Johannesburg: The Steve Biko Foundation and Macmillan. 51-72.

Chapter Three

'Mapfupa angu achamuka' (My bones will rise again): Spirituality, History, Memory and Ancestry in Land Ownership 'Debates' in Zimbabwe

Collen Sabao

Introduction

The name 'Nehanda' in Shona spiritual cosmology is synonymous with the Chimurenga liberation wars – the battle for land ownership in Zimbabwe. 'Nehanda, Nyakasikana', a spirit medium who organised and led the 1896-7 uprising against the White colonialists (Pasura 2010), is historically acclaimed as one of the greatest and most revered spirit mediums in Zimbabwe. She is credited with further playing a magnanimous role in the second Chimurenga, albeit from the grave – spiritually guiding liberation fighters in their quest to reclaim land stolen from them by British colonialists. Guillotined for her defiance of white colonial rule and its accompanying land appropriation, Nehanda is credited with having predicted that Zimbabwe's children would someday rise and defeat the colonialists and reclaim their land. She is credited with, before her murder, having exclaimed *'Mapfupa angu achamuka'* (My bones will rise again) – meaning there would be more rebellions in the future. Her words. *'Mapfupa angu achamuka'*, (and supposed spiritual leadership) are literary taken as the motivation for the liberation fighters during the war. The Second Chimurenga within Zimbabwe's history is metaphorically and literally viewed as a fulfilment of Nehanda's warning to her killers – the rising of her bones. As Makaudze and Gudhlanga (2014) would argue, 'the second Chimurenga (liberation) that culminated in the advent of independence for Zimbabwe was also partly due to the inspiration that Zimbabweans got from Nehanda's promise that her bones would rise'. Land ownership and identity are thus inseparable in Zimbabwean collective cultural and spiritual memory. The ancestral link to one's land is embedded in the cultural baggage one inherits at birth. Within Zimbabwean cultural cosmology, claims to land ownership often evoke ancestral historical ownership. At birth, a new born baby's umbilical cord is buried on the soil/land of his/her ancestors, mingling him/her with the soil and joining him/her with the ancestors (Dzvairo 1981). However, it is necessary to note that the baby itself is not interchangeable with the umbilical cord. Critically examining selected and liberation war and postliberation war songs, the chapter discusses the nexus between spirituality, ancestry and land ownership in Zimbabwe.

Liberation War: Multidimensional Concepts of Land among the Shona and/or Zimbabwean People

The period of colonialism in Zimbabwe, beginning in the early 1890s was characterised by displacements of natives from 'the lands of their ancestors'. The Black natives were forcefully removed from fertile lands which the White colonialists arrogated to themselves. The First Chimurenga (first war of resistance) of 1896 marked the initial defiance to White colonial robbery. It was a resistance to land dispossession and displacements of African people. It was a battle for land. Land was central to the Black man's fight against White colonialists in both the First and Second Chimurengas. It also become central to the operationalisation of the land redistribution of 1999 and early 2000s in Zimbabwe, dubbed the Third Chimurenga. But what is land?

Land, particularly among the Shona speaking people of Zimbabwe, can be conceptualised in multitudinous ways and a multifarious number of spiritually and ideological positionings. There are however three basic ways in which 'land' can be thought of. Firstly, land can be thought of in its most basic and primal ways – as *ivhu* 'the soil' that gives life through agriculture. The sustenance of Shona families is largely through land. The Shona, and by extension the Zimbabweans, generally speaking, are an agro-based community and as such subsistence farming is the source of livelihood for most families. Before the period of colonial dispossession and

66

displacement, Shona societies were largely communal and rural [with some towns - and industries such as mining, smelting, weaving, carving, trading and so on (Posselt 1935; Ellert 1984; Nhemachena and Dhakwa 2017)] and hence largely agro-based. One would then understand why the land theft by colonialists constituted a serious blow to African sources of food and livelihood. Thus, the colonial theft of African land and other resources was a cause of discontent and anguish and thus agitation and hence the desire for war.

Secondly, land can be thought of as *nyika* 'country or territory'. African communities are demarcated and identified through chieftainships which often border on "tribal", dialectical or "ethnic" identities. For example, in what is now called Manicaland Province of Zimbabwe, traditional precolonial boundaries are still recognised. One finds such descriptions as *nyika ya Mambo Zimunya* 'the territory of King Zimunya' and *nyika ya Mambo Mutasa* 'the country of King Mutasa', among others. With regards to these particular two for example, Musaemura Bonas Zimunya (personal communication 2018), explains that they are bordered by rivers which then signal the demarcations of the specific territory particular kings have dominion over. Envisioning and conceptualising land in this way has a spiritual import. Kings inherited these lands from their forefathers and ancestors and thus needed to protect this spiritual and cultural hieroglyph – an ancestral inheritance. The liberation wars, fought over land were thus not just physical between the colonialists and the living but also spiritual – spiritual in the sense that the ancestors, as custodians of the land also had a stake and claim to it. Musiiwa (2008) explains thus:

> As the owners and guardians of the land, who lie in its soil, the ancestors wanted the land to be freed. The fight for liberation was therefore not only for the liberation of the living, but also the departed. Consequently, unity between the two was integral and symbolic to the liberation of both physical and spiritual Zimbabwe (Musiiwa 2008: 20).

Displacements from such lands through forced removals were thus tantamount to culturally and spiritually unanchoring a people, disconnecting them with the land of their ancestors and forefathers – the land that all their forebears owned, productively lived on and passed on to them as inheritance. In an interview, one of the most prominent spirit mediums in Zimbabwe's history and spiritual cosmology, Chief Rekayi Tangwena makes an interesting narration of the oral history of his land and people. Overall, in explaining his resistance to forced removals by White colonialists, he gives out a line of his ancestors from which he had inherited the land. Hence it is no surprise that the refrains *nyika yamadzitateguru* 'land that belongs to the ancestors' featured prominently in the liberation war discourses, including even in Zimbabwe's current national anthem which refers to the country as such. The Fast Track Land Reform Programme (popularly known in Eurocentric scholarship as the Zimbabwe Land Grabs of the late 1990s and early 2000s) dubbed in Zimbabwean and ZANU PF discourses as the Third Chimurenga evinces such ideological convictions of reclaiming the land of the ancestors.

Land can also be thought of in the spiritual sense – a link between the dead and the living. It is an emblem for the collapse of time by connecting the dead and the living. Traditionally, though the custom has faded away, when a child was born, their umbilical cord was buried in the soil in the homestead, the same soil in which the forefathers and ancestors' remains were buried. In the words of poet Godfrey Dzvairo, in Kadhani and Zimunya (1981:13) 'in the poem "Birth right" views the ritual performed at birth as a commission given to the African to guard jealously the land as an infinite heritage'. He says,

> They took my umbilical cord
> And buried it
> In the fertile soil of the field nearby
> Mingling me with the soil
> On which blood was to fall
> Giving me birth right
> To guard dutifully and jealously
> With pride and reverence.

The ritual becomes a sacrosanct symbol for the oneness of the ancestral remains and umbilical cord with the soil. The umbilical cord bonds the child to the ancestors whose remains are already interred in the land. In some instances, ceremonies are conducted to introduce the new born baby to the ancestors. Such ceremonies can oftentimes be so elaborate and quiet spiritual. This evinces the deep rooted belief that the dead and the living can commune within such cultural belief systems. This belief, part of the Zimbabwean spiritual cosmos is for example the reason why each time the government relocates people, they also exhume the graves and reburials of remains are done in the new location. This is in a bid to ensure that the connection between the dead and their living is not cut off. However, on the other hand, widows and widowers are enjoined to undergo rituals to separate themselves from their dead spouses. In this regard, the Shona people do not only value connections with the dead but they also desire separation from the realms of the dead or some of the dead people.

The Role of Spirit Mediums and Ancestors in Life amongst the Shonas

Death amongst the Shona speaking people, and by extension within most African cultures' spiritual cosmology is not thought of as the ultimate end to all human life. In fact, it is conceived of as a graduation to the afterlife, *nyikadzimu* (the spiritual/ancestral realm) in which the deceased joins the ancestors, the departed forefathers in their role of watching over their earthly progeny. The existence of *nyikadzimu* means that African ancestors are not necessarily imprisoned in the soil/land where their remains are interred – ancestors are not interchangeable with the soil/land but rather they own the land/soil. The dead (revered as the living dead in this case), have power, control and authority over the living who are constantly seeking guidance and help through prayers and incantations. So profound is the believed power of the living dead (ancestors) over the living that ceremonies are held in their honour to beseech them for rains, good luck, and protection from enemies (physical and spiritual) among other things. Benyera (2016: 7171) explains this dialogic relationship between the unborn, the living and the dead as follows:

> Death occupies a special space in the Shona cosmology. It is a central part of the three realms of life, the 'living unborn', the 'living living' and the 'living dead'. It connects these three life forms together by ensuring the passage of life from the realm of the 'living living' to that of the 'living dead' (Benyera 2016: 7171).

The ancestors (living dead), are thus all seeing and have the power to peep into the futures of the living and guide them through their earthly life. For example, when a child is leaving home to go to school or start a job in a distant place, ceremonies are held to beseech the ancestors to guide his/her way and protect them from all harm, physical or spiritual. At the onset of each agricultural season, ceremonies are held to ask the ancestors for adequate rains so that 'their people' do not starve but instead receive bumper harvests. After harvests, ceremonies are also held to thank the ancestors for the produce. Ancestors are thus believed to have control over our daily lives, be it in our economic, social, political or spiritual existences. In explaining this role of ancestors in daily lives of the Shona specifically focusing on one spirit medium known as Chaminuka, Gelfand (1951: 13 – 14) opines that:

> The Mashona do not know Mwari (God) or approach Him directly, but only through Chaminuka the great messenger, the link between God and the people. No one dare show disrespect to Chaminuka for when he is annoyed there is no rain…

What then is the role of ancestors in life? Ancestors encapsulate the totality of a person. Each aspect of a person's life (private or public) is governed and determined by the ancestors. They influence each aspect of our lives, acting as guides and counsel through the journey of earthly life. In the spiritual sense, they act as gods, to be consulted at every turn. The Shona people generally believe in the afterlife and generally have a strong conviction about the role of the dead in the affairs of the living living (earthly living). For example, following Lifton's (1976) view on life and death as biosocial, the Shona people believe that they are and continue to be 'part of [their] children, family, and other groups, and this provides a continuity to [their] lives despite our own personal death'. This explains for example the *kurova guva* ritual performed by the Shonas in which after at least a year has passed after the death of a person, a ceremony is conducted to 'graduate' the spirit of the deceased into the afterlife and join the ancestors. As Benyera (2016: 7175) explains, 'Shonas are characterised by their ability to survive bodily death as exemplified by the various forms of communication that exist between the living living and the living dead. Without death, the living dead would not be in a position, not just to communicate with the living living but to play their role of protecting and sometimes punishing the living living'.

The Link between Land and Ancestry: Spiritualism and the Liberation Wars in Zimbabwe

There is an ancestral link between Africans and their land. Wars have been fought over territorial disputes. Within most African communities' spiritual and cultural cosmologies, the connection between human beings and land goes beyond the grave. Land is conceived of among many African cultures as a form of property, identity and cultural inheritance. To own a piece of land is considered, for example, among the Shona people as a symbol of growth, maturity and source of pride. It is an inheritance from the forefathers – the ancestors. There is temporal complexity within African cosmologies. The past, present and future can sometimes be collapsed into one. There is always the ancestral presence in our lives and we trust them to predict the future and protect us from harm. The ancestors protect our lands (our inheritance from them) and provide for us through the land – which explains why we petition them for rains and bumper harvests (Nhemachena 2017). This relationship between ancestors and their land as well as their ability to protect it and us, is why during the second Chimurenga the freedom fighters consulted with spirit mediums (ancestors) for guidance and prognostication of future battles.

Ranger (1982: 351) gives an example of the role played by another prominent spirit medium in Zimbabwe's liberation history, Chaminuka, in the war. He argues that the Shona fighters also moved towards the 'nationalist use of the Chaminuka myth ... in the 1950s Mashona reaction looked to the past for comfort and took as tribal hero the tall bearded prophet Chaminuka... a great prophet and symbol of... resistance... a binding factor in resisting the settlers'. This rallying behind Chaminuka was a result of his earlier prophecy that his spirit would come back and help fight the White settlers. Apart from Chaminuka, two other prominent spirit mediums are pivotal in the understanding of the role of ancestry in land disputes in Zimbabwe – Nehanda and Kaguvi. According to Chiwome (1990: 243):

Nehanda, the first Shona politico-religious leader to be executed for trying to oust the whites, is another historical and legendary figure. The most memorable hero of the first Chimurenga, she is said to be one of the daughters of Murenga Sororenzou Pfumojena, a progenitor of the Shona from whom the name Chimurenga is derived. Her spirit came to Mazoe Valley from Dande with Nyamita. Tradition has it that her spirit possessed Charwe, whose nickname is Nyakasikana, the Chiweshe spirit medium who, together with Kagubi, was executed by the whites in April 1898 for organizing the Shona against white settlement. It is said that the spirit of Nehanda lived on until the second Chimurenga, in which it was often the guide of guerrillas operating from the Mozambique bases. Before her execution, Nehanda is said to have foretold the coming of the second Chimurenga in the well-known phrase *mapfupa achamuka* (bones will reincarnate). She also symbolizes the indomitable spirit of the oppressed people.

Because music was one of the most popular modes of propaganda and morale during the wars, it is also important to observe how allusions of ancestry and spirit mediums were used in the songs. As Sabao (2018) explains, the role and power of music within Zimbabwe's liberation wars is historically recorded and the production of songs that historicised and conjured the 'spirits' was pertinent to the continuity of the struggle:

> The role of music in Zimbabwean politics during and post the liberation wars can never be overemphasised. The use of the popular culture of music as a political, ideology-spreading tool can be seen as an ingenious innovation by protagonists traversing a complex political context. The history of the use of ... music and ... in Zimbabwe... spans far back to the times of the Chimurenga Wars (wars of liberation against the British colonial settlers). Within these contexts, songs and jingles were used as a form of moral boost as well as a recruitment mechanism. Songs were also used to historicise colonial processes and their inherent evils in order to encourage natives to take up arms. In this regard, music performed commissariat duties, entertained and boosted the morale of the fighters and acted as a reservoir of memory and history (Sabao, 2018: 111-112).

Musiiwa (2008) further explains that as the Shona people believe in an afterlife, they also seem to believe in the role of the dead in the affairs of the earthly living. In this regard, allusions to the power and influence of spirit mediums in the war of liberation are successfully embedded in the lyrics in order to motivate the freedom fighters to fight. Since they believed in the power of the ancestors, they would be susceptible to believe in the predictions the ancestors made about the war. I consider here the Harare Mamboes song *Mbuya Nehanda*.

> *Mbuya Nehanda kufa vachitaura shuwa*
> *'When Nehanda died, she spoke'*
> *Kuti tinotora sei nyika ino*
> *About how to regain this country/land'*
> *Shoko rimwe ravakatiudza*
> *The only word she told us'*
> *"Tora gidi uzvitonge"*
> *'Grab the gun, and rule yourself'*

73

(Harare Mambos, *Mbuya Nehanda*: Year Unknown)

In the song, the message is that Nehanda had foretold that the only way to regain the land is to take up arms and fight. This provided a powerful motivation to join the liberation war for most combatants because of their belief in the power of the ancestors and their spirit mediums. The word of the spirit mediums, specifically in this instance Nehanda, are powerful and true and need to be heeded. Ngoshi (2009) further explains the mystical and mythical roles that spirit mediums and ancestry played in the liberation wars. Nationalist discourses were punctuated by historical allusions to the words of the ancestors whose spirits manifested through various mediums over time. Ngoshi (2009) argues in this instance that:

> Nationalists constantly invoked the role of Nehanda's spirit during the second war of liberation in the country. Again this in itself was a way of authenticating the war of liberation as a continuation of that which Nehanda 'had started'. Her later medium was even ferried to Mozambique by the Zimbabwe African National Liberation Army (ZANLA) freedom fighters in the 1970s. There is no doubt that her presence in Mozambique was meant to establish legitimacy and ancestral-spirit approval of the war.

Invoking the names of these magnanimous spirits, Chaminuka, Nehanda and Kaguvi, made the 'fighters optimistic that victory was certain since, by the spiritual presence of [the ancestral spirits], the fighters were by proxy the reincarnation of the 1896 fighters. The religious significance of the legendary figures created greater conviction in the cause of the war than rationality alone could' (Chiwome 1990: 244). Musiiwa (2008: 19) further explicates the strong religious conviction the Shonas had on ancestors to help fight the wars. He argues thus:

> This is why there is a whole body of *pungwe* [night vigils], choral and folk songs that appeal for the intervention of Nehanda, Chaminuka, Kaguvi and other national spirits to protect the sons and

74

daughters fighting the war. Indeed, there were a number of spirit mediums inside and outside the country (e.g. in Mozambique) to whom guerrillas relied upon for advice concerning the whereabouts of the enemy.

When one examines for example the legendary poem *Nehanda Nyakasikana* (made more famous through its recitation by former vice president Simon Muzenda), one feels the level of belief that the Shonas had on the power of ancestry in assisting them to fight back for their land from White colonialists.

> *O Nehanda Nyakasikana!*
> *O Nehanda Nyakasikana!*
> *Kunozove riniko Isu VaNyai tichitambudzika?*
> *How long shall we the Vanyai groan and suffer*
> *Mweya unoera!*
> *Holy tutelary spirit!*
> *Kunozove riniko Isu vaNyai tichidzvinyirirwa?*
> *How long shall we the Vanyai suffer oppression?*
> *Ko, inga taneta wani nekumwa misodzi?...*
> *We are weary of drinking our tears...*
> *Vana vacheche vatinobereka,*
> *The young ones our women bear*
> *vawakatipa Iwe Samasimba,*
> *given us by you Great Spirit*
> *vanova ndivo vadyi Venhaka dzedu,*
> *who should be inheritors of our hard earned substance*
> *nhasi vokura vakasunzumara ...*
> *all have an uneasy time in their own land...*
> *Rusununguko Nehanda nderupi?*
> *Where is our Freedom Nehanda*
> *Hamungaburukiriwo kwatiri here?*
> *Won't you come down to help us?*
> *Harahwa dzedu dzobatwa sepwere*
> *Our old man are treated like children*
> *munyika yawakavapa, musiki wengoni!...*

75

In the land that you gave them, Merciful Creator...

Tine chitadzo chakakura sei?

What foul crime have we committed?

Chokubva matiramwa zvakadai?

That you should abandon us like this?

Nehanda Nyakasikana! Kunozova riniko

Nehanda Nyakasikana how long shall it be

Isu vaNyai tichitambudzika?

That we the Vanyai must suffer?

Mhondoro Tsvene!

Holy tutelary Lion Spirit!

Kunozova riniko

How long shall it be

Isu vaNyai tichidzvinyirirwa

That we the Vanyai must suffer oppression?

In the poem, a lamentation, the poet 'call[s] upon the spirit of Nehanda to redeem or liberate the suffering people.' (Makamani & Choto no date: x). The poet emotively begs for the intervention of Nehanda to deliver them from the bondage of colonialism to Freedom. Incantations of this nature, which also deify Nehanda to the level of God by referencing her as *Mweya Unoera* 'Holy spirit', evince a deep-rooted belief in the power of spirit mediums and ancestors to assist the living in the fight against colonial forces – and hence regain the land from them. Makamani and Choto (no date) further explicate the power of the poem in the recruitment and morale of freedom fighters. They postulate that:

> It is a historical fact that the poem "Nehanda Nyakasikana," was chanted in many rallies during the liberation struggle. The vividness of the metaphors and their emotional appeal galvanized many youths into taking the onerous decision of joining the struggle to wrestle the nation from the claws of the enemy (Makamani & Choto, no date: x).

The religious beliefs of the Shona people thus were an invaluable part of the war, as is evinced by the inimitable roles of Nehanda,

Kaguvi, Chaminuka and other spirit mediums. Postulated by Chiwome (1990: 245), '[t]he names of these territorial spirits (*mhondoro*) were frequently invoked for guidance and protection during times of crises. Spirit mediums were often consulted by guerrillas for direction in executing the war'. This unfettered belief in the role of the *mhondoro* and *vadzimu* in the fight against White settlers is proof enough that within the Shona spiritual cosmos, war, '…like any other important Shona activity, could not be separated from traditional religion. The guerrillas, their relatives and the people often made supplications to the spirits (vadzimu)' (245).

When the Sins of the 'Ancestors' Haunt the Grandchildren: Politics of Entitlement, The Third Chimurenga and the Discourse of Land Appropriation Without Compensation

In 1999 and subsequently the early 2000s, the Zimbabwe African National Union Patriotic Front (ZANU PF) led by war veterans, embarked on a massive reclamation of land that was stolen by colonialists. The exercise saw the forced removal of White farmers, who owned the larger part of commercial farms in Zimbabwe. The exercise was dubbed the Third Chimurenga, regarded as a continuation of the earlier two liberation wars (The First and Second Chimurangas respectively). Again, in the now common spirit of appropriating the national historical metanarrative, ancestral, spiritual and historical allusions to the liberation war are made. Indigenous people in various countries within the world are currently claiming back their land and other resources which were stolen by colonialists. Thus, the ZANU PF government has similarly embarked on land redistribution exercise to benefit indigenous Black people. The government of Zimbabwe justified its actions by drawing on the liberation war rhetoric. In fact, both liberation wars (the First and Second Chimurengas) are used as historical allusions to justify and legitimise the land restitution dubbed the "Third Chimurenga." Mbare Chimurenga, a musical ensemble that emerged around the period of the land redistribution produced several musical albums. In seeking legitimation, again the spirit mediums are invoked. Land redistribution is cast as a fulfilment of Nehanda's prophecy – repossession of the land, the land of the ancestors. An example can be drawn from the song Muri Musoja (You are a soldier) in which the legend of Nehanda is invoked.

> *Kana ndichiti Nehanda handireve kahanda,*
> When I say Nehanda, I don't mean a puppy
> *[the Shona word for a puppy is kahanda];*
> *Ndinoreva Nehanda mudzimu mukuru muZimbabwe*
> *I mean Nehanda, Zimbabwe's greatest ancestral spirit.*
> (Mbare Chimurenga, 2010)

Historical allusions are made by using positive resources to describe the liberation war heroes and the soldiers who died on the battlefield. Allusions to the spirit medium "Nehanda" are quite pertinent to the analysis of the "importance" of the liberation war. Nehanda, historically acclaimed as one of the greatest and most revered spirit mediums, is credited with playing a magnanimous role in the liberation war—spiritually guiding liberation fighters. Looked at from a different angle, empire also has its ideological and spiritual mediums in Africa – there are Africans that are animated by imperial ideologies and spiritualities that thwart African efforts towards liberation (Behrend et al 1999; Nhemachena 2017). Thus, Behrend et al (1999:13) observe that:

> The disenchantment of the modern world and the disappearance of spirits, as foretold by Westerners, has not taken place, either at home or in other parts of the world. In Africa as well as Europe, many spirits and their mediums are part of local as well as global or transglobal cultures. Thus, we find Christian spirits named Hitler and Mussolini or King Bruce after Bruce Lee, the Kung – Fu actor, in a pantheon of new Christian holy spirits in Northern Uganda, who are waging war against the government...

Musiyiwa (2008:19) explains the invaluable contribution that the ancestors and spiritual legends brought to the fight for Zimbabwe as follows:

> The liberation war was inspired by the legends of the First Chimurenga, especially Nehanda, Kaguvi and other important national spirits, such as Chaminuka. This gave the war a strong religions dimension. The nationalists and particularly the masses believed that they could not fight a successful war without appealing to their ancestors for protection.

Guillotined for her defiance of White colonialists, she is credited with having predicted that Zimbabweans would someday rise and defeat the colonialists and reclaim their land. She is credited with having said, as alluded to earlier on, *"Mapfupa angu achamuka"* ("My bones will rise again"—meaning there would be more rebellions in the future). Her words (and supposed spiritual leadership) are literally taken as the motivation for the liberation fighters during the war as well as the justification for the land redistribution exercise. Both instances are cast as the fulfilment of her alleged prognostication and vision. "The prophecy of Mbuya Nehanda that *'Mapfupa angu achamuka'* (My bones shall rise again) became the watch words of the gallant 'sons of the soil' who fought in the second Chimurenga" (Sibanda and Maposa 2014: 58).

Conclusion

The role played by spiritual legends and spirit mediums in the construction of the Zimbabwe land disputes metanarrative should not be downplayed. There is within the Shona spiritual/religious cosmos, a link between human beings and their land, as well as between ancestry and land. The constant allusion to the spiritual realm, especially the legends of Nehanda, Chaminuka and Kaguvi during and after the liberation wars demonstrates the unfettered belief that the Shona people have over the influence and power of the spiritual realm. The ancestors whose remains are interred in the land are guardians and owners of the land on which we live at their pleasure. As such, the liberation wars and the post-liberation discourses on land ownership in Zimbabwe evince both physical and spiritual dimensions. The deep seated belief in ancestry evinces itself in the manners in which during the liberation war (the second Chimurenga to be precise), allusions to ancestry and spirit mediums were used for morale and as a tool to recruit new soldiers. The manners in which freedom fighters constantly consulted spirit mediums for both guidance and war strategy speaks to the nature of religious/spiritual convictions that the Shona freedom fighters had towards the words and actions of the spiritual world. It also resonates with the general belief systems within most African cultures that there is a link between the dead and the living – in other words death is a mere graduation into the afterlife and thus the 'dead' still live amongst and within us, influencing and controlling our existence and fates. In this regard, the neoimperial forces, understood as having undergone social death at the attainment of African independence, continue to play roles among Africans.

References

Behrend, H. *et al.* (1999). *Spirit Possession: Modernity and Power in Africa.* Madison: The University of Wisconsin Press.

Benyera, E. (2016). Expected yet uncomprehendible: Unpacking death through Nikolas Zakaria's *Rufu Chitsidzo. Gender and Behaviour* 14(2), pp7171 – 7181.

Chiwome, E. (1990). The Role of Oral Traditions in the War of National Liberation in Zimbabwe: Preliminary Observations. *Journal of Folklore Research*, 27(3) pp. 241-247.

Ellert, H. (1984). *The Material Culture of Zimbabwe.* Harare: Longman.

Gelfand, M. (1959). *Shona Ritual with Special Reference to the Chaminuka Cult.* Juta, Cape Town.

Hood, R.W., Jr. and Morris, R. J. (1983). Toward a Theory of Death Transcendence. *Journal for the Scientific Study of Religion,* 22(4) pp. 353-365.

Khadhani, M. and Zimunya, M, (1981). *And now the poets speak.* Gweru: Mambo Press.

Lifton, R. J. (1976). *The Life of the Self: Toward a New Psychology.* New York: Simon and Schuster.

Lifton, R. J. and Olson, E. (1974). *Living and Dying.* New York: Praeger.

Musiyiwa, M. (2008). The mobilization of popular music in the promotion of national unity in Zimbabwe. *Muziki,* 5(1) pp 11-29. DOI: 10.1080/18125980802633011

Mutswairo, S. (1988). *Nehanda.* Harare: College Press.

Ngoshi, H. T. (2009). Recovering the tongue: memorializing grieved women through spirit possession and ritual in Zimbabwean literature. *African Identities,* 7:4, 451-461, DOI: 10.1080/14725840903223190

Nhemachena, A. (2017) *Relationality and Resilience in a Not So Relational World: Knowledge, Chivanhu and (De-)Coloniality in 21ˢᵗ Century Conflict-Torn Zimbabwe.* Bamenda: Langaa RPCIG.

Nhemachena, A. & Dhakwa, E. (2017). When Did the Rain Start to Beat Us? Discursive Dispossession and the Political Economies of Misrecognition about African Mining, in Nhemachena, A. & Warikandwa, T. V. (eds) *Mining Africa: Law, Environment, Society & Politics in Historical and Multidisciplinary Perspectives.* Bamenda: Langaa RPCIG.

Pongweni, A. (1982). *Songs that Won the Liberation War.* Harare: College Press.

Posselt, F. W. T. (1935). *Fact & Fiction: A Short Account of the Natives of Southern Rhodesia.* Government of Southern Rhodesia.

Ranger, T. (1982). The Death of Chaminuka: Spirit Mediums, Nationalism and the Guerrilla War in Zimbabwe. *African Affairs* 81(324) pp. 349-369.

Sabao, C. (2018). Hegemonising Zimbabwe? The polity of *Mbare Chimurenga* lyrics in perpetuating Mugabe's and ZANU-PF's rule. *Muziki: Journal of Music Research in Africa* 15 (1): 109 – 30.

Sibanda, F., and R. S. Maposa. (2014). Beyond the Third Chimurenga? Theological Reflections on the Land Reform

Programme in Zimbabwe, 2000–2010. *Journal of Pan African Studies* 6 (8): 54–74.

Discography

Harare Mamboes, (Year Unknown). Mbuya Nehanda. Harare: Gramma Records

Mbare Chimurenga Choir. 2010. Nyatsoteerera. Harare: Gramma Records

Chapter Four

Pegging Out Claims in Space and Place: The Theme of Land Redistribution in the Music of Simon Chimbetu

Charles Pfukwa

Introduction

Simon Chimbetu was a prominent Zimbabwean artiste who left a legacy in Zimbabwean arts where sungura music has become a national brand. This chapter traces one theme out of many in Chimbetu's music: land redistribution. The chapter first lays out a theoretical frame to underpin the argument then it goes on to examine Chimbetu's cultural context and the sources of his rhythms and lyrical content. It then analyses four songs namely *Zuva raenda* (The sun is setting), *Southern Africa*, *Ndarangarira Gamba* (I remember a hero) and *Hoko* (Peg) which clearly reflect Chimbetu's position on land redistribution in Zimbabwe. The historical and political context in which we situate Chimbetu's work is a necessary prelude to the discussion.

King Lobengula was tricked into signing a concession in 1888 and a group of European adventurers funded by Cecil John Rhodes marched into central Zimbabwe and proclaimed a colony in the name of the British Empire in 1890. They carved up large tracts of land, started farming and displaced the local populace whose terms of tenure and ownership were very different from that of the White settlers. Conflict over land led to the wars of resistance between 1893 and 1896 that have become known as the first Chimurenga. The Europeans took control of the land in the name of the British crown. The term Chimurenga is derived from an ancestor of the Shona people called Murenga Soro Renzou who is linked to Mambiri and Tovera.

Through a series of legal edicts such as the Land Apportionment Act of 1931, the Animal Husbandry Act of 1959 and the Land Tenure Act of 1969, Black people were displaced from the land and it was a traumatizing experience. These forced removals were never properly recorded but were memorialised through oral tradition, song and poetry. The White colonisers also passed laws that entrenched racial discrimination and the native people were reduced to wage earners and had to pay hut taxes, dog taxes, poll taxes and so on. Dissent and protest of the 1950s became militant in the early 60s and the first shots of the second Chimurenga were fired at Chinhoyi in 1966. Guns fell silent after the Lancaster House Conference in 1979 but the land question was not fully resolved (Bhebe 1999; Moorcraft and McLaughlin 1982). It is against this background that the peasants and war veterans of the second Chimurenga took it upon themselves to move into White farms in what became known as the Third Chimurenga and Government later formalised this (Jenjekwa and Barnes 2018).

Why Chimbetu?

Simon Chimbetu, along with his brother Naison, represents the first generation of a Zimbabwean music genre called Sungura or Dendera. The music has been taken up by a new generation; their children, Sulumani, Tryson and others. Dendera or Sungura has stood the test of time and canonised itself by reproducing itself and more importantly has been passed on to the next generation. This process qualifies Sungura to be an integral part of Zimbabwe's cultural heritage.

Simon Chimbetu was a talented artist who was known throughout the region and Zimbabweans in the diaspora also followed him closely. Along with Thomas Mapfumo, Oliver Mtukudzi, John Chibadura and James Chimombe, Simon Chimbetu managed to break away from colonial traditions of playing copycat music and instead became creative, drawing rhythms from Zimbabwean *jiti, mbira* and other traditional rhythms. When he went

84

outside the borders of the nation he drew from East African traditions of the Benga movement of East Africa (Pfukwa 2010).

Some Theoretical Considerations

Music is a critical cultural index of any community. Western scholars have often mystified its study and have kept it as a fortified domain that has limited interrelationship with other disciplines especially in the arts and humanities. Furthermore, western scholarship has often seen music of other cultures through a western lens and in some cases relegated it as some lesser art. Given the cross - disciplinary trends in scholarship, it is necessary to research on the possible links between music and other disciplines especially on the African continent. This study should therefore be seen as a vehicle that drives African scholarship from the unnatural boundaries created by colonial traditions and deliberate discourse practices that saw African history, culture and its total experience through the lens of the colonial axis of the francophone, Anglophone and Lusophone communities.

Every community creates and performs its own music. It is a cultural experience peculiar to *homo sapiens*. With time, besides the bare vocals, humanity has added different instruments developed from the environment to support the rhythms created by voice and kinetic movements of the human limbs. Similarly, through the ages, musical instruments have become sophisticated and like language, music has found its way into different communities and beyond into other continents. It is this international nature of music that has tended to eclipse local movements on this continent. The second reason for the eclipse is that scholarship has always seen the study of music and all other epistemologies through western traditions. African music has been conceptualised, documented and studied using western theoretical perspectives such as Berliner (1993), and Paterson (1996). This is a process that has occurred by default rather than by design because African scholarship itself has not clearly defined the scope of the problem and has been content to use western theory in its own work. Part of the problem lies in the fact that there is considerable disagreement in conceptualisation of African music and how to repackage it to fit into the cultural frames of its communities on the continent. The trained musician uses theory as handed down by western traditions as a point of departure: this will entail use of staff notation and other detailed analytical tools that sometimes do not fit into the cultural framework of the African communities s/he seeks to serve. There are new movements that are interrogating these western driven perspectives such as Matiure (2011), (2014) and Njoora (2000). These are scholars bringing Afrocentric approaches and rethinking African discourse in the 21st century. Maganga (2017), Tirivangana (2011), Cabral (2007) and Asante (cited in Tirivangana 2011) are good examples of these new trajectories.

Tirivangana (2011) citing Asante explores in some depth the concept of "Afrocentricity" and posits that it is "... a theory of social change denoting the study of African concepts, issues and behaviour from an African worldview as opposed to a Eurocentric perspective". Tirivangana (2011) points out that it is essentially an attempt to rethink and reshape African epistemology in every possible sphere of scholarly enquiry. He goes on: "...the way an African artist or critic sees, thinks, and feels, should be conditioned by Africa-centred values if he or she is truly African in sensibility." This is echoed by Cabral's (2007) call to return to the source. Cabral always saw liberation going beyond the political struggle to remove the physical shackles into the cultural emancipation: "...national liberation is necessarily an act of culture." (Cabral 2007: 174).

For Cabral liberation began with establishment of African identities which meant some kind of cultural recovery and reconstruction. It was not necessarily a return to the pre-colonial era but it was about carving African identities that are firmly rooted in African tradition and African values. This was especially important for Portuguese colonies where the colonial power literally erased language and cultures through the policy of assimilation. Hence it is important, as Tirivangana (2011) says, to take a philosophy of life and world-view that draws from the bottomless well of African traditions and cultural practices. This means distilling theories for Africa from conceptualisation to application and deployment across the disciplines. This process must start from an African perspective that is firmly rooted in the African continent. Other theories from other continents can only then be brought in to buttress or reinforce Afrocentric approaches. Tirivangana argues that the Afrocentric perspective stands on its own, complete in itself, from start to finish, not in relation to another theory or as some counter discourse. It should never be seen in some Manichean or bipolar perspective that is sometimes common in western thinking. It is a theory that stands on its own, for itself, any other perspectives only come in to complement, support or illuminate the Afrocentric idea. Thus, as we look at African music, we see it in this Afrocentric paradigm. Furthermore given that it is a form of cultural expression we must also study the lyrical content, its form and other elements that arise from it through this Afrocentric lens. It is on this foundation that the discussion examines the work of Simon Chimbetu.

Orality and the Past

Western scholarship has often seen the written form as the supreme form of text, whether this is deliberate or not is not our concern here. However, the oral is an equally powerful mode of narration and has so many different forms (Vambe 2007). These have also been explored in detail by literary scholars. Visual texts have been more difficult to theorise and there is some interesting work in that area as well. We can locate African music in song and performance in this domain (Njoora 2000; Matiure 2014; Ntsinga 2009). The Shona act of *Kudeketera, kudetemba* and in the Ndebele *imbongi* and *isitshikitsha* are elaborate performances but they are also rich in metaphor and other figures of speech. In them are layers upon layers of cultural experiences, histories, traditions and values of a people and form, part of a vast treasure of African cultural heritage.

Among other things, narratives can never be exact representations of pasts but a mere approximation of those experiences in relation to current circumstances (Javangwe 2012). It is not necessarily a full and accurate recount of the past but of particular moments illuminating aspects of a person's or a peoples' total experience. All stories of human experience are a fairly complicated process where the content is in fact a miniscule selection of a limitless archive stored in the memories of the narrator. Javangwe (2012) and other scholars maintain that these stories will always come in their own order. What is finally produced verbally or in some written form is a finer distillation of a series of a string of ideas, of thoughts or experiences some of which are chaotic and disjointed in the mind when initially conceived. Chimbetu's music can be seen as a sonic expression of the wider national cultural struggles which in turn are linked to the political or national struggle called Chimurenga.

The Zimbabwean Land Redistribution

The Zimbabwean land redistribution exercise (also known as the Third Chimurenga has been steeped in controversy as different players look at it from different perspectives. The former White farmers and the west call it *land invasion* and they called the new Black settlers *squatters*. At the other extreme the new Black settlers call it land redistribution and it is a part of the Third Chimurenga. Zimbabweans have always argued that liberation cannot be complete without the land. In between these two extremes is a profusion of views some for, some against, and few can be called neutral. Scholars of development and economics and related disciplines have also made their contribution but more empirical studies still need to be done.

Generally most of these studies have been political where debates were played out in the media – print and electronic and these trends continue. They have also been found in other narrative forms such as film and music. The music ranges from the politically driven Tambaoga and Brian Mteki to the artistically driven Simon Chimbetu and Oliver Mtukudzi at the other end of the pendulum. A note on the word 'chimurenga' is in order here because it holds the historical and cultural context in which Chimbetu develops his music.

Chimbetu's Cultural Context

Any narrative, including the sonic makes a strong representation of the cultures and traditions of the communities where it is created and "consumed" (Javangwe 2011). The songs are composed, narrated and performed collectively. The context or setting of these songs depends on its creator and his/her cultural context. Pfukwa (2012) expresses the same point when he says context is: "...a fairly complex matter in that a social context is seen through different eyes. Different narrators will have different narratives of the same event and this in turn is influenced by different variables."

In our case, the context within which Chimbetu lays out his music can be viewed from two perspectives. The first is a purely temporal context where he places his art in some historical time frame of the second and third Chimurenga. For Chimbetu the liberation struggle is a well from which he draws material for composition and performance. As a participant (apparently some say his brother Naison disputed this) many of his songs dwell on this historical epoch. It looms large in his consciousness, lyrical content, his rhythms and performance. Later on trial and incarceration colour Chimbetu's as well.

At a second level there is spatial context where Chimbetu draws deeply from Benga rhythms given that Chimbetu went as far as Tanzania during the liberation struggle so he was exposed to east African rhythms. Pfukwa (2010) explores Benga influences on Zimbabwean music and Chimbetu's rhythms reflect this. Chimbetu's lyrical content draws from Zimbabwean culture and this is spelt out well in some of his songs. So the traces of Benga signify East African links yet the name Dendera itself gives Chimbetu's songs a clear Zimbabwean identity. The Dendera (Southern African Ground Hornbill *Bucorvus leadbeateri;*) is a huge bird found in parts of southern Africa and has this deep booming call. The dendera sound became a trade mark of his deep throbbing bass which is very similar to the deep bass in Benga music.

This fusion of different rhythms is what some scholars in popular culture call "cultural hybridity" (Hall and Du Gay 1996). The strings draw extensively from other parts of the subcontinent and this is infused with Shona lyrical content. In addition the performance captures the *Jiti* rhythm and this gives it the distinct Zimbabwean flavour in his work. *Jiti* is best appreciated in performance and this is an integral part of Chimbetu's music. Dendera music was created in this *Jiti* setting and there is a lot of song and dance. *Jiti* is part of Shona celebration in different rituals be they rain petitioning (see Nhemachena 2017), harvest or any other ceremony. It was a shared experience – a collective creation collective performance and collective ownership. Chimbetu's rhythms follow these cultural traditions.

Performance and Entertainment

Song as a genre can be a bridge between the literary and the historical text. Historians are still struggling to come to terms with the fact that literary genres in their different forms can be historical representations. For a live audience the mode of narration is very important. Content is not necessarily the key variable but how the song is performed. Chimbetu's music was not for a gathering of music critics, scholars or politicians, it was an audience simply in search of entertainment. The music is a public narrative for the various places of entertainment and public gatherings. It is a script for all to "see" (in the case of music – for all to hear). It is not some private piece to be stored in some library. Music in performance can be seen as art in motion, an active narrative. Every performance becomes an active script with the stage, the template upon which the tale is played out. The audience becomes the reader-just like reader of a written text. This discussion looks at the artiste Chimbetu in this framework.

Sungura Rhythms

Chimbetu's music has been given several names, most prominent is Sungura and Dendera, This discussion uses the term Sungura and the word is also linked to the Swahili term meaning *hare*. While in Tanzania Chimbetu was exposed to Benga music which is characterised by soft vocals, few lyrics and long guitar solos (Pfukwa 2010). It is backed by so many vocal interjections such as ululations, laughter, yodelling, whistles, sighs, gasps of joy and sometimes sorrow.

Chimbetu: Some Bionotes

He was born in Chegutu in 1955 and in the liberation struggle went as far as Tanzania. He worked in the tobacco auction floors in the early 80s and started playing music with brother Naison. In his early years he played with John Chibadura's Sungura Boys and this is probably where the term Sungura develops. Together with brother Naison they set up Marxist brothers. Around 1987 he split with Naison and the latter went to create the G7 Commandos and Simon set up Orchestra Dendera Kings. In the early years of Orchestra Dendera Kings he sang the song *Samatenga* which was a huge success.

Probably he reached his height around 1989 when he was accused of receiving stolen property and he narrated these ordeals in songs such as *Ndouraiwa, Judas Iscariot* and *Hutete Ura*. This was followed by imprisonment at Khami for four years and his wife abandoned him during that period. Upon release in 1995 he sang *Pachipamwe* – which means business as usual. After imprisonment he went on to produce the album *Survival* which was followed by *Lullaby* with its songs of consolation. In the final stage of his career he became intensely political and openly declared his support for the land redistribution program in the song *Hoko*. He lost some of his following but he remained steadfast in his support for land redistribution. His last album was *Ten Thousand Dollars* and he passed away in 2005. The discussion looks at some songs that reveal his deep political convictions.

Metaphor in Chimbetu's Music

The phrase *Zuva raenda* (the sun is setting) in Shona is a metaphor that means time is running out. Here is someone looking into the sunset yet certain tasks remain unfinished. The sun is setting for this generation yet it remains landless. This again is linked to the Second

91

Chimurenga where the issue of land was central. So like many of his political songs, *Zuva Raenda* carries simple but very powerful lyrics: "big brother time is running out, share the meat."

In *Zuva Raenda* Chimbetu uses the metaphor of a meal to spell out his major concern to the powers that be: share out the land. He passionately expresses the need for land redistribution through the simple images of the meal and of sunset. Traditionally, in Shona communities males and females take meals separately and this is further divided into age groups. This ensured order and equitable distribution of food which was mainly sadza and some relish. When the relish was some meat dish it was the responsibility of the older ones to share out the meat in order to control greed. So the younger ones had to wait patiently for the elder brother to share out the meat. The brother is taking time to share the meat and the younger ones are getting impatient.

When he sings about land in *Zuva Raenda* he just mutters under his breath one single line that spells it all: ... *govai minda*... which means share out the land. It takes close attention to pick out the line amidst a string of lines that sing about sharing out meat during a meal - *govai nyama*. Hence the whole song is about a long overdue process: land redistribution and like an obedient junior he implores authorities: "Big brother share the meat time is running out. In one single line he spells it out: ...*govai minda*...*eee zuva raenda* (...distribute the land...time is running out).

This line is barely audible yet it encapsulates all of Chimbetu's political ideology and his position on land redistribution. It is another of those songs with long periods of instrumentation but the message gets through clearly – parcel out the land, time is running out.

It is worth noting *Zuva raenda* was released several years before the Third Chimurenga started in earnest. While *Zuva raenda* is mild and appealing *Hoko* is in the imperative mood and has little room for negotiation, it is a song that was created at the height of the Third Chimurenga.

Probably *Hoko* is the apex of Chimbetu's political discourse and his passion for the struggle for land. The song starts with a voice over in English: "The Third Chimurenga has already began, The *Hoko* has already been pegged, *Hoko* is blood. Because a lot of blood was shed no one is allowed to never ever, tamper with the *Hoko*"

The voice is solemn, baritone and oozes with authority. The lines are repeated several times amidst the rhythms.

In Shona *Hoko* literally means a peg or a stick that is driven into the ground to demarcate boundaries on a piece of land. It can be informal where a father parcels out a piece of land to a son or it can be a cadastral mark that marks out a space that has been surveyed. It is a symbol, a marker of physical space, it is a statement that this space is occupied. In Shona it is also called *mbambo*.

Hoko becomes a metaphor for the act of reclaiming the land – the Third Chimurenga. In the song Chimbetu maintains this peg is sacred and carries several attributes, it is a symbol of power and authority. The peg marks an arrival, the land at last. This is the fulfilment of a promise (*chirangano*) it is like arriving in the Promised Land. The peg assumes the attributes of a flagpole: it is sacred "... do not tamper with it..." - *siya iripo* (leave it there).

The peg becomes a memorial, a symbol that evokes memories of the days of the struggle and all its pain. It is a symbol of triumph, an arrival after a long journey and the long journey was the protracted struggle of the second Chimurenga. This peg is drenched in the blood of all those who died in the struggle to liberate the land. Many lives were lost for that peg to be where it is. It is peg full of painful memories, a long script written in blood. It is a stylus which writes the long and painful journey of Chimurenga. To get it meant a lot of sacrifice and many died to get this peg. His song such as *Ndarangarira gamba* (I recall a fallen Hero) is a moving symbolic rendition of the blood on the peg mentioned in the voice over in *Hoko*.

Ndarangarira Gamba a dirge overflowing with emotion as a fighter narrated the death of a comrade. Seeing a person die is always a traumatising experience which needs intense counselling and psycho-therapy. Chimbetu seems to relive trauma through song as he memorializes this painful experience. In a few heart rending lines we witness a tragedy unfolding as life ebbs away. In a moving eulogy despite the pain, the imminent death the comrade's last words are, "continue with the struggle to the end". The loss of a comrade in combat is always a traumatic experience for every soldier. The Second Chimurenga was no exception. In a few lines punctuated by long guitar solos the audience witnesses how a whole generation sacrificed their lives for that peg that marks a piece of land.

Some people started quarrelling with Chimbetu after *Hoko* but he had started talking about land redistribution long back. While this song can be called the centre piece of Chimbetu's songs on land redistribution he did not start singing about land redistribution in *Hoko*. His commitment to the national cause is unquestionable as we see him sing *Southern Africa*. We look at *Southern Africa* briefly as the last example of Chimbetu's concern with issues of the land and the people.

Chimbetu's nationalist passions do not begin in the post-incarceration period (1995 onwards), even from the early years of his career we encounter the intensely political *Southern Africa*. It is a bold reminder to the White people who took land by force and never revealed this to their descendants. This is an open address to a former South African President John Vorster (1915 -1983) a major architect of apartheid and the imaginary Heinrich who represents every White man in Southern Africa. Vorster and Heinrich made the mistake of not telling their grandchildren that the White people had seized land from the Black people. When the Blacks demand their land the Whites should return it. If not the White people would be wiped out. Some followers of Chimbetu were not aware of his strong ideological convictions and they saw him simply as an entertainer. The sentiments in *Southern Africa* and *Zuva Raenda* are similar to those in *Hoko* only that Chimbetu was still polite and courteous about it. In *Hoko* he pulls out all stops and becomes aggressive.

As observed earlier, Cabral (2007) argues that liberation is incomplete without cultural liberation and this is also Chimbetu's song. Without the land which is the primary means of production, liberation is incomplete. He was an entertainer *par excellence* but he went way beyond that. His political template made entertainment, culture and politics inseparable. His music and performance was a strong expression of cultural values, contemporary issues and problems that the community he was living faced.

Chimbetu was not a lonely voice in this genre. Oliver Mtukudzi sang about land from a neutral perspective and he was very clear about the value of land redistribution: *"murimi we tora kapadza urime ...nyika ivhu, ivhu ndiyo nyika ...murimi munhu..."* On the other hand others such as Tambaoga and Bryan Mteki were bluntly partisan.

In conclusion we need to see Chimbetu's treatise in the broader context of the national debates on land redistribution that have so many complexities.

Conclusion

This chapter demonstrated how Chimbetu, through his songs, directly and indirectly championed the cause of the displaced Black people in Zimbabwe and called for redressing the situation through land redistribution programmes. Chimbetu's songs reveal that there are limitless possibilities of telling the Zimbabwean story through an artistic medium that is often underrated. In other words, through Sungura music and other musical genres, we get multiple interpretations and images of Zimbabwean pasts, their triumphs and tragedies. This discussion shows that there are many ways to document, narrate and celebrate the histories, cultures, literatures and all forms of cultural heritage of a people.

References

Asante, M. K. (1998). *The Afrocentric Idea*. Philadelphia: Temple University.

Cabral, A. (2007). *Unity and struggle*. Pretoria: Unisa Press.

Hall, S. and Du Gay, P. (1996). *Questions of Cultural Identity*. London: Sage.

Javangwe, T. D. (2011). "Contesting Narratives: Constructions of Self and Nation in Jenjekwa, V. and Barnes, L. (2018) Changes in the Linguistic Landscape Resulting from Zimbabwe's Post 2000 Land Reforms: Recasting the First and Second *Chimurenga* Narratives, *Language Matters*, 49:3, 67-85,

DOI: 10.1080/10228195.2018.1539119

Matiure, P. (2011). "Mbira dzavadzimu and its space within Shona Cosmology: tracing mbira from bira to the spiritual world" *Muziki,* 8(2): 29-49.

Matiure, P. (2014). Archiving indigenous and contemporary cultural legacies of Shona *Mbira Dzavadzimu* in the context of *kurova guva* and *dandaro* practices. PhD Thesis, University of KwaZulu Natal, Durban. Unpublished Thesis.

Nhemachena, A. (2017) *Relationality and Resilience in a Not So Relational World? Knowledge, Chivanhu and (De-)Coloniality in 21ˢᵗ Century Conflict-Torn Zimbabwe.* Bamenda: Langaa RPCIG.

Njoora, T. K. (2000). "Guidelines for Incorporating Kenyan Traditional Music in the General Music Curriculum", PhD Dissertation. Eugene: University of Oregon.

Ntsinga, T. (2009) Song Texts and the ambiguities of oral performance. *Muziki* 6.1 pp36-47.

Paterson, D. B. (1996). "Trends in Kenyan Popular music" in http://hometown.aol/comdpaterson/ (accessed 3 October 2009).

Paul. F. B. (1993). *The Soul of Mbira: Music and Traditions of the Shona People of Zimbabwe.* Chicago: University of Chicago Press.

Pfukwa, C. (2010). When cultures speak back to each other: the legacy of *benga* in Zimbabwe *Muziki._*7 (1), pp 172-181.

Tirivangana, A. (2011) "Towards a Theory of Africa– Centred Metaphysics: A Critical Exploration of the Ngozi theme in Selected Zimbabwean Fiction," Unpublished DPhil thesis Department of English University of Zimbabwe.

Chapter Five

Of Mothers, Umbilical Cords and Tongues: Land Ownership, Language and Identity in Chirikure Chirikure's *Rukuvhute*

Angeline Mavis Madongonda & Enna Sukutai Gudhlanga

Introduction

The woman in Zimbabwean and Rhodesian literature has often been portrayed as a second-class citizen and her role in society has received limited literary attention. To add to this, a significant number of scholarly works in Zimbabwe harp on the woman being a victim rather than dwelling on her strengths. Yet the woman's place in Zimbabwean society and indeed in Africa is undoubtedly that of giver of life, language and most of all an identity - attributes that are often taken for granted. Her role has been that of a pillar without whose existence a significant number of things would not have been the same. The importance of women is underscored by some scholarly works such as Davy Mutasa's *Sekai Minda Tava Nayo* (2005) that show women in a more positive light. Such literary works in indigenous languages have challenged the deeply entrenched Eurocentric beliefs of the woman's inferior status – the scholars demonstrate women's significant stakes in Zimbabwean society.

Ngugi (1981) has highlighted the importance of one's own indigenous language to communicate issues that affect one's society. The mother tongue in literary works has thus played a significant role in shaping society's perceptions and worldviews. The term 'mother tongue' invites a serious and thought-provoking debate over the significance of one's first language and its intricate ties with the mother figure. A linkage of the three, the mother, the tongue and the umbilical cord are undeniable. The umbilical cord is another life-giving connecting tendon between the woman and humanity. The woman in this regard is seen as giver of life, teacher of a language and therefore an identity. However, such links between the woman, identity and land ownership have been underplayed. Chirikure Chirikure captures this link between the mother tongue, umbilical cord and identity which subsequently connect one to his/her land ownership. This chapter demonstrates that intricate relationship between the umbilical cord, land ownership and the tongue as well as the linguistic wealth that lies in the indigenous language of Shona in capturing what could take scholars and historians volumes of research to arrive at. Several selected poems by Chirikure (in his anthology *Rukuvhute*) serve to demonstrate how he utilises the umbilical cord motif to explore issues to do with land ownership and identity as well as the cycle between life and death. A textual analysis of the selected poems is done to bring this to the fore. Afrocentricity, African Womanism and Post-Cartesian theories are used to shape this research and open new avenues to interpreting the selected poems. These theories provide a framework which is useful in analysing the cultural practices of the Shona people and resistance to dominant Western discourse on land and language use. They therefore offer an alternative reading to the presentation of women in fostering identity and some connection to land ownership. Connections between the literal and metaphoric mother and umbilical cord to the land ownership issues, ancestry and hence identity cannot be under-estimated. This chapter therefore unravels the positive cultural perceptions of women and identity in general and how this is bolstered through the use of the indigenous Shona language in Chirikure Chirikure's *Rukuvhute*.

Background

Zimbabwean contemporary society is highly gendered. In traditional Shona society women occupied important positions - an aspect which was usurped through colonialism. With the colonial influence, women lost some of the positions and significant roles they played in traditional societies. Colonial influence meant that men assumed a superior status while conversely, the woman in most Zimbabwean societies was regarded as a second-class citizen and her role in society has received limited attention. Codified customary law which is heavily loaded with Victorian values relegated African women to the fringes of the family and society. Colonialism then brought with it feminist perspectives that relegated women to the fringes of the society which was contrary to the significant roles that women played in traditional Shona society. The adage *musha mukadzi* (a home is given significance by a woman) point to the critical roles that women play in Shona society. Women also have significant roles in families as mothers, aunts and influential societal figures as demonstrated by Queen Nzinga of Angola, Nehanda of Zimbabwe and the Makoni female warriors of Rusape (Gudhlanga 2013). Sadly, this important role of women seems to be absent in most creative works of literature particularly indigenous literature. Zimbabwean cultures place importance on the role of women in socialising children and fostering identity. Chirikure Chirikure through his poetry anthology *Rukuvhute* demonstrates women's importance in fostering identity and fostering in children very close ties with their land ownership regimes from a tender age.

Women have traditionally been accorded a significant role in Shona communities. Gudhlanga (2016) aptly underlines that even in landownership patterns in Shona traditional culture, women were considered as players in society's wellbeing. Land ownership then was not the preserve of men for they could only be allocated land after getting married. Bachelors were not allocated land (Gudhlanga 2016) thereby placing the importance of the woman in the institution of marriage. It therefore only follows that research recognises women as having greater affinity to the land for they are the ones who worked the land (Gudhlanga 2016). As a result, connections between women and land ownership go beyond merely working the land and this dates back to centuries before colonisation. However, not many literary studies associate the woman with land ownership and identity, yet in real life the connections appear so glaring almost to overshadowing her male counterpart. Sadly, the change of status of the woman as a significant player in society was assumed upon colonisation whereupon the balance between genders was overturned in favour of the patriarchal one (Gudhlanga 2013; Schmidt 1990; 1993).

There are, however, a few representations of women's connections to land ownership, language and identity in a number of literary works such as Chenjerai Hove's *Bones* (1988) and Davie Mutasa's *Sekai Minda Tave Nayo* (2005). As a result of not having enough literature on this subject, women's representation continues to be overlooked, with limited voices that do not clearly bring out the critical roles they play in society. It is not surprising that contemporary works by Zimbabwean writers focus more on Eurocentric versions of women's liberation and feminist discourse. Through colonialism, the women's undisputed dominant role at the fireplace has been dislocated and side-lined to the peripheries, yet the oral folktales that they told constitute part of the oral traditions that form part of history and day-to-day teachings that included imparting a language and culture. Studies indicate that women have been side-lined and their works (and works representing their experiences) continue to fight the perennial struggles against subjectification (Kambarami 2006; Stratton 2006). Chirikure Chirikure's anthology is one rare collection, coming from a male writer, attempting to retrieve the woman's dignity and place in Shona society. As a result, this chapter examines the connections between the woman, land ownership and identity through the use of the mother tongue and umbilical cord motif in selected poems in Chirikure Chirikure's *Rukuvhute*. The chapter also examines how Chirikure utilises the umbilical cord motif to explore issues to do with the connection between life and death. The chapter also evaluates Chirikure's success at using the indigenous language, Shona, thereby harnessing resistance to the adulteration of indigenous culture that has suffered the onslaught of colonial incursions.

The chapter is qualitative in outlook and is grounded in critical appreciation of Chirikure's poetry anthology *Rukuvhute*. It relies heavily on textual analysis of some selected poems in the anthology, *Rukuvhute*, critiquing Chirikure's depiction of the connections between the woman, the tongue and umbilical cord in some of his selected poems and how these foster identity and affinity to land among people of African descent.

Theoretical Framework

This chapter is informed by the Afrocentric theory, Africana Womanism and post-Cartesian theories. Women's struggles from the feminist perspective, place patriarchy at the centre of women's struggles; that by virtue of being a woman biologically, women find themselves at the receiving end of men (Oyewumi 1997). This however is deeply entrenched in Western feminist conceptions of patriarchal societies where the women persistently view the man as an enemy who should be fought. In this sense, feminist theoretical pretensions setting African women against African men are a strategy by colonialists and imperialists who are keen to divert African attention away from fighting for reparations, restitution and restoration of what was stolen during the colonial era. (Nhemachena, Warikandwa and Mpofu 2018). The neoimperial logic is that if African men and women waste their time fighting each other, then they will not have time to fight for restitution, restoration and reparations for enslavement and colonial wrongs. In essence, feminism is a diversionary ideology meant to detour African men and women from struggles to decolonise and recover reparations, restitution and restoration for colonial and enslavement wrongs. This study is therefore Afrocentric in outlook. Afrocentricity is a theory "which calls for all African phenomena, activities and way of life to be looked at and be given meaning from the standpoint and worldview of Africans" (Gray 2001: 3; Asante in Hudson-Weems 2007: 29). Using Afrocentricity allows for an understanding of women's connections to land ownership and how they play a critical role in defining the African people's identity as depicted by Chirikure in the selected poems. The Afrocentric discourse helps to separate the African woman from the European perceptions of the African woman.

Afrocentricity is a paradigm based on the idea that African people should re-assert a sense of agency in order to achieve a sense of being.

Afrocentricity enables us to decipher how Chirikure is preoccupied with reclaiming and dignifying the past linguistic wealth that lies in the indigenous language of Shona as well as retrieving experiences of the indigenous people in terms of how they value their identity and their connections to land ownership, *mwana wevhu* (child of the soil) which clearly demonstrates the Shona people's identity and land ownership. Chirikure's poems demonstrate an avid awareness of the social, psychological and cultural inferiority of the formerly colonised. With the use of Shona language, Chirikure is appealing for the shared cultural heritage of the use of this indigenous group. The poet also uses this language to demonstrate linkages between women and identity as well as subsequent linkages with the African land ownership regimes. He also attempts to show "where the rain began to beat us" (Achebe 1958) by persistently referring to the ideals of the war of liberation to confirm how contemporary society, through the influence of colonialism now looks down upon women. Yet the woman used to occupy significant spaces in traditional Shona society. This is augmented by using Africana Womanism (Hudson-Weems 2007) as this theory is a departure from the mainstream feminist approach which is Euro-centric. Hudson-Weems's (2007) contribution in the Afrocentricity discourse helps to separate the African woman from the European woman. The Africana womanist philosophy brings out the uniqueness of the African woman and it is underpinned by the African culture which has the family as its core. Unlike the feminists whose struggle is independent of men, the Africana womanist invites men in her struggle. Africana womanists believe that "emancipation is unattainable until the basic rights are provided to all people (Ajai cited in Ntiri-Quenum 2007). Thus African women are family oriented hence the seeming oblivion of injustices perpetrated to them by their African men. African women realise that in order for society to be functional it emanates from the basic unit of society, the family. A functional family results in a functional society. The theory therefore works well in an African set up in which women occupy significant spaces in forging the African identity.

Post-Cartesian theory is also utilised to understand the inexplicable relationship between the physical and metaphysical among the Shona. While the thinker Rene Descartes's dualism separated the body and the mind, there is a way in which the two somehow connect when issues of identity are brought up. Identity relates to one's consciousness of one's personhood which appears to be in tandem with Descartes's maxim "I think therefore I am." However, Descartes's Cartesianism fails when it separates the body and the mind as well as individualise one's consciousness of the self. Atwood and Stolorow (2011) critique how Cartesian theory disregarded context (that isolates individual consciousness) when they state that Post-Cartesian theory "is contextual in [as it] holds that such organizations of emotional experience take form, both developmentally and in the psychoanalytic situation, in constitutive relational or intersubjective contexts." Therefore the body and the mind are not always separated and this is applicable to Shona metaphysics. Through the connection of one's umbilical cord to the physical land, one (according to Shona philosophy) is connected to his/her people or his/her ancestral spirits and hence his/her identity and connections to the metaphysical world are forged. One's being and becoming therefore subsume the physical body as he/she literally and metaphorically are connected to the physical and metaphysical world through the umbilical cord which is dug into the ground and connects one to land ownership. It is a connection best understood by the Shona people and mostly made possible by the mother figure who facilitates the link between one and his/her land ownership regime through the umbilical cord. The Shona and other African ethnic groups realise the significance of the woman in their societies- a role equivalent to Chinua's Achebe's reference to "Mother is supreme" adage in Igbo culture. One's identity takes into cognisance familial ties that recognise the past, present and the future through both the physical and metaphysical interconnectedness of human experiences, experiences that are best understood by other Post-Cartesian thinkers.

Chirikure Chirikure, by using the indigenous Shona language in writing his poetry, retrieves and appropriates a language that was and still is being shifted to the peripheries of society by the global nature of the world today. Owing to the psychological damage caused by colonialism that infused the inferiority of African languages, Shona is one of the many languages that are slowly being discarded in favour of the more preferable English language. Africana Womanism also retrieves the harmonious co-existence of men and women that Chirikure engenders the previously colonial induced lack of importance of the female figure in Zimbabwe's cultural heritage. He recreates and gives emphasis to traditionally accepted role of the woman in Shona society in which women had a critical role in forging one's identity and attachment to the land. Chirikure challenges the now normalised debased perceptions of woman stemming from the colonial legacy through his anthology *Rukuvhute*.

Of Mothers, Language and Identity

For one to be called a Zimbabwean, it has a lot to do with variables such as the location where s/he hails from - the place of origin or his/her ethnic roots, the language s/he speaks and his sense of being - that is, what appeals to his consciousness about who she/he is. It is prudent to note from the onset that this identity is made possible through the mother figure or the woman who inculcates it in every child from a tender age. It is the female figure who connects the newly born child with his/her land ownership regime through the burying of the umbilical cord into the ground. This act symbolically ties one to their land and is a tie that cannot be easily severed. This explains why African and Shona people in particular are connected and tied to the land.

A significant number of literary works in Zimbabwe such as Tsitsi Dangarembga's *Nervous Conditions* (1988), Lutanga Shaba's *Secrets of a Woman's Soul* (2013) and Tendayi Westerhoff's *Unlucky in Love* (2005) harp on the woman being a victim rather than on positive images that she portrays. Issues to do with identity are fostered through the woman who socialises the child into any given society. It is the mother figure who teaches the child about his/her ethnic identity and introduces him/her to their cultural roots and gives them their identity. Male figures do not play this critical role in the life of children. This leaves the woman with so much in terms of the role she plays in identity formation in her society. The woman's place in Zimbabwean society and indeed in Africa is undoubtedly that of giver of life, language and an identity from the very foundations of life to adulthood. Through marriage, a woman in Shona culture joins the husband's family but always retains her identity and does not belong to her husband's people. This explains why even in death it is only her people who can come and perform burial rites because she perpetually belongs to her family where she was born. However, despite being a *mutorwa*, someone brought in to her husband's family, she still plays a critical role of giving her children their identity and linking them to their culture and land. The wife in traditional African societies was not necessarily a stranger, but she was someone who was brought in (*kutorwa* and hence *mutorwa*) to her husband's family where she could even secure a medium upon her death. Colonial culture is silent on this role which is quietly appreciated and brought out in Chirikure Chirikure's poetry anthology.

To add to this, one's indigenous language is vital in one's identity and sense of "ethnic" being. The world over, one's "ethnic" origins are usually brought to the fore through one's language. It is therefore imperative that one uses his/her indigenous language when expressing ideas. In *Decolonizing the Mind*, Ngugi (1986) states that ideas expressed in English or in a foreign language by an African writer result in a writer being enmeshed in a culture that is not his/her own. This translates into what Ngugi describes as "being made to stand outside himself to look at himself" (Ngugi 1986: 17). This therefore has implications on one's identity and cultural heritage.

Scholars such as Descartes have pointed out the separation of the physical body and the mind, that is, one's consciousness. Shona mythology suggests a holistic connection of one's being and identity. However, spirit mediums set their spirits traveling – their spirits detach from their bodies so that they are able to follow events at a distance and then advise their clients accordingly (see Nhemachena 2017) Through the umbilical cord, one's physical connections to his/her spiritual roots and ancestry are not debatable. Thus, post-

Cartesianists allow for and believe in such connections between the body and soul through metaphysics. This is what forms one's identity. At the centre of Shona cultural heritage is the metaphysical belief that man's consciousness and being are connected to his/her land ownership. In this way, both men and women play a significant part in the identity formation of any individual. Wilson Katiyo's (1989) novel *Son of the Soil* succinctly captures this belonging and becoming of a liberated Zimbabwean as lying in the repossession of the land. Katiyo has envisioned the centrality of the land and how the future of Zimbabwe lay in reclaiming what it had lost through colonialism. Unfortunately, colonialism deprived women of the centre stage they previously enjoyed in Shona traditional culture. Shoko (2004) underlines this when he describes the relationship between man and the land as a special gift from the ancestors. In this chapter, an exploration of the mother figure in Chirikure Chirikure's poetry is done.

The Mother Tongue and Identity in Chirikure Chirikure's *Rukuvhute*

A significant number of Zimbabwean writers prefer using English to Shona in their writings. According to Achebe using a colonial language empowers the writer and offers him/her an alternative way to express oneself. However, this has been castigated by Ngugi (1986) who underlines the importance of the mother tongue in any form of communication. Failure by writers to use indigenous languages has resulted in some of these languages becoming extinct and most of those disappearing languages are in Africa. Debates also abound on the use of indigenous languages in creative writing. Some scholars such as Ngugi (1986), in *Decolonizing the mind*, have highlighted the importance of one's own indigenous language to communicate issues that affect one's society. However, Ward (1997) has defended Ngugi who is often misquoted as indicating the use of the indigenous languages in their pure original form.

Okpewho (cited in Kizza 2010) also pointed out the altering "ethnic" landscape, with people continually migrating globally and into urban centres and even intermarrying and how this has impacted on indigenous languages. Chirikure's collection of poems therefore embraces the indigenous language, Shona and his writings and ideology are clear markers of Ngugi discipleship. As previously mentioned, one's language has strong links to one's identity. Any language has its origins and is often localised in a certain area hence linkages between languages within certain regions or countries. In the anthology *Rukuvhute*, Chirikure Chirikure demonstrates how the retrieval of one's cultural heritage and identity can only be salvaged from the rural setting. The country's urban area is an epitome of the destruction of the cultural heritage while the village represents culture in its purest form. Connections with one's origins for most urbanites are lost and identity becomes problematic. The navel loses its significance and hence connections to the land owing to the dispossession and subsequent dislocation of the people from their land through colonialism which violently severed the ties that people had with the land ownership by uprooting them and relocating them into new areas in which they did not have any ties with.

The concept of the tongue is aptly captured by Chirikure's use of the mother tongue- *rurimi rwaamai*. Nnaemeka (1997) shows how the concept of mother defies the colonial odds which redefined women as being the insignificant "other" in Africa. Nnaemeka demonstrates how several concepts are prefixed by "mother" (In its articulation of the many "faces of "(m)other"— mother tongue, mother wit, motherhood, mothering" (Nnaemeka 1997) thereby underlining the centrality of the mother figure in Africa. However, by appropriating the mastery of the mother tongue and using it in his poetry, Chirikure creates a synergy between orality whose guardian was traditionally the female in Zimbabwe and the predominantly male in the written arena. Chirikure insists on delivering his poetry orally thereby recreating a space that has originally been colonially associated with women's spaces as is demonstrated below.

The Land and Umbilical Cord in Chirikure Chirikure's Poetry

The umbilical cord is a recurring motif in the collection. Literally, *rukuvhute* is the umbilical cord. Mawere (2014: 7) alludes to the centrality of *rukuvhute* when he says this:

> In Zimbabwe, they would call such knowledge as IK "*ruzivo rwevana vevhu*" (literally: knowledge of the children of the soil) which means knowledge of the people with African origin. *Vana vevhu* (children of the soil) therefore do not only mean people of Zimbabwean origin but can also be referred to mean people of the African origin as all these people have special relationships with the African land: African land is the land where their *mikuvhute* [singular: *rukuvhute* in Shona] (umbilical cords) as well as their ancestors were buried.

The umbilical cord thus makes vital connections of the child before and when it is born to its mother and its land – therefore its ancestry. Through the umbilical cord, there are common characteristic traits between the mother and land ownership. In its pre-natal state, the child is nourished by the mother and at birth the vital life giving force is severed. Its interment in the soil thus serves as a symbol of the land now taking over post-natal and lifelong nourishment of the remains of the newly born. It is thus not surprising that one's language of origin is referred to as his/her mother tongue. In a symbolic way, the child "belongs" to the soil through that symbolic connection. The image on the cover of the anthology *Rukuvhute* signifies this although according to Wasosa (2012) it takes a Pan-African flavour when referring to one's identity, roots and Africanness.

Chirikure gives a concise description of the vitality of the umbilical cord in the title poem "Rukuvhute" (p. 9) *Chaivapo chaindisunganidza naamai* (There once was that which tied me to mother). *Mwedzi mipfumbamwe kudya ndichiwana* (For nine months with enough nourishment provided). In a similar fashion the same umbilical cord is what is critical in family ties (*mhuri*), connection with the ancestral world (*vadzimu*) with God (*Zame/ Musikavanhu*) and that which ties him to the land – "Afrika" – aptly spelt in Shona. Chirikure underlines the literal and the metaphoric nourishment that the umbilical cord serves in the different levels of existence. In several of the poems, the persona underlines how the umbilical cord was interred within the bowels of the earth (*"kutsirwa"*) by the midwife or the mother thereby connecting him to those who have departed. The critical duty of linking the living and the departed by burying the umbilical cord in the ground was done by women. This demonstrates that women in Shona or African cosmology play a significant role of making sure that the newly born are connected to their land and this gives them their identity and entitlement to ownership of land. The woman in the form of the mother is a critical identity maker in African society even though western thinking has tried to subvert this and marginalise them to the periphery of societal activities.

References to the umbilical cord as an identity maker are made in such poems as *"Tiri ropa rimwe chete"* (We are of the same blood p. 28), *"Kunemi VaDevera"* (To you the Devera people) p. 28 and *"Nzira Kurukuvhute"* (The Way to the Umbilical Cord). Musiiwa (2004) refers to the umbilical cord as the values, life-giving forces and blood ties that are not supposed to be broken. The umbilical cord gives this metaphysical connectivity between the living and the departed and it is the woman who performs such rituals of making it possible that the critical stage in a *muShona* or an African's life is done.

The Land and the Umbilical Cord in Chirikure's *Rukuvhute*

In the poem *"Nzira Kurukuvhute"* (p. 28) Chirikure underlines this aspect when he says, *"Imomu makatsirwa rukuvhute rwangu/ Ndimo makatsirwa madzisekuru angu/ ndimo muchatsirwa wangu mutumbi"* (p. 28) (Among the Devera people). That is where my umbilical cord was buried/ that is where my ancestors were buried/ That is where I will be buried). The umbilical cord is that which connects the close relationship between indigenous traditional religion, land ownership and the people. It is women who have the duty of burying the umbilical cord in the ground. Women have an immense responsibility in making sure children have close ties with their land, as a heritage,

109

as understood in Shona worldview. The umbilical cord becomes that which connects a people's identity, hence the adage *"mwana wevhu"* (a child of the soil). Through the umbilical cord, "as a foetus is connected to the mother by this coil in the womb, so the African is tied to his/her cultural and material heritage" (Musiiwa 2004). Zhuwarara (2001: 12-13) confirms this when he says:

> African societies regarded the land as the home of ancestral spirits who…acted as intermediaries between the living and God….the land functioned as a geographical and metaphysical, the world at whose centre was entrenched the roots of African belief systems, systems which denied a stark division between the sacred and the secular, man and his environment.

In the same vein, Chirikure makes these connections (linkages between the land, the living and dead) in the poem *"Kunemi VaDevera"* (To you the Devera people). *"Rwangu rukuvhute makatsira pasi/ …Wenyumutumbi takatsira pasi/ Asi mweya wenyu tinawo pano pasi/…Muchibatanawo nevamwe pasi ipapo/ Kutitungamirira isu vana tiripanze/…Kusvika tazoyaruka, tatiwo go pasi."* (My own umbilical cord you buried in the ground/…Your body we buried in the ground/ But we have your spirit here on earth/…Unite with fellow spirits in the ground/ Leading us children who are on earth/…Until we go and reside with you in the ground). Again it is the women who bury the umbilical cord underground. What is missing in this excerpt is how the role of the woman is subsumed in those of the Devera people whose mention here seems to take on a patriarchal tie but in African culture the issue of the importance of the complementarity of roles by men and women has to be taken note of. Krog (2001) speaking from the perspective of female oral artists, captures this dilemma when he states that the silencing of women particularly in public spaces began with the location of women's voices and activities. Through colonialism women in Africa are therefore associated with quaintness and their activities located within the confines of the home and the domestic sphere. Chirikure in his poetry redeems women from the marginal roles they have been condemned to by colonialism and gives them their significant role of fostering identity and link to the land among the children and people of African descent.

Chirikure Chirikure demonstrates this significance of the mother figure in identity formation and linkage to the land when he dedicates a number of poems in *Rukuvhute* to mother figures as he cherishes their love, their role in procreation and the preservation of cultural values. The poem *"Mai vangu MaMoyo"* (p. 28) (My mother MaMoyo) is a dedication to the persona's own mother. *"Mbuya Ndakasharwa"* (p. 42) (Grandmother Ndakasharwa) he dedicates this poem to his grandmother who dies before seeing his child- her grandchild. The persona emphasises that she would watch over his children as an ancestor who would continue to look after him and his family; thus he demonstrates the various responsibilities that the dead have even in death (p'Bitek 1986). The grandmother will continue to look after his family as an ancestor. *Tetendoenda* (p. 44) (Auntie I am going) is a poem dedicated to his aunt. In the poem the persona informs his aunt that he is leaving to start his own family. He brings to the fore the importance of women in African identity for they direct and guide family members in crucial rites of passage such as marriage. Marriages are sanctioned by such aunts whose role in such cases is indispensable.

Post-colonial Hybridity and Identity in *Rukuvhute*

Chirikure Chirikure's insistence on the retrieval of the mother tongue is consistent throughout his writing *Rukuvhute*. Yet with the global nature of the world today, his retrieval and insistence on the use of Shona cannot go unchallenged. While he has managed to retrieve even the performative component of the traditional poetry, this is no longer in its purest form. One cannot ignore the hybrid nature of his poetry and performance especially in the post-modern world stage. While the Shona language is a dominant marker of his Shona cultural heritage, his style of presentation is undeniably hybrid. Although trying to retrieve and appropriate the original mode of presentation of his poetry-oral performance, his style is a far cry from

111

the oratory skills drawn from his home area (Wasosa 2012). Chirikure has managed to linguistically penetrate the modern world stage of a plural audience while still performing in Shona. One would have expected him to address the indigenous Shona language speakers as Ngugi (1986) would insist but through translation (into English, German etc.) at his live shows, for example, and of his other poetry collections such as *Hakurarwi* (We shall not Sleep), his audience base has grown. Not only has he placed the Shona language on a world stage, but his fusion of his poetry with background mbira music has cut him out as an innovative poet par excellence.

He, like Chenjeral Hove, albeit his collection being in Shona, fractures normative expectations of placing the woman at the centre. Chirikure vindicates the woman whose role in identity formation is ignored and has often been located on the peripheries of society. Using his mother tongue, Chirikure hopes to change the mind-sets of those appreciating his poetry to also value the aesthetic pleasure derived from use of the Shona language. Not only that, the language itself creates some form of agency from the insignificant language it has been to a force to reckon with on the literary arena. Chirikure through the use of the Shona language forms the basis from which to combat colonialism and neo-colonialism. However, despite Chirikure's use of the Shona language, he has also adopted Western style of writing infusing it with his use of the oral roots of his indigenous poetry. This is supported by Ojaide (1996) who says:

There is a symbiotic relationship between the oral and the written in modern African poetry in which the poetic aim, vision, and practice have fused to produce a poetry that is distinctly oral though written. The oral character of written poetry is generally strong because of the vocal nature of its transmission, being essentially composed to be read aloud.

Chirikure emphasises the oral nature of African poetry and joins other African oral poets and griots who fuse their poetry with music (Finnegan 2012). Apart from his exploration of the indigenous Shona language as well as the mother and umbilical cord motifs, Chirikure's style of presentation is thus without doubt hybrid fusion of music, poetry and other folk forms (Muponde 2009). His renowned style is far from the original oratory skills of the traditional Shona performance poets of his home village (Musiiwa 2004). With the backing of his band Detembira, "garnished with song and dance, drum and percussion" (Musiiwa 2004) Chirikure has placed the Shona language on the global stage consequently growing his audience base. He joins other renowned poets such as Kofi Anyidoho whose poetry is "no longer a textual art bound to the written page... [but] fully distanced from the distancing effort of print technology" (Selina 2015).

Chirikure invites some pertinent reminders to one's roots and identity. With a significant population in the urban areas, roots to the land and identity and original locations have been lost. Chirikure's concept of the umbilical cord retrieves the cultural heritage of what it means to be Zimbabwean and claims to place, ownership of resources and nationhood.

Conclusion

The chapter has demonstrated that through his poetry anthology *Rukuvhute*, Chirikure Chirikure has managed to bring to the fore the significant role of women in fostering identity and linkage to land ownership among the people of African descent. He has further demonstrated that in Shona cosmology women are not second class citizens but are in concert with their men through complimentary roles in identity formation. Chirikure Chirikure successfully integrates the umbilical cord, language and the mother figure to delineate the connections within Shona oral culture and cosmology. The umbilical cord motif clearly demonstrates the ties between the mother, land ownership and identity as well as the connections between life and death. He managed to tap from the rich repertoire of Shona folklore and mythology showing how the woman is held in very high esteem. The umbilical cord motif was also successfully used to denote the Shona people's identity, their connection to land ownership and ancestry. Chirikure's use of the indigenous Shona language concretises the identity question and also directly connects one to his place of origin, and to property that constitutes heritage among Africans.

References

Atwood, G. E., Stolorow, R. D. & Orange, D. M. (2011) The Madness and Genius of Post-Cartesian Philosophy: A Distant Mirror, in *Psychoanal Rev Jun; 98(3): pp. 263-85.*

Chirikure, C. (1989) *Rukuvhute.* Harare: College Press.

Finnegan, R. (2012) *Oral Literature in Africa* Cambridge: Open Book Publishers

Gray, C.C. (2001). *Afrocentric Thought and Praxis: An Intellectual History.* Asmara: Africa World Press.

Gudhlanga, E. S. (2013). Shutting them Out: Opportunities and Challenges of Women's Participation in Zimbabwean Politics. *Journal of Third World Studies.* 30(1): 151-170.

Gudhlanga, E.S. (2016). Gender and Land Ownership in Zimbabwean Literature: A Critical

Appraisal in Selected Shona Fiction. D Phil Thesis, University of South Africa, Department of African Languages.

Hove, C. (1988). *Bones.* Harare: Baobab Books.

Hudson-Weems, C. (2001). Africana Womanism: The Flip Side of a Coin. *The Western Journal of Black Studies,* 25(3): 141-145.

Hudson-Weems, C. (2004a). *Africana Womanism: Reclaiming Ourselves (4th Revised Edition).* Troy, Michigan: Bedford Publishers.

Hudson-Weems, C. (2006) "Africana Womanism" in Layli Phillips (ed.) *The Womanist Reader* New York: Routledge.

Hudson-Weems, C. (2007). Nommo/Self-Naming, Self Defining, and the History of Africana Womanism. In C. Hudson-Weems (ed) *Contemporary Africana Theory, Thought and Action: A Guide to Africana Studies.* Asmara: Africa World Press, pp. 289-308.

Kambarami, M. (2006) Femininity, Sexuality and Culture: Patriarchy and Female Subordination in Zimbabwe. Africa Regional Sexuality Resource Centre in collaboration with Health Systems Trust, South Africa & University of Fort Hare Understanding Human Sexuality Seminar Series

Katiyo, W. (1989) *A Son of the Soil.* Addison – Wesley Longman Ltd.

Krog, A. (2001) Women's Voices: African Poetry in Motion *Journal for the Study of Religion, Vol. 14, No. 2, Transition and Transformation in South Africa: Aspects of Women's Spirituality*, pp. 15-24

Mawere, M. (2014) *Culture, Indigenous Knowledge and Development in Africa: Reviving Interconnections for Sustainable Development* Cameroon: Langaa R PCIG

Musiiwa, M. T. (2004) The Poetry of Chirikure https://www.poetryinternationalweb.net/pi/site/cou_article/it em/5735/The-poetry-of-Chirikure-Chirikure/en

Nhemachena, A., Warikandwa, T. V. & Mpofu, N. (2018) Transitology as Cannibalism/Cannibalism as Transitology: An Examination of (Neo)Imperial Processes of Consuming African People, in *Africology: The Journal of Pan African Studies* vol 12 (6) ff

Nhemachena, A. (2017) *Relationality and Resilience in a Not So Relational World: Knowledge, Chivanhu and (De-)Coloniality in 21ˢᵗ Century Conflict –Torn Zimbabwe*. Bamenda: Langaa RPCIG.

Nnaemeka, O. (1997) *The Politics of (M)Othering: Womanhood, Identity and Resistance in African Literature*. London: Routledge.

Ojaide, T. (1996) Orality in Recent West African Poetry *College Language Association Journal*, Vol. 39, No. 3 (MARCH 1996), pp. 302-319.

Selina, B. S. (2015) Poet-Performers in Contemporary African poetry. *International Journal of English Language, Literature and Humanities* Vol III Issue IX November. Pp140-147.

Schmidt, E. (1990). Negotiated Spaces and Contested Terrain: Men, Women and the Law in Colonial Zimbabwe, 1890-1939. *Journal of Southern African Studies*, 16(4): 622-648.

Schmidt, E. (1992). *Peasants Traders and Wives: Shona Women in the History of Zimbabwe, 1870-1939*. Portsmouth: Heinemann.

Shoko, T. (2007) *Karanga Indigenous Religion in Zimbabwe: Health and Wellbeing*. Farnham: Ashgate Publishing.

Stratton, F. (2002) *Contemporary African Literature and the politics of Gender*. London: Routledge.

Wasosa, W. (2012) Chirikure as a writer in politics: a study of selected poems Africana. June/July.

wa Thiongo, N. (1986) *Decolonising the Mind.* Harare: Zimbabwe Publishing House.

Zhuwarara, R. (2001) *An introduction to Zimbabwean literature in English.* Harare: College Press.

Chapter Six

Discourses of Colonial Displacement: The Impetus of Selected Historical Novels

Colleta Kandemiri & Nelson Mlambo

Introduction

During colonial times, the majority of Zimbabweans were confronted with adversities that include displacement which brought about far-reaching consequences that upset the fundamental life patterns, cultural mores, and norms of the Black people. Some traditional African families consider fore-parents, networking several generations earlier, and these fore-parents can also be referred to as ancestors and they form part of the family. The ancestors, who are spiritual beings are said to be powerful and they are above human beings (Mbiti 1990). Their presence in the community is accepted and respected among some traditional African groups. The ancestors and the living belong together, with the ancestors' graves being situated on the physical environment and they are considered as sacred to some African societies. Thus, the displacements brought about by colonialism become sacrilege as this displacement actually promoted the separation of African people from their ancestors' remains and their ancestral lands. Ancestral lands are lands that belong to ancestors and that are passed on to progeny as heritage. More so, the displacement resulted in the degradation of the land which is a colossal consequence. It is against this background that this chapter sought to discourse on displacement emanating from the colonial milieu, explicating its arguments by relating to two historical literary novels: *The Grass is Singing* by Lessing (1950) and *Waiting for the Rain* by Mungoshi (1975). The selected novels provide a defined representation of the impact of displacement on both the displacer and the displaced in the process of displacement. Lessing (1950) shows how the displacers ravaged the land they had dispossessed of

117

Black people through the character Slatter, while Mungoshi (1975) presents how the displaced expose the levels of land degradation through the Manyene Tribal Trust Land resettlement as a result of colonial displacement as well as other pertinent issues that radiated thereafter as a consequence of dispossessions. The chapter found out that displacement during colonial times resulted in the development of some of the contemporary struggles faced by some Zimbabweans even after close to four decades of independence and these include loss of cultural footing, loss of identity, loss of ownership of resources including land, landlessness, environmental degradation, among others.

Theoretical Framework

Ecocriticism is the theoretical framework applied in this study as it deals with humans' environmental experiences of pleasure, distress, ownership, uncertainties, anticipations, desires and adversities, to name but a few, as reflected in the works of literature. Barry (2009) observes that from an ecocritical perspective, all the artistic expressions and human experiences are primarily shaped by the natural and cultural environment. Buell, Heise, and Thornber (2013: 421) also argue that, "ecocritics had emphasised ties to place, post-colonialists had foregrounded displacements". In a way, natives' connections to land ownership in Africa got disturbed and de-centred by displacements that were instigated by colonialism. Also, colonialism disrupted the relations, connections and ties between indigenous people, God and spiritual beings that exercise guardianship and control over nature (Nhemachena 2017). Oslund (2011: 5) comments that, "Colonial and postcolonial history certainly provide many examples of high modernism at work and of this ideology's disastrous effects on the environment". Thus, as Fenn (2015) argues, literature cannot separate characters from nature as these interact either by being destructive or productive to the environment. The problem with the ecocritical theories is however that they do not address the issue of land ownership by Africans – all it emphasises are equivocative notions of "relations", "connections" and "ties" between human beings and environment. In so doing, the theories deny Africans the history of ownership over their land and other environmental resources – preferring as they do to focus on "relations", "connections" and "ties". The impact of colonialism on the environment is one of the major concerns of *Waiting for the Rain* (1975) and *The Grass is Singing* (1950). However, when looking at impacts of human beings on the environment in postcolonial Africa, it is also necessary to ask questions about ownership of the environmental resources because ownership of African resources is what colonialism denied African people.

Humans and Environmental Degradation

Reser (2007: 2) asserts that "environmental degradation is in large part caused by human behaviours and it directly affects human health and well-being". Such complications resulting from human negligence and ignorance are reflected and highlighted in the novels *The Grass is Singing* (1950) and *Waiting for the Rain* (1975). Environmental degradation largely refers to the exploitation of the environment through different modes which are especially rooted in human greed and the *libido dominandi* of some other races; for instance the African environment has experienced diverse forms of exploitation and degradation, especially with the arrival of the colonisers into the continent (Owhofasa 2013). Colonisers robbed Africans of their ownership and control over the environment and therefore Africans lost the motivation to conserve the environment that had been stolen by colonisers – ownership is central to conservation measures because people conserve what they have a sense of ownership and control over. Some examples include the destruction of trees, pollution of water, pollution of farmlands, loss of pastoral beauty, the destruction of naturally occurring water bodies, and diverse health problems, which before were alien to Africa (Owhofasa 2013). These viewpoints concur with Ojaurega (2013) who proffers that the non-preservation of forest trees and wildlife as well as the natural seashores in the wake of modern architectural developments are also key factors responsible for the on-going environmental despoliation being experienced in some parts of the world.

Moreover, with regards to colonialism and its subsidiaries, aspects of environmental degradation include the non-preservation of forest trees as depicted in *The Grass is Singing* (1950) and *Waiting for the Rain* (1975), which is a major concern for this chapter in particular. Of interest is the way the environment is polluted and degraded through powerful and vicious forces of neocolonialism as seen through some of the repercussions of displacements. Pollution and degradation of the environment have negative effects on human beings.

Nature as an Agent of Destruction

From a Eurocentric perspective, "nature" has always been a chief ingredient in the survival of human beings. However from a traditional African religious point of view, spiritual forces and God control the natural world – therefore Africans hold that spirits and God are the chief ingredients in the survival of human beings. Thus, arguing from a Eurocentric perspective, Shikha (2011) contends that "nature" [and not spiritual beings and God] tends to be stronger than man. This, for Shikha, is when humans have to face the catastrophes caused by "nature" and these vengeful catastrophes are argued to be beyond human control and manipulation. Shikha (2011) further affirms that "nature" has often shown its power by controlling manpower through natural calamities like famine, droughts, floods, earthquakes and so on. Man's life and "nature" are interlinked (Ojaide 2012) and for that reason, it becomes impossible for human beings to separate themselves from its influence. However, it is also necessary to notice that African human beings are also connected to God and spiritual beings that have guardianship and control over "nature" (Schoffeleer 1999; Bourdillon 1979; 1991; Gelfand 1959; Nhemachena 2017). However, in Eurocentric thinking, humans have no choice but to accept both "nature's" bounty and adversity (Shikha 2011). Droughts are a common feature in *The Grass is Singing* (1950) and they adversely impact Dick Turner and Mary Turner. On the

120

other hand, the vengeful relationship may be explained as a nemesis of the White colonialist who has brutally dispossessed the Black African; and since the African is momentarily unable to take up arms, "nature" itself fights man's battles. Actions like the wanton exploitation of resources through activities such as resettlements in uninhabitable and fragile landscapes emanating from colonial displacements are irresponsible actions that mostly cause irreversible destructions to nature. Thus, according to Shikha's (2011) Eurocentric views, the reciprocity is more of an ecosystem in the way it works in which everything is related to each other and therefore it affects each other. The author therefore, as a liberal White writer, uses the metaphor captured in the title where "the grass is singing" as if to imply that colonial dispossession is not only evil but also unnatural such that even if the native Africans themselves might not fight for it, the grass itself will voice and "sing" its concern.

Convergence of Post-colonial and Environmental Issues

Post-colonialism in its broadest sense entails the times during colonialism as well as the times after independence of the colonised (Ashcroft *et al.* 1995). It focuses particularly on the way in which literature by the colonising culture distorts the experiences and realities of the colonised, and inscribes the inferiority of the colonised people on literature by colonised peoples, who attempt to articulate their identity and reclaim their past in the face of that past's inevitable otherness (Lye 1998). The way the environment was in Africa before colonialism, changed drastically upon the insertion of the colonisers and their ways of extensive capitalist farming that was production and profit oriented, which is consequentially detrimental to the environment as reflected in historical novels like *The Grass is Singing* (1950) and *Waiting for the Rain* (1975). Ikuenobe (2014: 2) argues that "the activities that have raised environmental concerns in Africa [even to this day] did not exist prior to colonialism because Africans had conservationist values, practices, and ways of life". In this regard, precolonial Africans had ownership and control over their environments and so they were motivated to conserve it – on the other hand, colonialism dispossessed the Africans of their environments and so it demotivated them from enacting conservational practices. Precolonial Africans did not necessarily have ties, connections or relations with the environment but they, *a fortiori,* owned and controlled the environment that was part of their heritages. Thus, colonialism to a greater extent has a major hand on environmental issues which are distressing Africa.

To the coloniser, colonialism is 'development' to Africa, but to the African environment, it is the draining of resources and degradation of the environment. Such colonial acts of disfiguring the environment are thus highlighted and criticised in literary works such as *The Grass is Singing* (1950) and *Waiting for the Rain* (1975). This therefore corroborates Huggan and Tiffin (2010: 27) who note that, "one of the central tasks of postcolonial ecocriticism as an emergent field has been to contest – also to provide viable alternatives to – western ideologies of development". However, the weakness of ecocriticism is that it does not explicate the historicity of African ownership and control over their environments and other resources – ecocriticism unduly focuses on relationships, connections and ties supposedly existing between human beings and the environments – it neglects connections between human beings and God who has created, and owns and controls nature. The denial of and neglect of African ownership and control of environments and other resources is common to both colonialism and ecocriticism (Nhemachena, Kangira & Mlambo 2018). Decolonial theories have to interrogate the commonalities between ecocriticism and colonial denials of African ownership and control of their resources. Colonialism did not deny African connections to nature – in fact Darwinist theories as well as colonial theories on animism attributed connections between African human beings and nature including animals. The enslavement and colonisation of Africans were preceded by the framing of and popularisation of Darwinist and animistic theories whose import is similar to contemporary ecocriticism theories (Nhemachena 2017). Animistic theories connect African human beings to nature/animals in ways that legitimised the use of Africans as beasts of burdens for imperial purposes.

General Colonialism in Africa

Europe colonised Africa simply for the exploitation of its natural resources, getting raw materials for the European industries and the need to get markets for the products from European industries. Africa had and still has natural resources in abundance, and from a European perspective, Africans lacked the intellect or initiative to exploit them to meet their needs (Ikuenobe 2014), and as such, Europeans exploited Africa under the disguise of bringing civilisation to Africa and Africans. In this regard, contemporary theories of ecocriticism also assume that Africans cannot have mastery, ownership and control over their resources – the ecocriticism and animism theories assume that all that Africans have are connections, relations and ties with the environments which they supposedly cannot own, control and use or have sovereignty over. Thus, Africans were displaced in order to pave way for colonial agendas.

The way the African people interacted with their African environment was, according to Ikuenobe (2014: 12), further "seen by Europeans as a sign of savagery, barbarism, and lack of intelligence and rationality, which was supposedly reflected in the African's inability to see the utility of natural resources in order to exploit and use them for human interest". Thus Moffat (2010: 23) comments that, "African peoples have often been dehumanised and marginalised". Furthermore, Falola (2007: 3) underscores the arrogance in the colonisers when for example British geographer, James MacQueen made a proclamation that, "If we really wish to do good in Africa, we must teach her savage sons that white men are their superiors".

Europeans implemented a variety of colonising stratagems by settling in some areas and then creating institutions that protected private property and in some areas they only targeted the extraction of minerals and raw materials, as much as they could. According to Hrituleac (2011), the colonisers empowered the elite in African countries such as Congo, Burundi, Ghana and Ivory Coast, to extract gold, silver, cash crops and other commodities. The colonisers included the British, the French and the Portuguese. Ferreira (1974)

123

states that Portugal formerly proclaimed that during the five centuries in which it dominated African territories; it was engaged in a civilising mission. In a way Portugal was justifying European colonisation of Africa, but it was insensitive and inconsiderate about the way the civilising mission was polluting and degrading the African environment.

By purporting to bring civilisation, the colonisers perceived themselves as agents of change. Hrituleac (2011) attests that the establishment of modern export systems, infrastructure and education facilities by the colonial powers necessitated the profitability of the whole colonisation venture. This was advantageous to the Europeans but it was detrimental to the colonised as colonialism encouraged competition and conflicts between "ethnic" groups amongst Africans (Hrituleac 2011). Bulhan (2015: 240-241) attests that "colonialism left behind enduring legacies including not only political and economic, but also cultural, intellectual, and social legacies that keep alive European domination". Colonialism is thus a continual process and its effects are impacting African societies to this present day as evidenced in the two novels. Ikuenobe (2014: 13) remarks that, "Some economists and political scientists have argued that the many economic, political, and social problems in Africa [today] can be traced to their colonial experience and environmental problems as epiphenomena of these [current/prevailing] social, political, and economic problems". As such, the waves of colonisation are still manifesting and impacting present day Africa.

Power Structures

In order to provide a context of the possible ways in which colonial invasion contributed towards environmental degradation in Africa, there is need to consider how the repressive system disrupted some of the African systems that were already in existence and functioning. With the advent of colonialism, power setups and structures of the African indigenes were interrupted by the new systems that were implemented by the European settlers. African

124

spiritual, physical and ritual ways of controlling nature were eroded by the colonialists who are now ironically claiming that nature cannot be controlled by human beings. According to Hampton and Toombs (2013: 6), "In colonisation, power relationships are established as the result of domination of another culture". With that, social structures transformed from indigenous African pre-colonial conventions to conform to the coloniser as highlighted by Ikuenobe (2014: 15) that, "within the context of the new meanings and symbols of colonialism and the new socio-cultural system it created". This conversion however, had an impact on the moral fabric and social hierarchy that existed for the African people, thereby making them to adopt and adapt to the new practices. Ikuenobe (2014: 115) remarks that, "The new powers and functions of traditional rulers and government functionaries in Africa are examples of such transformed social structures". In a way, power was tactfully seized from the Africans through the new systems brought about through colonialism, as well as proprietorship of land was removed from local communities to the government of colonialists. Such is evidenced in *Waiting for the Rain* (1975) particularly when the Black people are displaced and forced to stay in the dry and infertile colonial "reserves" like Manyene Tribal Trust Land and in addition to that, they are forced to pay hut tax. In other words, the coloniser had control over the land and Black people as well – Black people were effectively put on the same level with nature: they were regarded as tied to or connected to nature as postulated in contemporary ecocriticism and animism theories.

There is a marked observation in the reverence accorded to the land before and after colonialism. Ikuenobe (2014: 15) observes that:

> When the land was owned by communities, it was respected and preserved based on the traditional values that saw nature as something with intrinsic value that must be reverenced. When the land became government's property, it became something to be used and not cared for; in some sense, it did not belong to anybody because land was removed from the primordial public realm of the local communities to the civic public realm of the state.

This line of thought is expressed by Lessing through Charlie Slatter in *The Grass is Singing*. Charlie Slatter represents a breed of colonialists that is ruthless, self-centred and unrepentantly abusive. Slatter's prime motivation is individualistic financial gains at the expense of nature. He is a capitalist who can do anything to satisfy his insatiable appetite for more and his greedy has no limits as indicated by his desire to even dispossess Dick Turner to take over his farm and enlarge his grazing lands. This is opposed to a situation where native Africans were conscious of their environment and they highly preserved it as it was embedded in their traditional values which demanded that the land had to be appreciated, owned, controlled, cherished and preserved. Hrituleac (2011: 24) also notes that:

> The British and the French searched for African collaborators in order to better control their colonies. In this matter, the British adopted a strategy of indirect rule, using indigenous chiefs to exercise power. On the other hand, the French granted "assimilation status", where the Africans benefiting from this privilege were expected to be loyal to the state and follow the pursuit of colonial objectives. Most of the African leaders used violence to impose themselves and maintain order and law.

From that perspective therefore, it can be seen that distorted power structures are prevalent in *The Grass is Singing* (1950) through the treatment of the native Africans by the White society and in *Waiting for the Rain* (1975) it is mainly through the differences between Hampshire Estates and Manyene Tribal Trust Lands.

The Significance of Land Ownership and Identity

Land ownership is very important as it extrapolates on the idea and sense of place of attachment. Okolo (2013: 23) acknowledges that "Land is held on to as a sign of belonging to a particular community, a link to one's roots and source". The strand of identity and linking it to land ownership is presented as well by Nfah-Abbenyi (2007: 713) who argues that, "belonging to the land gives one identity

126

and a history that is deeply grounded in culture as well". Furthermore, Huggins (2010: 5) comments that, "Land is essential to most rural livelihoods, but it is also bound up very strongly with issues of identity and power". Peters (2007: 1) also observes that "Indigenous people's relationship with their traditional lands and territories is said to form a core part of their identity and spirituality and to be deeply rooted in their culture and history". Thus, the interconnectedness between land ownership and identity is established; however colonial exigencies brought about totalitarian estrangements whose conventions disrupted the African setups as presented in both *Waiting for the Rain* (1975) and *The Grass is Singing* (1950).

In a research carried out in Mashpee Wampanoag in Nepal, Peters (2007: 1) states that "Not being in control of the land, or not being able to protect it or have access to the natural foods and medicines that grow on it, gives us a really shaky future". In other words, this corroborates the idea of guarding the environment jealously as it contributes to human sustainability (Okuyade, 2013), which are some of the core tenets of ecocriticism. Okolo (2013) attests that African literature gives attention to the relationship existing between humans and the land through different cultural ceremonies like festivals and other rituals that are enacted from time to time in order to sustain such a link. Such ceremonies are distinctive in *Waiting for the Rain* (1975) and the Old Man, Sekuru Mandengu's role in the novel is to serve as a traditional vestige that constantly remind us of the ruthlessness through which colonial dispossession took place. His reliance on the drum and his sense of creativity and craftsmanship are indicative of his will to own, control and conserve nature. However, owing to how they have been displaced from the places which had abundant forests to the arid Manyene Tribal Trust lands, his actions can easily further land degradation as he has to cut down big trees. Yet still, for him to stop making the symbolic drums means that he has been severed from his spiritual, cultural and economic connections, thus meaning that colonial dispossession had huge implications for the native Africans' psycho-social wellbeing.

Furthermore, Hampton and Toombs (2013) assert that identity provides a sense of belonging to a specific group at family, community or national level and that individual identity relates closely to cultural and social identity, which incorporates roles in a social setting. Once such conditions are infiltrated by pervasive forces like colonialism, entities become disoriented and such disorientation is discernible in the Old Man, which further demonstrates how dispossession de-centred him. More so, Hampton and Toombs (2013: 6) observe that "Identity arises from the adoption of social roles through personal experience. The individual negotiates the meaning of his or her identity with family and society members". In this instance, identity is not only within an individual, it infuses the family and society as well.

As established earlier that colonialism amongst other agencies is to a great extent responsible for land degradation (Owhofasa, 2013), land degradation has a colossal consequence. ELD (2015: 8) declares that "Land degradation jeopardises ecosystem services globally, including agricultural products, clean air, fresh water, disturbance regulation, climate regulation, recreational opportunities, and fertile soils". Some of these consequences are presented in both *The Grass is Singing* (1950) and *Waiting for the Rain* (1975).

Man and the Environment in *Waiting for the Rain* (1975)

The Old Man's dream in Chapter 1 of *Waiting for the Rain* (1975) acknowledges the "complementarity" that exists between humanity and the surrounding environment. Human activities revolve around the environment such that even in their sleep, their ancestors through the environments influence their dream as evidenced from the Old Man's dream:

> The air trembles with roaring thunder and the earth grumbles with earthquakes and shrieking lightning splits the darkness into quivering shreds of light and he is a lonely whirling little dot who has to hold his own to stay alive… (Mungoshi 1975: 1).

The Old Man's frightening dream may be alluding to the restlessness that is stimulated by colonialism. The description of the roaring thunder and the earthquakes may be illustrative of the uncertainty of Black people's lives under colonial bondage where they have been displaced from their ancestral lands. To show this sense of unease, it is the "natural" environment that the author uses to show that there is a symbiotic "relationship" between man and the land; a "relationship" that manifests itself even through the spiritual world as represented by the dream. Nonetheless "The chilly morning air and the quietness clean the sleep out of his [Old Man's] head and eyes" (Mungoshi 1975: 4). Thus, the environment is multifunctional as in this case it cleanses the Old Man from the terrible dream, providing him with a consoling and comforting dose, and it serves as a refreshing tonic. The environment is there to purify and cleanse humanity both spiritually and physically, which is indicative of its role in human affairs, thus to dispossess man of this critical life-giving entity is to actually commit a slow and painful genocide.

. *Waiting for the Rain* (1975) testifies directly to the effects of colonialism particularly on the colonised and the environment. To start with, colonialism promoted racialism thereby allowing the painful germination of segregation, with Black people being affected most, regardless of the fact that land was rightfully theirs. They were driven into reserves like the Manyene Tribal Trust Land, which was infertile and life-less (Mungoshi 1975). Thus, through colonialism, there was displacement of Black people and Magaisa (2010) highlights how the creation of native reserves initiated segregation and the compulsory supplanting of Africans from their familial lands.

The Land Tenure Act of 1930, as noted by Magaisa (2010), Raftopoulos and Mlambo (2009) and Ndlovu-Gatsheni (2009), was an initiative for total spatial segregation, thus resulting in the enormous chasm between the barren Manyene Tribal Trust Land and the lush Hampshire Estates. The juxtaposition of these two places reveals the imbalances fashioned by colonialism as noted in *Waiting for the Rain* (1975):

The sudden transition from the rolling ranches of Hampshire Estates with their tall dry grass and the fertile soil under the grass; into scorched nothing-here-and-the-horizon white lands of Manyene Tribal Trust Land, with the inevitable tattered scarecrow waving a silent dirge in an empty field, makes a funeral intrusion into the bus. And those who have been singing all the way from Salisbury with drunken excitement of going home seem to be regretting their having come at all (Mungoshi 1975: 39).

The comparison of Manyene Tribal Trust Land to Hampshire Estates articulates the deplorable circumstances of Black people stirred by repressive systems like the colonialism as experienced at that particular time and the present moment. In *Waiting for the Rain* (1975), the characters express their grievances that "this is our country, the people say with a sad familiarity (Mungoshi 1975: 39). The "empty fields" signal barrenness and they are indicative of how denuded the land is, which makes it enormously difficult for the Black people to erke a living in the Manyene Tribal Trust Lands.

The segregation does not just end in separating Black people from White people but rather, it is an extension of the negative effects manifesting and impacting on the environment. The Manyene Tribal Trust Land is a colonial construct and an agonising situation as many Black people got cramped in the reserves which in turn could not sustain such a huge and progressively expanding population. That could be the reason why the "scarecrow" is waving a "silent dirge" which makes a "funeral intrusion on to the bus" (Mungoshi 1975: 39). If the environment is likened to a 'funeral' then it may be interpreted that the environment is futile and gives back nothing. The funeral metaphor that has been employed refocuses our ways of thinking towards the novel *Waiting for the Rain* (1975). There is an unavoidable sense of disaffection and there is no feeling of attachment towards the land, and notable being that Manyene Tribal Trust Lands is a colonial creation – it is product of colonial dispossession. Thus there is no sense of belonging as evidenced in the novel where it reads:

Not until you look towards the east and see the tall sun-bleached rocks of Manyene Hills casting foreboding shadows over land beyond like sentinels over some fairy-tale land of the dead, are you really at home (Mungoshi 1975: 40).

The visibly 'sun-bleached rocks of Manyene Hills' could signify deforestation and the excessive cutting down of trees hence leaving the rocks bare and visible. This concurs with Reser's (2007: 2) assertion that "environmental degradation is in large part caused by human behaviours". In this case, colonialism is the human behaviour and force behind the activities evident in Manyene Tribal Trust Lands.

The reserves like Manyene are unproductive and unyielding, and these are the places that the Black majority were driven and forced into. In their deplorable state, the situation about the degradation of the environment escalated as instigated by the colonial move of restricting Africans into the so-called reserves. Noted is the destruction of rivers through siltation where Mungoshi (1975) states that:

And here now the bus turns west, following the line of the old village, and you look across Suka - which has given up flowing - and see the line of the new village stretching like an interminable snake in the sun from the southern bank of the river, on and over the rim of the earth to the other end of the world, with the Ancient Rain Tree - now impotent - standing guard in an empty landscape (Mungoshi 1975: 40-41).

The above quotation justifies Ikuenobe's (2014) argument that the activities that have raised environmental concerns in Africa did not exist prior to colonialism as Africans had conservationist values, practices and ways of life. Thus the forceful and uncaringly violent colonial settling methods along Suka River resulted in the river 'giving up'. This impacts on the environment as the river will not be able to provide people, animals and nature with water. The whole natural system and the water cycle are disturbed. The people along

131

Suka River had to adopt and adapt some tactics in order to survive. The forceful resettlement of people without care and concern by the colonial forces has had and continues to have disastrous effects on the environment, hence the river is now failing to "reciprocate" and "complement" the relationship that exists between humanity and the environment. This is evidenced in *Waiting for the Rain* (1975) as:

> She [Betty] crosses Suka River, now almost dry - a mere trickle of rusty water on a bed of sun-browned sand. She digs in the sand till water begins to sip into the hole through the grains of sand. She waits until there is enough water to fill a mouth. She takes a drink and moves on (Mungoshi 1975: 37).

Nature provides for the sustenance of human beings and any form of disturbance to the natural resources results in nature failing to provide for humans. Life becomes difficult for humans as their life is dependent on the providence of nature. Also, Garabha "kneels down to drink from the river, his open palms pressed hard against- and his fingers digging into – the hard packed sand" (Mungoshi 1975: 81-82). This somehow proves how bad the situation is; the impact that environmental degradation had on humanity such that they had to struggle to get water to drink. On a symbolical level, water is an important natural resource and its lack is detrimental to human life.

Because of colonialism, other agencies of denudation are also highlighted in *Waiting for the Rain* (1975) where Mungoshi (1975: 81) states that "He [Garabha] drops the stunted bush, down the cattle-and-rain deepened stony path to the river". The stony paths are a sign of environmental degradation which will eventually transform into gullies, thereby degrading the environment. Furthermore, the state of Suka River and its surroundings evokes Garabha's "childhood memories, as he sees the helpless silvery trickle in the sand that is the mighty Suka in flood time, but now, in dry season reduced to begging for a passage through sandy wastes" (Mungoshi 1975: 81). It may therefore be concluded that colonialism (and colonial greed) is one of the, if not the worst force responsible for the deplorable state that Suka River is. Manyene Tribal Trust Lands is a microcosm of

Rhodesia, implying that the pervasive colonial measures may have been uniform through-out the country and natural resources like rivers were threatened.

The repressive system was structured in a way that the colonisers would enjoy most of the "natural" resources at the expense of the indigenous people. Suka River along which the Black people were forcefully settled succumbed to siltation and other forms of denudation resulting in it now failing to provide water to the inhabitants. This is unlike "the mightier Munyati in the plains of Hampshire Estates" (Mungoshi 1975: 81) which is forever flowing and Black people no longer have access to it, owing to racist and evil colonial rules that segregated them but granted the colonisers a superfluous form of dominance. Childhood memories to Garabha are such that "Munyati River: the memory is hunting at night and the vision of quick, tail flickering reed buck drinking water at dusk-fall" (Mungoshi 1975: 81). These are just nostalgic and sweet memories that are unfortunately disturbed by colonialism and some of its subsidiaries. The memories are there to provide a reflective glimpse into balanced nature where there is water in abundance for use by both humans and animals; and the environment would provide game for hunting for meat. But all this has been distorted, destroyed and denied to the Black man due to colonial dispossession.

When the reserves like Manyene Tribal Trust Land were created, Black people were forcibly moved to these areas together with their large herds of cattle. However, the large herds of cattle could not be sustained by the strained and barren lands, thereby posing a danger and further threatening the land, thus leading to environmental degradation. According to Bhebhe (1989), by 1943, most reserves were in a deplorable state due to overstocking and destructive methods of cultivation that were happening in those settlements. *Waiting for the Rain* (1975) thus contains sufficient and powerful utilitarian prototypes on how inhumane colonial practices led to environmental mortification.

In *Waiting for the Rain* (1975), the Old Man feels betrayed and he is melancholic as he wonders as to what used to be the number of his herd of cattle but now reduced to nearly nothing because of the

Native Land Husbandry Act of 1951, where the colonial statute required Black people to have a limited number of livestock. Mungoshi (1975: 5) describes the Old Man thus: "Here again he [Old Man] stands and thinks of his once hundred head of cattle – when grass was still Earth's grass – now reduced to ten". This kind of manifestation is contradictory to the coloniser's way of perceiving themselves as "agents of change" (Hrituleac 2011) and being "engaged in a civilising mission" (Ferreira 1974). Rather, the manifestations are the justification of the intended mission to Africa for "extreme exploitation and manipulation leaving the land in anguish and poverty" (Weilin 2011: 115), which the researchers deem a devastating formula of vandalism and destruction.

The devastating state of the environment represented in *Waiting for the Rain* (1975) may mostly be attributed to colonial forces that came and intervened by interrupting and emasculating the organised African systems that were in place and were functional. According to the Old Man, "Everything was the earth's" (Mungoshi 1975: 116), implying that there were structures in place but that did not reflect on ownership of the land and the environment, as by that time, land literally belonged to 'Earth'. So the advent of colonialism and consequently the imposition of the Land Apportionment Act of 1930 altered this kind of approach and introduced the grabbing of land and the "ownership" of land by a few who could use and abuse it.

When the land was originally in the hands of Africans, as highlighted by Ikuenobe (2014), that it was owned, controlled, respected and preserved, based on the traditional values which saw nature as something with intrinsic value and thus which must be reverenced. Thus, Africans were conscious of their environment and highly preserved it since it formed part of their traditional values. In a way, *Waiting for the Rain* (1975) is a novel that confronts post-colonial concerns by exposing the impact that colonialism had on the environment. The Old Man laments how the land was stolen from Black people and insists on "what comes of playing someone's drum" (Mungoshi 1975:117), which is his mantra to decry the effects of dispossession, deposition and the attended feelings of helplessness and rootlessness.

Moreover, nature's way of "giving" sustenance and provisions to the day to day lives of human beings shows nature's "kindness". In *Waiting for the Rain* (1975), there are numerous instances where nature "provides" for human beings, proving how humans are dependent on nature as shown here: "Later, after taking Old Mandisa her firewood, the Old Man sits smoking in his semi-circular grass-and-branch workshop on the edge of the yard. The log he left burning last night is still alight" (Mungoshi 1975: 7). Trees are used for firewood and together with grass for construction of different infrastructure. This is also noted when Betty "pulls out a handful of grass and rolls it into a circular cushion, puts it on her head and then balances the pot on top of the cushion" (Mungoshi 1975: 89). The pot she is carrying has water that has been "provided" by the environment and the pot itself is made from the clay which is also "provided" by nature. The cushion she makes is from the grass, again showing how heavily dependent humans are on the environment. However, in Shona annual rituals of thanks giving after harvests, they expressed the gratitude not necessarily to nature but to the *mhondoro* spiritual being that would have made it possible to get rain - it is, for the Shona people, God and *mhondoro* that provided for the sustenance of human beings (Gelfand 1959; Bourdillon 1979; 1991; Nhemachena 2017).

Another instance is noticed when Raina uses cow dung as floor polish. The use of cow dung is an indicator of how natural resources can be recycled and be used without impacting on the environment. This is evident from the novel when "She [Raina] will do Lucifer's room. She will sweep out the chicken curt, smear the floor with cow dung to stay the dust and clean the cobwebs in the corners (Mungoshi 1975: 19). Cows eat grass and they produce cow dung as a by-product, other than serving as manure the cow dung may also be used for floors to get rid of dust in some homes, further reinforcing the interaction and interdependency of humanity and the environment.

Also, in the novel the land is seen to "provide" food, when people cultivate and grow different types of plants which in turn provide an assortment of food. For instance, from *Waiting for the Rain* (1975), along Suka River, Betty "can hear the noise of some boys fishing" (Mungoshi 1975:37). Other than that, the environment additionally "provides" for the medicinal needs and sustenance of the humans. The medicines that were meant for Lucifer to carry overseas with him for protection, which he refuses to carry at the end of the novel, were also "provided" by nature. Again it confirms the dependence and connectivity to the environment that humans are. In *Waiting for the Rain* (1975), the Old Man says, "My own grandfather showed me the shrub. But it's the bulb of that shrub that makes this medicine. It's a cure for low spirits, severe pains, lack of energy – anything" (Mungoshi 1975: 93), in other words the land "holds" the cure for anything. This conversation between Old Man and Garabha reflects on passing on of a people's knowledge from generation to generation by word of mouth thereby drawing in the aspects of indigenous knowledge systems. Thus, despite the colonial context in which they are, this scenario is more of a powerful statement to protest the severance of the people from their land.

Moreover, the environment cannot talk but it communicates by some kind of indication as a means of "retaliation" or "acceptance". The reactions are what humans interpret for them to comprehend nature's response. However, in Shona cosmologies, environmental changes including droughts were interpreted as signifying the anger of *mhondoro* spirits and God - who therefore needed appeasement (see Gelfand 1959; Bourdillon 1979; 1991; Nhemachena 2017). Tongoona's wife, Raina, is described as an untidy woman who seems not to care about the environment that she lives in. Raina and Tongoona's sleep and sleeping environment is infested "…crossing the dangerous and lonely night-river of bugs, fleas, lice and the other not-so-easily-named things…" (Mungoshi 1975: 8). In a way, the presence of the bugs and fleas and so forth, may be a signal from the environment that Raina is failing to "reciprocate" with the environment. The untidiness is further described when Tongoona remarks:

> At least you could dust the room. Each time I have to sleep I must wade through a foot of dust, a jungle of rags, stumbling through a battle of pots, plates, spoons and what-not-else as if this were a kitchen,

clawing my face trapped in spider-netting. Expect a body to live long (Mungoshi 1975:8).

The untidiness is symbolic of the chaotic colonial imposition. The parasites may literary represent the colonisers whose presence exhibit distinctive features of the humiliation of the colonised, hence the parasites distressing Tongoona and Raina through every night.

The presentation of Raina's everyday untidiness and bedroom which are interior, juxtaposed to the way she prepares the room for Lucifer, say volumes about colonial infiltration. This may be interpreted as a way to show that Lucifer is being venerated as a figure of distinction by virtue of acquiring the White man's education. Comparing Lucifer to the elderly brother Garabha, it appears that the brothers have exchanged birth rights with Lucifer usurping his senior brother's position, which is all symptomatic of the extensive and exclusive functioning of colonialism. Through Tongoona, revelations of such insignias are distinguished where he says "But, because I have appointed you Father of the Family, don't you think that I am throwing Garabha out" (Mungoshi 1975:158).

The truth is that Garabha is considered as nondescript as he is not educated, and as such the father feels that Garabha deserves to be sacked. Even the Old Man is equally shocked as he says, "You want to disinherit the eldest son while he is still alive" (Mungoshi 1975: 152). Tongoona goes further to comment on Garabha that, "He is only a fool and you will have to care for him until he dies" (Mungoshi 1975: 158). Thus, the parents' behaviours (Tongoona and Raina) are equally contaminated by colonialism and for that resolve to propelling the veneration of Lucifer.

Additionally, it can be further argued that the environment communicates with humans as the Old Man confirms that in the battle of the First Chimurenga, a number of people died and as such, "That year there was no rain" (Mungoshi 1975: 115). The environment was probably "retaliating" to the uninviting actions done by human beings. The Old Man goes further to justify why the environment had but reacted thus as "The earth was angry with so much spilling of blood" (Mungoshi 1975: 115). It may therefore be commented that the fighting that happened in the First Chimurenga did not conform to nature's expectations of human beings. As such the humans were being punished as there were no rains and the Old Man confirms that, "We were hungry" (Mungoshi 1975: 115). It can therefore be concluded that within Mungoshi's setting nature does not "approve" of violence and for that it can "punish" humans through droughts and other forms of disasters hence nature can be an agent of destruction.

Induction and Ramification of Colonialism in *Waiting for the Rain*

Waiting for the Rain (1975) is a novel that attests to life's disrupting setbacks instigated by colonialism and its subsidiaries. Mungoshi's deft integration of the environment aids in articulating the subsequent realisations of colonialism. *Waiting for the Rain* (1975) may be described as a kind of dystopia as highlighted by Baccolini (2004), that it is actually a negative utopia where dehumanisation and poverty are ubiquitous. However, it has to be borne in mind that the dystopian feature of *Waiting for the Rain* (1975) is routed and anchored in colonialism and expressed through the use of metaphors pertaining to the environment.

The effects of colonialism are even felt in almost all spheres of life and they can intrude into the victims' dreams just like the distress in the Old Man's dream. The apt ability of literature to capture and expose those qualitative and intricate features affiliated to colonialism aid in realising the impact of colonialism as well as in comprehending the novel deeply.

Colonialism impacted on the social life and way of thinking of the colonised people. In *Waiting for the Rain* (1975) such disruptive change is discernible and noted through the way the characters converse. The language itself is immensely influenced such that even in the act of pacifying children grains of colonialism are assertive. This is noted when Lucifer says to his younger brothers:

Grown up as you are. I won't take you on the bus to Salisbury to see the cars and the shops and ride the big wheel at Lunar Park. And there won't be any sweets or biscuits or shoes or any nice clothes for any cry-babies (Mungoshi 1975: 113).

Such words have power that is anchored in colonialism forcing one to think on the retooled language and culture, since language and culture are compatibles. It promotes Black invisibility and promotes the coloniser's ways to the fore. The Old Man is able to ascertain the presence of a problem by questioning the way Lucifer tries to pacify the little ones where he says "Well, what do you think of that? This new language - this new way of pacifying crying children" (Mungoshi 1975: 113). The Old Man is concerned as this is an indication of the ailing and eventual death of their culture, language and identity hence he talks about "playing someone else's drum".

The Old Man can see that their life is changing as they are moving away from their traditional African language, culture and ways of life. He makes a comparison of how the differences come to be where he says, "In our day, our parents frightened us with threats of monsters that would come and eat us. Today the child stops crying with promises of the new life: sweets and biscuits" (Mungoshi 1975: 113). In a way, the Old Man's salient observation denotes the dynamic operations of colonialism.

Similarly, to ascertain the dynamism in colonialism, the Old Man highlights some of the indications that are following colonialism and how they are extending to almost all avenues of the African people's ways of life. For instance, the Old Man says, "Each time my wife Japi take in a handful of sugar, I know how complete and final the white man's conquest has been" (Mungoshi 1975: 115). That craving for sugar may be suggesting the infiltration and perpetual settling of colonialism in the African people, and again it is an indication of "playing an enemy's drum". This includes the radio that John brought for Lucifer for his farewell and other material things that are deeply rooted in colonialist establishments.

Furthermore, the refusal of Lucifer to carry traditional medicine meant to "to protect" him when he goes overseas is another example of how colonialism infiltrates in almost all facets of the colonised people's life. One of the unnamed characters in *Waiting for the Rain* (1975) comments on how people like Lucifer no longer take their culture and traditions seriously and says, "That was wrong. You should have given him some pills. You will never get these educated children drinking any roots" (Mungoshi 1975: 121). This comment was passed after Lucifer was said to have been attacked by a headache and one of the grandmothers had prepared traditional medicine which Lucifer refused to take. Again the preference of pills to traditional medicine is as good as "playing someone else's drum".

The constant reference to the drum by the Old Man is a deep metaphor and when he says "playing someone else's drum" there is much to be desired as the statement gives away the complete meaning of *Waiting for the Rain* (1975) in just a few words. The few words encapsulate the literary meaning, that of moving away from one's specificity by embracing others' way of life. This then results in ambivalence and jeopardising of one's own culture and tradition.

Man and the Environment in *The Grass is Singing*

In *The Grass is Singing* (1950), reference is instantly made that attests to the existence of a "relationship" between man and the environment. The coming of colonial settlers to Rhodesia, who established as farmers, is an indication on how humanity interacts with the environment, though colonialism was not really for the development and care of the Rhodesian lands. The construction of settler networking defaced the appearance of the Rhodesian terrain probably disturbing the natural environment and its ecosystem, evident from the novel where it says:

> As the railway lines spread and knotted and ramified all over Southern Rhodesia, along them, at short distances of a few miles, sprang up little dorps that to a traveller appear as insignificant clusters of ugly buildings but which are the centres of farming districts perhaps a couple of hundred miles across. They contain the station building, the post office, sometimes a hotel, but always a store (Lessing 1950: 36).

The infrastructure mentioned in the above quotation may be what Hrituleac (2011) has commented as a facility that necessitated the profitability of the whole colonisation venture, as the motive behind colonisation was hinged on exploitation of natural resources in Africa. The establishment of these centres meant cutting down of trees and paving way for the rail and road networks. It may have been a good idea in terms of development but it was detrimental to the environment. Thus, human actions are responsible for environmental degradation.

Other than that, the White farmers probably had a deficiency in caring for the environment observed as they propelled the colonial agenda with diligence. On the huge chunks of land that they designated to themselves through the Land Apportionment Act of 1931 which instigated segregation (as mentioned already by Magaisa 2010; Raftapoulos & Mlambo 2009; Bhebe 1989), there was malpractice seen through their operations. On those farms land degrading activities were evident as presented when Lessing (1950: 98) notes that, "Mr Slatter's farm had hardly any trees left on it". It could be that when Mr Slatter first came to the farm, the land had trees on it and the place was probably environmentally healthy, however the exploitative farming methods resulted in it being "a monument for farming malpractices, with great gullies cutting through it, with acres of good dark earth gone dead from misuse" (Lessing 1950: 98).

The Slatter farm may be a replica to The Hampshire Estates in *Waiting for the Rain* (1950), in which Mungoshi (1975) just contemplates on the outside appearance leaving much to be desired whilst other writers like Lessing (1950) deliberate on the expositions of what really transpires on those farms. However, the White farmers like Slatter "made the money, that was the thing" (Lessing 1950: 98). In other words, the purpose of the White farmers was fulfilled as their mission was on exploitation and none about the welfare of the environment. Therefore, Lessing (1950) subtly attacks colonialism by not pointing to it directly but rather using characters such as Slatter in *The Grass is Singing* (1950) to bring out the environmental concerns.

Ramification of Colonialism on the Coloniser

The whole motive behind colonialism was to enrich the White people by subjugating the African people and their land. Colonialism brought suffering on the Black people and issues such as those discussed in the analysis of *Waiting for the Rain* (1975). However, the complications of colonialism did not impact on the Black people alone, the colonised; it extended its tentacles to distress on its agents, the colonisers. *The Grass is Singing* (1950) allows a glimpse into the sufferings that the colonisers endured under their own masterminded colonialism. The novel successfully articulates with bluntness the coarseness of colonialism on the colonisers.

Segregation is one of the colonial tendons that was also noticed within the White colonisers as "Long before the murder marked them out, people spoke of the Turners in the hard careless voices reserved for misfits, outlaws and the self-exiled" (Lessing 1950: 10). So the White communities were susceptible to isolation just like they isolated Black people from the White communities. As for the Turners, the segregation was a contagious type as they "were disliked, though few of their neighbours had ever met them or even seen them in the distance" (Lessing 1950: 11). However, the Turners knew they were disliked and in return "They were never seen at district dances, or fete, gymkhanas" (Lessing 1950: 11), where the White society mingled and socialised. Their excommunication signalled instability and solitary life in a colonial context, they neither belonged to the White community nor the Black community, even the environment "spurned" them; their farm never produced enough to sustain them.

It appears the Turners' segregation was rooted in them being poor "though the arguments were unanswerable, people would still not think of them as poor Whites. To do that would be letting the side down" (Lessing 1950: 11). In a way reducing the status of the White people was not acceptable as they had the 'right' to prestigious life. So even if the Turners were not well up, they were not supposed to be referred to as "poor whites" because "The Turners were British, after all" (Lessing 1950: 11).

The description of the Turners' house "a small square building" (Lessing 1950: 62), with corrugated iron roofing and "looked shut and dark and stuffy" (Lessing 1950: 63), though few of the natives "had houses as good" (Lessing 1950: 11). Inside the house "there was a strong musty smell, almost animal like" (Lessing 1950: 63). As if not enough, their farm never produced anything profitable therefore rendering the whole idea of farming futile. Their poor life on the farm "for years they provided the staple of gossip among the farmers round about" (Lessing 1950: 208). Again this points to disunity amongst the colonisers, though the first law of White South Africa stated that "Thou shalt not let your fellow whites sink lower than a certain point" (Lessing 1950: 221) but for the Turners, they had been sinking, never to rise again.

Another issue, which is more of a peculiar and of personal deportment, on the part of Mary Turner and her enduring relationship with Dick Turner, expounds on the absence of love. The relationship between Mary and Dick is for convenience; they never got to fall for each other but had to get married to cover up certain discrepancies that had arisen in their individual lives. For Mary it was "all the time, unconsciously, without admitting it to herself, she was looking for a husband" (Lessing 1950: 51). For Dick "He was lonely, he wanted a wife, and above all, children" (Lessing 1950: 56). For that, "they were married by special licence two weeks later after the proposal. However, even Dick himself was surprised by "her desire to get married as quickly as possible" (Lessing 1950: 60) and surprisingly the marriage was not properly seasoned that it was tasteless and distasteful.

Dick failed to provide and satisfy Mary's material, sensual and probably spiritual needs as well, which resulted in a problem that was way beyond expectations of the coloniser community; that of Mary resorting to a Black servant who indeed successfully filled in the gap that was created and left void by Dick. Moses had genuine love for Mary but the motive behind him killing Mary is not stated though there may be a number of possibilities such as that of helping Mary to stop suffering and also that of being jealous of Mary going away with Dick on holiday and highly not to return. However, another possible perception could be that to satisfy colonial typecasts as:

> The newspaper did not say much. People all over the country must have glanced at the paragraph with its sensational heading and felt a spurt of anger mingled with what was almost satisfaction, as if some belief had been confirmed, as if something had happened which could only have been expected. When natives steal, murder or rape, that is the feeling white people have (Lessing 1950: 9).

This stereotype is what Lessing (1950) attempts to clarify that Black people had no voice in the colonial setting and that it was partly if not wholly the White people's responsibility in creating a dystopia (Baccolini 2004) characterised by a society that is undesirable and frightening; where there is dehumanisation, poverty, societal collapse and where humanity suffers from a lack of true freedom and liberty. The death of Mary did not spring from Moses wanting to rape or steal from the White woman, but the account of how it all began gives a basis to argue like Lessing (1950) that the truth could be something else shocking other than the prevailing and common stereotypes levelled against Black people. Besides, all the ills, be it on human beings (the victims and the victimisers) or the natural environment, has the roots in colonialism.

Lastly, the death of Mary brought with it some transformations at the farm as "After that, the Turner's farm was run as an overflow for Charlie's cattle. They grazed all over it even up to the hill where the house stood" (Lessing 1950: 34). The environment could not "give" and "sustain" Mary and Dick but after they were gone, cattle benefitted from that farm. The house, "it was left empty; it soon fell down" (Lessing 1950: 34). At a symbolical level, the falling down of the house could mean the natural environment trying to "restore" its naturalness and by letting the house fall, it could be signalling that nature is "conquering" colonialism which is human made. Even the environment does not stand colonialism, hence Mary and Dick failing to stay at their farm much longer.

Conclusion

The analysis of the chosen two novels *The Grass is Singing* and *Waiting for the Rain* provided a defined representation of the impact of displacement on both the displacer and the displaced in the process of displacement. *The Grass is Singing* shows how the displacers ravaged the land they had dispossessed of Black people through the character Slatter, while *Waiting for the Rain* presents how the displaced contributed to land degradation through the Manyene Tribal Trust Land resettlement. Furthermore, as a result of colonial displacement other pertinent issues such as loss of cultural footing, segregation, stereotyping, subjugation and humiliation of Black people, Black invisibility, creation of dystopia, violence, environmental concerns, to name but a few radiated thereafter as consequences. It may therefore be concluded that the displacement that took place during colonial times resulted in the development of some of the contemporary struggles faced by some Zimbabweans even after close to four decades of political independence and these include loss of cultural footing, loss of identity, loss of ownership of land and other resources, landlessness, environmental degradation, among others.

References

Ashcroft, B., Griffiths, G., & Tiffin, H. (1995). *The post-colonial studies reader.* New York: Routledge.

Baccolini, R. (2004). The persistence of hope in dystopian science fiction. *Modern Language Association, 11*(3), 518-521.

Barry, P. (2009). *Beginning theory: An introduction to literary and cultural theory* (3rded.).Manchester, UK: University of Manchester Press.

Bhebe, N. (1989). *B. Burombo: African politics in Zimbabwe 1947-1958.* Harare, Zimbabwe: The College Press.

Bourdillon, M. F. C. (1979) *The Shona People: An Ethnography of the Contemporary Shona with Special Reference to their Religion.* Gweru: Mambo Press.

Bourdillon, M. F. C (1991) *The Shona People. Gweru:* Mambo Press.

Buell, L., Heise, U. K., & Thornber, K. (2013). Literature and environment. *Annual Review of Environment and Resources, 36*, 417–440.

Bulhan, A. H. (2015). Stages of colonialism in Africa: From occupation of land to occupation of being. *Journal of Social and Political Psychology, 3*(1), 239–256.

ELD Initiative. (2015).*The value of land: Prosperous lands and positive rewards through sustainable land management.* Retrieved on 16 January 2017 from http://www.eld-initiative.org/index.php?id=111

Falola, T. (2007). *The Amistad's legacy: Reflections on the spaces of colonisation.* Fourth Annual Distinguished AMISTAD Lecture, Central Connecticut State University, 14(2). Retrieved on 25 July 2017. http://web.ccsu.edu/afstudy/upd14-2.html

Fenn, V. (2015). Roots of ecocriticism: An exploration of the history of ecocriticism, a literary theory of the post-modern world. *Journal of English Language and Literature, 2*(2), 115-119.

Ferreira, E. S. (1974). *Portuguese colonialism in Africa: The end of an era.* Paris, France: The UNESCO Press.

Gelfand, M. (1959) *Shona Ritual with Special Reference to the Chaminuka Cult.* Cape Town: Juta & Co.

Ndlovu-Gatsheni, S. J. (2009). From the Second World War to UDI, 1940–1965. In B. Raftopoulos & A. Mlambo (Eds.) *Becoming Zimbabwe: A history from the pre-colonial period to 2008* (pp. 75-114). Harare: Weaver Press.

Hampton, R., & Toombs, M. (2013). Culture, identity and indigenous Australian people. In R. Hampton & M. Toombs (Ed.), *Indigenous Australians and health: The wombat in the room* (pp. 3-23). South Melbourne, VIC, Australia: Oxford University Press.

Hrituleac, A. (2011). *The effects of colonialism on African economic development: A comparative analysis between Ethiopia, Senegal and Uganda.* Aarhus University,Retrieved on 20 July 2016. http://pure.au.dk/portal-asb-student/files/41656700/

Huggan, G., & Tiffin, H. (2010). *Postcolonial ecocriticism.* New York: Routledge.

Huggins, C. (2010). *Land, power and identity: Roots of violent conflict in Eastern DRC.* Retrieved on 14 July 2016 from www.international-alert.org

Ikuenobe, P. A. (2014). Traditional African environmental ethics and colonial legacy. *International Journal of Philosophy and Theology, 2*(4), 1-21.

Lessing, D. (1950). *The grass is singing.* London, UK: Heinemann Educational Books Ltd.

Lye, J. (1998). Contemporary literary theory. *Brock Review, 2*(1), 90-106.

Magaisa, A. T. (2010). *The land question and transitional justice in Zimbabwe: Law, force and history's multiple victims.* Retrieved on 16 January 2017 from https://www.law.ox.ac.uk/sites/files/oxlaw

Mbiti, S. J. (1990). *African religions and philosophy.* London, UK: Heinemann.

Moffat, R. (2010). *Perspectives on Africa in travel writing: Representations of Ethiopia, Republic of Congo and South Africa, 1930–2000.* (PhD thesis, University of Glasgow).

Mungoshi, C. (1975). *Waiting for the rain.* Harare: Heinemann Books.

Nfah-Abbenyi, J. M. (2007). Ecological post-colonialism in African women's literature. In T. Olaniyan & A. Quayson (Eds), *African literature: An anthology of criticism and theory* (pp. 233-246). Oxford, UK: Blackwell Publishing.

Nhemachena, A. (2017). *Relationality and Resilience in a Not So Relational World? Knowledge, Chivanhu and (De-)Coloniality in 21st Century Conflict-Torn Zimbabwe.* Bamenda: Langaa RPCIG.

Nhemachena, A., Kangira, J. & Mlambo, N. (2018). *Decolonisation of Materialities or Materialisation of Recolonisation? Symbolisms, Languages, Ecocriticism and (Non)Representationalism in 21st Century Africa.* Bamenda: Langaa RPCIG.

Ojaide, T. (2012). *Contemporary African literature: New approaches.* Durham, England: Carolina Academic Press.

Ojaruega, E. (2013). Eco-activism in contemporary African literature: Zakes Mda's *Heart of redness* and Tanure Ojaide's *The activist.* In O. Okuyade (Ed.), *Eco-critical literature: Regreening African landscape* (pp. 31-46). New York, NY: African Heritage Press.

Okolo, I. (2013). Landscaping as a plot and character development medium in Ngugi wa Thiong'o's *Wizard of the crow*. In O. Okuyade (Ed.), *Eco-critical literature: Regreening African landscapes* (pp. 15-30). New York, NY: African Heritage Press.

Okuyade, O. (2013). Introduction: African cultural art forms, eco-activism, and (eco) -logical consciousness. In O. Okuyade (Ed.), *Eco-critical literature: Regreening African landscapes* (pp. ix-xviii). New York, NY: African Heritage Press.

Oslund, K. (2011) Introduction: Getting our hands dirty. Retrieved on 16 July 2016 from http://www.ohioswallow.com/extras/9780896802827_intro.pdf

Owhofasa, O. D. (2013). Women as victims, environmentalists and eco-activists in Vincent Egbuson's *Love my planet*. In O. Okuyade (Ed.), *Eco-critical literature: Regreening African landscapes* (pp. 123-138). New York, NY: African Heritage Press.

Peters, R. (2007). *Indigenous peoples - lands, territories and natural resources*. Retrieved on 22 January 2017. http://www.un.org/esa/socdev/unpfii/en/session_sixth.html

Raftopoulos, B., & Mlambo, A. S. (2009). *Becoming Zimbabwe: A history from the pre-colonial period to 2008*. Harare: Weaver Press.

Reser, J. P. (2007). *Psychology and the natural environment*. A position statement prepared for The Australian Psychological Society. Retrieved on 16 July 2016. https://www.psychology.org

Schoffeleers, M. (ed) (1999). *Guardians of the Land*. Kachere Series.

Shikha, K. (2011). *Ecocriticism in Indian fiction*. Retrieved on 10 January 2017 from http://worldlitonline.net/ecocriticism-in.pdf

Shoba, V., & Nagaraj, P. (2013). Ecology in relation to ecocriticism – A theoretical approach. *Indian Journal of Applied Research, 3*(1), 85-86.

Weilin, L. (2011). An ecological analysis: The sense of loss from *Heart of darkness*. *Studies in Literature and Language, 2*(3), 153-160.

Chapter Seven

Spatial Marginalisation: (Re)reading Musaemura Zimunya's Gendered Space and Place in *Country Dawns and City Lights*

Angeline Mavis Madongonda

Introduction

Land ownership in Zimbabwe is gendered in that ownership patterns from a colonial perspective reflect the same. Since colonial (Western) and patriarchal discourses on land predominate in most studies, little consideration has been given to how African women were colonially dispossessed. Therefore, African women have hardly been factored on loss of land and related issues. While colonial urban space provided an alternative for the many who were displaced and flocked to towns, there was no consideration of spaces to accommodate displaced African women. This chapter focuses on two main issues; first, how the urban space has not been adequately interrogated as running back to back with land dispossession. The urban space vividly gives us the flip side of the effects of land dispossession. A significant number of studies focus on land dispossession from a rural perspective, which is in the light of agricultural land (Moyana, 2000; Mafa, Gudhlanga, Manyeruke, Matavire & Mpofu, 2015; Gudhlanga 2016; Zhuwarara, 2001). Secondly, the gendered space variable has not been factored in most critical works of literature as the land issue was viewed in general rather than specific to any gender. Few analyses have hinted on the urban men and women who lost their livelihoods and shifted to alternative homes in the city space where the gendered effect on the men has been largely promulgated. This chapter looks at selected poems by Musaemura Zimunya in a bid to discern the hidden dimensions of urban men and women's loss of land during the colonial era. The chapter utilises qualitative and interpretivist research methods; hence a textual analysis of selected poems from Zimunya's *Country Dawns and City* lights is done. Zimunya's anthology offers rare gendered perspectives on land and the rural/urban divide. The chapter is shaped by Feminist Urbanist Theory. The theory explains the settlement of people from rural to urban capitalist centres. The chapter also utilises Cleonora Hudson-Weems' Africana Womanism (1987) which debunks colonial and Western patriarchal myths that posited the discourse of men being the owners and workers of the land (and conversely losers during land dispossession), suffering the worst effects of land loss. It explores how dispossession is reflected in the city spaces of colonial Salisbury and demonstrates how women (like their male counterparts) who ended up in the city were also losers through the dislocations caused by colonialism.

Background

This chapter has been framed by the historical context around Musaemura Zimunya's works. Colonialism, marginalisation, dispossession and disempowerment of the people by the colonial pieces of legislation such as the Land Apportionment Act (1930) and Land Tenure Act (1965), Land Husbandry Act (1951) and other laws that led to the creation of Tribal Trust Lands/Reserves, commercial farms, towns and cities (Mapanzure 2014). The laws were enacted supposedly to correct bad traditional agricultural practices and techniques that were used by the indigenous peoples. In reality however, the laws were used as a smokescreen meant to justify the illegal land grabs that the colonial system imposed against the Black population. The land degradation that society is grappling with today has roots in colonialism and therefore is to a large extent a White and colonial creation. The expropriation of land and the resultant overcrowding in the reserves or Tribal Trust Lands is confirmed by Little (1974) when he states that one of the push factors in the rural-urban migration was increased pressure of population upon land resources and reduced fertility of the soil which failed to sustain the population density of the Black people. The land issue became the bone of contention in Zimbabwe between the minority White colonial government and the Black majority (Manyame-Tazarurwa 2011; Ranger 1985) leading to the protracted war of liberation. However it appears that focus on the effects of dispossession was on land largely located in the rural areas which was mainly used for agricultural purposes. The discourse around the Tribal Trust Lands is testimony to this. Works covering the overcrowding in the cities is largely overlooked and more so the gender dimension of the city space is ignored. Little (1974) has expounded on the migratory basis of urban growth in Africa. He cites European partitioning of Africa as the real reason that kick-started the colonisation resulting in traditional life being invaded by Western economic enterprises and the capitalist market economy. Scholars such as Lefebvre (1996) have highlighted that in the discourse to do with the city, the point of departure should be colonialism when the country comes into conflictual relationship with the development of criminal colonial industrial centres. Of this, Little (1974: 8-9) says:

> Naturally workers were needed to provide labour and services for these various economic enterprises although at first the idea made little appeal to the ordinary villager. Working for money and wage-labour was foreign to the tribesmen of the late nineteenth century. It savoured somewhat of slavery. Usually he had resources of his own, showed little interest in the trade goods procurable by money and so had little desire to earn it.

The historical perspective embraced in this study by Little (1974) does not see men and women as co-participants in the improvements of their livelihoods. Yet women and men had traditionally been known to work together hence by preferring men for waged labour in the developing industrial town, a chasm was created resulting in the fragmentation of family life and other ensuing challenges. The government's imposition of taxes (that were supposed to be payable in cash) saw the Black man with no option but seek waged labour. It meant the man (as the head of the family) leaving his rural home for the city. The city space, however, did not accommodate woman and at its worst was even hostile to her. In this chapter I argue that,

151

removed from the shared space with the man, the dehumanising effects of urban migration had left the woman more discriminated against than her male counterpart; not along spatial or racial lines alone but gender as well.

Not many scholars and social critics have discoursed the issue of women as having born the brand of dispossessions and dislocations of colonialism particularly to do with the rural-urban migrations. Women's issues are subsumed in the racial discourse yet they had their own kind of challenges emanating from the loss of land and consequently loss of accommodative space particularly in the urban areas.

Contextualising Space and Place

Scholars such as Moretti (2005) have emphasised the study of physical surroundings to interpret texts. Simply put, setting refers to the place and time and scholars like Watson (1991) bemoan the teaching of literature for example, where the component of setting is overlooked. He says, "Stressing plot development, recognising character delineation and growth, and uncovering hidden meaning all too frequently take precedence over realising how setting may aid the interpretation of all the components in a holistic manner" (ibid. p. 638).

As far back as the late twentieth century, interest in the landscape in literary texts was already gathering momentum with scholars such as Pocock (1981) observing an interest by geographers in literature in a bid to demonstrate the interconnectedness of human beings and their landscape. Soja (1971) also agrees with Pocock on the importance of human space when he talks of boundaries that are created and maintained by man. Like Pocock, Soja recognises how political organisation is firmly rooted in the geography of a country thereby underlining the spatial relations between man and his environment. Soja (1971), however, distinguishes political geography as "catalogues of states and their characteristics...with incidental notes about current events." In other words what Soja is implying is that political geography is inadequate in giving a holistic picture of human habitation and activity. Literary study therefore, covers this gap. Azizi and Afroughed (2013: 641) underline this when they say, "A literary writer tries to give a new picture of life to the reader by combining a represented place of the real world in imaginary spaces, sometimes representation of spaces (place) are mere copies of the real places but sometimes they are wholly imaginary."

To Salter and Loyd (1977) studying literary landscape "relates to the concept of landscape signatures, or specific imprints people or peoples have made upon' the earth in their use of geographical space." The study of space assigned to women in the city is most likely to deal with spaces that have escaped the intentional glare of the author as he or she attempts to steer through relationships and experiences. Yi-fu Tuan has also brought in the significance of space in people's lives. He however has deliberated on the space-place binary where space is the unlimited expanse of geographical bearings, unknown and not tied to any individual identity, while place is defined by human habitation. To him space is freedom while place is constricted. This paradigm is used in this research to explain the inhabitation of space by women. Since women appeared unaccommodated in the city, the chapter adopts the concept of space to explain the habitation or lack of it of women in the city of colonial Rhodesia- Salisbury. Tally (2013) has highlighted how the discourse on spatiality has been male dominated and this is the case with both literary and critical works. A study of women's spaces, therefore, might offer newer insights into gender relations in the colonial urban centre of Salisbury.

Notable discourses have also revolved around the woman being confined to the kitchen/home while the man enjoys more public space at his disposal (Spain 1992; Massey 1994; Bulbeck 1998). This has culminated into the public and private space debate where the home is seen as confining and constricting place when juxtaposed with the perceived masculine space of the public sphere (Jeater 2000). In this chapter the constricted space in the city space has been taken to mean prohibited space in the colonial city that appears largely populated by men. This space is further constricted for the females who attempt to invade this space.

Separate spheres along gender lines have been influenced by the then world power Britain and its Victorian values where "[m]en's place was in the public sphere - in politics, in the economic world which was becoming increasingly separate from home life as the industrial revolution progressed, in public social and cultural activity"(Lewis 2016). Such ripple effects are felt in pre-independence Zimbabwe where Black women, due to the establishment of colonial urban centres, are confined not just to the kitchen but to the rural home. Unfortunately for the woman in colonial Rhodesia, in trying to reinvent her relevance alongside her male counterpart, she had to experience the vagaries of city life which sadly have been attributed to her presence in the city rather than the colonial system at hand.

Theoretical Framework

This chapter is informed by Feminist urbanism theory which focuses on the effects that the environment has had on women. The theory is a strand of the larger urban theory often associated with the fields of human geography. It is the most suitable theory as it accounts for the inequitable distribution of city space along gender lines. The Black female in the colonial Rhodesian era is not factored in in the capitalist structure of the White colonial system. Proponents of this theory posit that the construction of space has historically excluded women in both decision-making (planning) and the design of urban spaces. Feminist urbanists are critical of the masculine nature of the construction of the city (van den Berg 2017). The theory was found suitable as it demonstrates how women have been excluded from power and participatory dynamics in the construction of the city space. This, as has been highlighted before, can be traced to dominant patriarchal hegemony largely imported from the West. The lack of women's involvement in the production of space has therefore had serious consequences to their welfare as this chapter shows. Lefebvre (1996) has emphasized the interplay between space and patterns of behaviour, that is, physical spaces and their design play a role in constructing identity. Writers like Zimunya, due to their patriarchal orientation, have their works in the text under study

154

showing serious bias against women. The physical environment reflects and reinforces social norms and patterns of behaviour in both the man and the woman.

The chapter also uses Cleonora Hudson-Weems's Africana Womanism Le theory (1997) to demonstrate how African women have traditionally partnered with their men although colonialism subsequently disrupted this partnership thereby fostering the dominant patriarchal ideology of the West. Colonialism re-defined the African woman as a housewife (Gaidzanwa 1994), a characterisation that was unheard of in traditional society since women partnered with their men for the well-being of their families and societies. The African woman has traditionally been recognised in traditional Shona culture as a significant partner – a fact that is demonstrated by the married women who were left in the rural areas to fend for the family while the absent father is in the city. In spite of her prohibition from the city and the resultant negative activities, the woman demonstrates her capacity to reinvent herself and scrounge for survival- a quality that she is revered for in traditional Shona culture.

The Country in *Country Dawns and City Lights*.

When dealing with the city, it is hard not to juxtapose it to rural space. This is also unavoidable considering Zimunya's deliberate juxtapositioning of the two- aptly captured in the title of the anthology and the sections within. The country/city space debate has been in existence from time immemorial and people relate to these spaces in almost similar voices- the country being a place of peace and tranquillity and the city representing the hustle and bustle that accompanies city life. Writing from the perspective of the English, Williams (1975: 1) has this to say about the country and the city:

> On the country has gathered the idea of a natural way of life: of peace, innocence and simple virtues. On the city has gathered the idea of an achieved centre: of learning communication, light. Powerful hostile associations have also developed: on the city as a place of noise,

155

worldliness and ambition; on the country a place of backwardness, ignorance and limitation.

This according to Williams (1975) has been varied along historical lines. What is generally agreed upon and among scholars are the feelings of yearning and nostalgia for the utopian country and rural life to the extent that in spite of the English society having become predominantly urban, for example, " its literature for a generation was still predominantly rural" (p. 2). However, Williams's description of the hive of activity of the city, its noises and buildings are done from the perspective of an English citizen and an insider with a sense of pride and belonging to the culture and reality of its people. It however does not give perspectives from the point of view of the marginalised and those racially discriminated against. Starkly contrasted to the almost romantically presented rural life, hostility towards the city by Victorian writers such as Thomas Hardy and Charles Dickens is evident in their works. Zimbabwean writers such as Dambudzo Marechera (in *House of Hunger*) have demonstrated the negative side of Rhodesia's high density areas and city life.

Zimunya's poetry section of "country dawns" is largely romantic in its portrayal of the countryside. His absence from the Zimbabwe's socio-political scene in the 70s is glaring. His portrayal of the country appears stultified to reflect the peaceful and tranquil rural landscape of Zimbabwe which can be traced back to the pre-colonial era or the era when struggles against colonialism were still in their infancy. Yet the period that is reflected in the anthology has a lot to do with the colonial period at the height of general discontent and the actual war of liberation. The struggles of the Zimbabwean people in the rural area against colonialism are almost concealed in this anthology as if everything was well. Yet the rural area was the hot bed of the liberation struggle that consequently ushered in independence in 1980. As a result there appears a gap in his depiction of the socio-historical processes that saw Rhodesia transform into the Zimbabwe we see today particularly in his portrayal of the country. Ziwira (2018) underlines this when he says the country:

...encompasses beauty and embraces pastoral innocence and serenity. It is about the vulnerability of the fragile – women and children; untainted love and freedom. In his depiction of the rural landscape, which espouses home – the real home, Zimunya, like Hove, is inspired by the untainted Eastern Highlands, from whence he comes; and grew up before the advent of colonialism.

Zimunya also appears to dwell largely on the transitional period of the Black man's movement from the rural area into the city and the ensuing challenges. This is reflected in the city space where the Black man is grappling with the colonial socio-economic system. The political atmosphere of the 1970s is omitted. While this may be a strength portraying the transitional period, the greatest weakness of his poetry collection is its failure to depict the central political struggles, a subject that other poets such as Tafataona Mahoso, Chenjeral Hove and Freedom Nyamubaya attempt to deal with in their writings. His absence from Rhodesia's political scene appears to have led him to speculate what was transpiring on the ground for the ordinary Black man.

The space that is under investigation in this chapter is the city space of Harare, or the then Salisbury, as it was known in the colonial period. The rural space in this chapter is used as a backdrop of the city area to demonstrate how the Black man after being uprooted from his rural home loses his bearings once placed in the city. In Zimunya's works the Black man appears docile helpless and hopeless -unable to transpose and re-contextualise himself once he moves to the city; that is to turn it to his advantage. As a result, the male figure in Zimunya's poetry is a flat character who appears unable to shift himself from the doldrums of city life such as poverty and squalor of the space assigned to him by the colonial system. Being the victim that he is, worse is the case of the female counterpart as shall be shown in this study, the man's space denotes victimhood to the colonial system as well as the woman's sexual advances.

157

The Woman and the City

The woman in the city of colonial Rhodesia cuts a lonely figure. She is often unaccompanied and rarely is she found accommodated or claiming any of the spaces in the city. While it was a fact that the Black man did not have any decent accommodation in the city, for the woman it was worse. In Zimunya's collection, men are the accommodated while the woman is associated with the outdoors and the streets. The poem "On the Streets" (p.50) the lonely sick vagrant reflects the challenges of the city against the background of the streets that point to the source of the "sick" he is suffering from. Zimunya is unapologetic as he assigns this space to the woman whose harshness does not spare even a male vagrant. The desperation of both the man and the woman are underlined. The poem "City lights" (p45) also portrays the woman on the streets with dreams of city luxuries doomed as employment evades her; she resorts to vending in the white suburbs for a living.

The woman's place of habitation is also located in the dark city lanes selling her body for survival. Poems such as "I couldn't believe it," (p.51) "Beneath the glare," (p.36) among others testify to this. The city lights may be alluring from the distance of the village yet under the direct glare of the city lamp posts is a rot that is revolting. Under the city lights the woman and her partner chose to accommodate their ephemeral activities both demonstrating the lack of privacy and shelter that the Black people endure in the colonial era. The woman has to wait "until darkness comes" ("The Lane" p. 52). The married woman also falls victim to the system. Not only is she banished to the rural area but her husband is swallowed by the city bringing her the grief of lonely nights and lack of financial support. The poem "Lost and Found" (p.70) reflects this. The cordial gender relations in Zimbabwean culture often reflected in the popular adage *"mushamukadzi"* – a home cannot be a home unless there is a woman (Chigidi & Tembo 2013) are lost. While this saying appears to confirm the woman's domestic space from a Western sense, the Shona culture is appreciative of the role of the woman in the home demonstrating a peaceful co-existence between the sexes before colonialism disrupted it. Women who are often unaccommodated are left to fend for themselves and exposed to the nocturnal violence of the outdoors often associated with rape, muggings and murder. Women who venture out are indeed desperate; under normal circumstances no woman would go out at night as highlighted in "I wouldn't" (p. 58). The persona wouldn't dare risk stepping out to walk on the streets in the evening and be exposed to the underlined violence of the city. Other negative experiences are reflected in the woman predicament in the city are succinctly captured in the poem "In the Capital City" (p. 61) where an aged prostitute laments:

> I wandered the streets
> and struggled to keep an emotion
> because I was alone in the largest city...
> only felt the cold rain and the wet pavements...
> I took [a man] in but he rose to go
> As though my bed were full of gravel...
> I am too old to begin
> too ignorant to know where
> I am stuck where I know the most:
> the loneliest street corner in Harare.

Apart from the streets, other common hangouts for women are the city bars with dizzying disco lights where they provide company and entertainment (p.70). If at all they are accommodated it is not dignified and is frowned down upon, that is, for fleeting moments when they steal moments of pleasure from their male counterparts for the much sought after dollar as reflected in the poem "Monthend" (p. 39).

The next space is the delivery lane which becomes a running motif in Zimunya's anthology and all for the negative reasons it represents. Like goods or commodities women are confined to the delivery lanes of the city again where their clandestine activities are done and this reflects the mental disposition of their male counterparts towards their trade. Not only are women treated as outcasts but as goods that are acquired as and when they are needed. Beyond that there are no relationships that surpass this rule of supply and demand. The delivery lane is also literally known for the delivery of goods and at the same time housing the rubbish and rubble discarded from the shop front. It houses the back space that is known for the waste from the shops and therefore associated with the rubbish trucks. Thus the women play the binary role of a commodity that one can use or discard at will. When unwanted she degenerates into the category of the unwanted of society belonging only to the rubbish heap. The metaphor of the rubbish trucks connotes how women are the scam of the unwanted in society which is supposed to be cleared from the system. The rubbish metaphor is also associated with women and their genitalia ("Please Stay p. 54, "Nine Months" p. 69). From the colonial system's perspective this is apt but from Zimunya's it gives an interesting reading. He appears to share the same sentiments with the coloniser regarding women around the city and around men. He believes they are an unnecessary nuisance which should be rid of.

To underline the dehumanised state of the woman by the system, she shares the same space with animals in the delivery lane. "The Lane" (p. 52) exposes the intricately linked and interchanged activities of both humans and dogs. Associated with the unattached woman is the dog imagery that demonstrates Zimunya's perception of women in general and their sexual activities as notoriously equated to those of dogs in the delivery lane. To this effect, women are regarded the scam of society; Zimunya constantly refers to the dog in the delivery lane in such a revolting manner meant to repulse any reader. The dogs are mangy, disease ridden just like the women prostitutes who spend much of their time there. In other words, the anthology portrays the city as dehumanising to the Black man in general but surprisingly the woman appears to exacerbate the woes of the man and is held accountable for the troubles.

Spatial Marginalisation: The Woman, the Man and the City

Where the married woman appears to be secure in her home, it is not a comfortable home. Accommodation for the woman in the city space is constricted and denies the man the freedom of association with his married partner resulting in him soliciting the comforts of the street walker- the prostitute. Or he forgets his rural home resulting in a broken home and familial bonds. Not only is she responsible for the serious consequences that ensue; either the man's pockets are "cleaned out" resulting in him failing to settle his bills and care for his family ("Wonder, p. 68, "Month-end" p. 39). In the poem "Wonder" (p.68) the delivery lane is lurking with prostitutes and thieves who waylay the hapless man resulting in him getting

> Cleaned out of the month's grocery
> Cleaned out of the month's rent
> Cleaned out of the credit instalment
> ...the month's bus fare
> ...child's pencil and book
> ....with a broken jaw
> And toothless pain
> Cleaned out of all words

Therefore for want of space in the city, the woman becomes a home wreaker and is responsible for the ruin that befalls the man. However, the anthology fails to demonstrate that women in this case are the victims of a system, not just a gender based discrimination instigated against them, but a racial, social and economic system that locks out the Black man in general.

The man is a perennial victim of the constricted space of the city which begets other undesirable consequences. Muchemwa (2013: 12) has this to say about the colonial city, "Violence produces the trauma of black urban (un)belonging. The colonial city starkly inaugurated the spatial politics of dispossession, displacement and exclusion....". While women do not occupy the core but share the racial peripheries of the city with their male counterparts, they go a yard further by occupying the physical margins of the city through their gender. To add to this the Black man and woman are thus alienated from the culture they are used to and at the same time alienated from each other.

The city home thus becomes an epitome of fragmented lifestyles where the harmonious existence of the married Black man and woman are disrupted. Women largely stay in the rural home while the man scraps for a living in the city. Thieves are ready partners with prostitutes also wreak havoc in the city. In reality, the city constrains and oppresses both men and women leading them to find other forms of survival.

Weaknesses of Zimunya's Anthology

The Zimbabwean literary terrain has been gendered with the male writers and critics dominating that terrain (Veit-Wild 1992; Kahari 1990; Stratton 1994). Zimunya's anthology is indicative of this dominant patriarchal disposition. His anthology therefore is not representative of the ordinary Zimbabwean woman. His is a biased depiction of the woman in the city especially in colonial Rhodesia. Zimunya does not seem willing to show the negative circumstances that force the woman into prostitution. Whether intentionally done or not, he would rather portray the man in the city as a victim; unable to display any form of agency to his situation in the city. The unwanted woman does albeit through the frowned upon profession. The man's victimhood (to the larger colonial system and the clutches of the woman) is omnipresent in Zimunya's collection. In an undertone, most likely inadvertently expressed, Zimunya's message is that women find ways of survival in the city despite the proscriptions that lurk in every corner. Men have a ready space created for them in the political economy of colonialism and hence are catered for. Women have to find ways to factor themselves into a system that readily rejects them.

Typical of an observer, Zimunya appears to look at the society with eyes of the outsider he was while in exile. He has no sympathy for the female inhabitant of the city but the male. At the same time

162

he appears to look at the metropolitan city minus the hub of activity of township life. The delivery lane that he subscribes to throughout most of his poems is located either in the city centre or business areas where beerhalls are likely located. Such locations reinforce the lack of freedom of movement and association the colonial city has been known for. We get little in terms of the dusty township streets of the ghetto. However, the dumped babies, infanticide as well as sex escapades in the delivery lane (often associated with shop backyards) do fit the location where women find themselves space, which sadly they cannot claim as their own. The mangy dogs and the rubbish dumps compete for space with the women and the deplorable habitation of humans in general of colonial Rhodesia. This demonstrates the battle for the scarce resources- space being chief amongst all. This way Zimunya concretises the lack of space. The assigned space for Black people, the township however, appears insignificant or Zimunya evidently lacked exposure to capture the experiences of township life of the Western Rhodesian suburbs owing to his exiled status or it was a deliberate omission. To add to this, Zimunya's poetry reflects the same victimhood of the man to the extent of ignoring his well-documented agency in his struggles against colonialism. His obsession with the predicament of the man in the colonial city almost blinkers him from that critical stage in Zimbabwean history- Zimunya is almost silent, in this anthology, on the war of liberation. It takes one to read the history of Zimbabwe and poems from other anthologies to complete the picture.

Conclusion

Zimunya's recreation of home appears to be where his heart belongs in the rural Eastern Highlands where he grew up. For him the city is repulsive and unaccommodating meant to destroy the Black man and woman. However, Zimunya's sympathy lies with the Black man and appears to attribute his suffering to the activities of the woman, yet the woman is worse with colonial laws that bar her from areas of industry and commerce. The woman claims the city space in her own way, exposing the various ways the city has impinged on her freedom and that of her male counterpart. Through his anthology *Country Dawns and City Lights*, Zimunya unravels not just the racial segregation of the city but the spatial marginalisation of the city. His anthology also demonstrates the gendered dimension of both his poetry as well as the spatial relationships in the city. His exclusion from this poetry collection of political events and struggles of his day, however, may have afforded Zimunya the opportunity to focus on other aspects of the socio-economic experiences of the Black man in colonial Rhodesia.

References

Chigidi, W. and Tembo, C. (2013) Traditional oral literature and the socialisation of the Shona (Zimbabwe) girl child: An agenda for disempowerment. *Madirativhange: Journal of African Indigenous languages and literature vol. no 2.*

Gaidzanwa, R. (1994). Women's Land Rights in Zimbabwe. *Journal of Opinion*, 22(2): 12-16, http://www.jstor.org/stable/1166726.

Kahari, G. P. (1990). *The Rise of the Shona Novel*: A Study in Development, 1890-1984. Gweru: Mambo Press.

Lefebvre, H. (1996) *The Production of Space*. Oxford: Blackwell Publishers.

Little, K. (1974) *Urbanization as a Social Process: An essay on movement and change in contemporary Africa.* DOI: 10.4324/9781315017327

Mafa, O., Gudhlanga, E. S., Manyeruke, N., Matavire, E. H. M. and Mpofu, J. (2015) *Gender, Politics and Land Use in Zimbabwe 1980–2012*. Dakar: Council for the Development of Social Science Research in Africa (CODESRIA).

Manyame-Tazarurwa, K. C. (2011) *Health Impact of Participation in the Liberation Struggle of Zimbabwe*. Author House.

Mapanzure, R. (2014) Mapping the Terrain Zimbabwean literature, like most ... – WIReDSpace wiredspace.wits.ac.za/jspui/bitstream/10539/13520/2/MAIN%20REPORT.pdf

Massey, D. (1994) *Space, Place and Gender.* Minneapolis: Polity Press in Association with Blackwell Publishers.

Moyana, H. V. (2000) *The Political Economy of Land in Zimbabwe.* Gweru: Mambo Press.

Muchemwa, K. Z (2013) Imagining the City in Zimbabwean Literature 1949 to 2009 Unpublished PhD thesis. Stellenbosch University.

Pocock, D. C. D. (1981) *Humanistic Geography.* London: Croom Helm LTD.

Ravengai, S. (2013) Reimagined rural-urban landscapes and Zimbabwean Cultural Identities in Zimunya's *Country Dawns and City Lights African Identities* Vol 11 Issue 4 Nov pp381-394.

Saunders, D. (2010) *Arrival City: How the largest migration in history is reshaping our world.* New York: Pantheon Books.

Soja, E. (1971) The political Organisation of Space. Association of American Geographers. Resources Paper No. 8. Washington: Commission on College Geography.

Stratton, F. (1994) *Contemporary African Literature and the politics of Gender.* London: Routledge.

Tally, R. T. (2013) *Spatiality. The New Critical Idiom.* London and New York: Routledge.

Tuan, Y. F. (2000) *Space and Place: The Perspective of Experience.* London: University of Minnesota Press.

van den Berg, M. (2017) *Urban Theory: Feminist Urban Studies and the Gender Revolution in Gender in the Post-Fordist Urban.* London: Palgrave Macmillan.

Veit-Wild, F. (1992) *Teachers, Preachers and Non-believers: A social History of Zimbabwean Literature.* London & Harare: Hans Zell Publishers in Association with Baobab Books.

Williams, R. (1975) *The Country and the City.* New York: Oxford University Press.

Zimunya, M. (1985) *Country Dawns and City Lights.* Harare: Longman.

Ziwira, E. (2018) Unpacking Zimunya's 'country dawns and city lights' The Herald. Harare Zimpapers.

Chapter Eight

The San People of Zimbabwe: Decades after Land Dispossession

Shuvai Chingwe

Introduction

For much of the 20th century, national governments around the world sought to integrate indigenous minorities into mainstream society by way of following policies of assimilation. Efforts of assimilation of indigenous people into the mainstream economy were meant to improve the well-being of indigenous minorities but these efforts to assimilate them into mainstream economy have failed in most countries the world offer. The last two decades of the past century up to present day have resulted in a growing dominance of a global discourse on the rights of indigenous people which has led to the ratification of the United Nations Declaration for the rights of Indigenous Peoples in 2007. The declaration established the basic concepts of self-determined development which encompasses indigenous people's rights to self-determination, land, resources and culture. Despite such international developments on the promotion of indigenous peoples' rights, many indigenous peoples and communities have totally lost their ancestral lands and resources which have relegated them to marginal positions in the society. This is traced back to the history of many indigenous communities which resulted in the loss of ancestral lands and the erosion of indigenous culture and their impact on the livelihoods of indigenous peoples. This chapter therefore focusses on indigenous people's loss of land and the erosion of their culture with specific reference accorded to the Tshwa (San) people of Zimbabwe.

A Historical Background of the San People of Southern Africa

The term "San" is commonly used to refer to a diverse group of hunter-gatherers living mainly in South Africa, Angola, Botswana, Namibia and Zimbabwe who share historical, cultural and linguistic connections. The San people of Southern Africa are among the region's best-known people despite their small overall population. Today the San people are iconified as an archetypal hunting and gathering society. They are the subject of numerous ethnographic studies, documentaries, feature films, coffee-table books and postcards (Suzman 2001a). The San of Zimbabwe make up only a small portion of the total San population of Southern Africa, which is estimated to be between 85 000 and 90 000 people in six countries (Suzman 2001b). The San in Tsholotsho District of Zimbabwe generally identify themselves as the "Tshwa". The Tshwa in Zimbabwe have a population of approximately 2,500 people residing in Matabeleland North Province (in Tsholotsho District) and Matabeleland South Province (in Bulilima-Mangwe District) (Hitchcock, Murwira and Clench 2016). The Tshwa are divided into a number of different groups, some of whom have long occupied the same land, while others have either moved to new places on their own or they have been resettled.

Globally, the issues of the San may be equated to the Aboriginal discourses and struggles and they fall under the generic term 'indigenous people'. The history and struggles of indigenous people are wide and varied. The history of Latin America's indigenous people is one of a long struggle that started with the European invasion and conquest in the fifteenth and sixteenth centuries when an estimated 90 to 95 percent of the native population was wiped out by the colonialists (Dosch 2012). According to the International Work Group for Indigenous Affairs (IWGIA) (2006), the situation of indigenous people in Africa is extremely serious because of the high prevalence of bad governance, corruption, impunity, violent conflict and poverty. This chapter therefore looks at the effects of land dispossession, loss of ancestral lands and the loss of hunter-gatherer livelihoods for the San people of Southern Africa

The San people are members of various indigenous hunter-gatherer people of Southern Africa found mainly in South Africa, Namibia, Botswana, Zimbabwe and Angola. Tomaselli (2012:41) notes that the San are stereographically 'assumed by media and journalists … to have been a pre-modern people living in the past'. Historical evidence shows that the San people lived in the Kalahari Desert from as early as 2500 BC and they are believed to be the original human inhabitants of Southern Africa and are the oldest culture in the world as noted by Lee and Hitchcock (2001).

Despite being hunter gatherers, the last century saw an almost complete integration of surviving San populations into the lowest echelons of the regional political economy and with it their growing dependency on others. Finlay and Barnabas (2012) note that the San were a source of cheap labour in the farms from as early as 1800. With neither White nor Bantu immigrants considering hunting and gathering to be a legitimate form of land use, San people were spuriously declared nomads and thus they could not exercise objective rights over land or natural resources as observed by Suzman (2001a).

The San people of Southern Africa have also been frequently referred to as the "bushman". Simoes (2001) notes that the label Bushman was a colonial construct, along with the category of "tribe" created to control subjugated peoples in manageable, depoliticised, arbitrarily bounded enclaves of homogeneity in a previously flourishing landscape of political and social diversity. Lee and Hitchcock (2016) further note that in the late 1960s, the term Bushmen was considered pejorative and was replaced in scholarly circles by the seemingly more neutral Indigenous term 'San'. The term San also had derogatory connotations of 'worthless vagabond' or 'people without cattle'. In Botswana they are called the Basarwa while Namibia has adopted the name 'San'. Despite different connotation attached to the term "bushman", to the San, it is an identity which they happily embrace as it identifies them as kings or experts of the bush which has been their main source of livelihoods.

All of the governments of Southern African states where the San live in large numbers; that is in Namibia, South Africa and Botswana, follow integrationist and assimilations policies as observed by Sapignoli and Hitchcock (2013). The objectives of all the governments are to encourage 'marginalised and vulnerable communities' to enter the mainstream society as a way of improving their livelihoods. This essentially means to get them to be more involved in livestock, agriculture, small businesses and the formal industrial economy. Sapignoli and Hitchcock's (2013) study on Indigenous people of Southern Africa came to a conclusion that in some ways, there is continuity between colonial and post-colonial states' oppression of Indigenous people in Southern Africa. This chapter will concentrate on the San people of Zimbabwe because there has been little research about the San people of Zimbabwe. Of all the San people of Southern Africa, the Tshwa are the least known "tribal" grouping. Hitchcock, Murwira and Clench (2016) note that the San people in Zimbabwe prefer to use their own name for self-identification, and whilst sometimes known as Amasili or Abatwa (the Ndebele word for Bushmen or San), most San in Zimbabwe identify themselves as Tshwa. Their identification as the "Tshwa" like other different San and Bantu groups, translates directly as "person". The traditional language of the Tshwa is Tshwao, but the vast majority of the Tshwa San in Western Zimbabwe are multilingual, speaking several different languages. Many Tshwa today consider themselves to be indigenous to Western Zimbabwe. Their claims are supported by the existence of archaeological materials which date from the Early Stone Age, around 1 million years ago (Hitchcock, Murwira and Clench (2016). This is similar to the other San groups in Namibia and Botswana who claim to be the indigenes of the present day Namibia and Botswana respectively. However, the issue of being indigenous is a debatable as discussed below.

Are the San People of Zimbabwe Indigenous to Zimbabwe?

Indigeneity is an essentially contested concept in many parts of the world as noted by Tomaselli (2004). Tomaselli (2004) views indigeneity as contemporary performance of self, enacting a restoration of relations for historical purposes. In the same line of thinking, Corntassel (2003) proposes four criterion for defining Indigenous people. The first is that of people who believe that they are ancestrally related and identify themselves, based on oral and written histories, as descendants of the original inhabitants of their ancestral homelands. The second criteria proposed by Corntassel (2003) includes people who have community based institutions which reflect ceremonial cycles, kinship networks and cultural traditions. The third criterion according to Corntassel (2003) includes people who speak or once spoke an Indigenous language, often different from the dominant society's language. The final criterion for defining Indigenous people as put forward by Corntassel (2003) refers to people who distinguish themselves from the dominant society and other cultural groups while maintaining a close relationship with their ancestral homelands and sacred sites, which may be threatened by economic or political encroachment or may be places where indigenous people have been previously expelled, while seeking to enhance their cultural, political and economic autonomy. Tomaselli (2004: 47) agrees with Corntassel (2003)'s final criterion by referring indigeneity as a status usually accorded to 'remnant prior peoples living on their former lands in the margins of the nation states'.

The above criteria put forward by Corntassel (2003) was summed up in a fairly broad definition by the African Commission's Working Group of Experts on Indigenous Populations/Communities which summarised the overall characteristics of groups which identify themselves as indigenous peoples as follows:

> Their cultures and ways of life differ considerably from the dominant society and their cultures are under threat, in some cases to the extent of extinction. A key characteristic for most of them is that the survival of their particular way of life depends on access and rights to their traditional land and the natural resources thereon. They suffer from discrimination as they are being regarded as less developed and less advanced than other more dominant sectors of society. They often live in inaccessible regions, often geographically isolated and suffer from various forms of marginalisation, both politically and socially.

They are subject to domination and exploitation within national political and economic structures that are commonly designed to reflect the interests and activities of the national majority. This discrimination, domination and marginalisation violate their human rights as peoples/communities, threaten the continuation of their cultures and ways of life and prevent them from being able to genuinely participate in deciding their own future and forms of development (African Commission on Human and Peoples' Rights 2005: 89).

The above definition concurs with Sarivaara, Maatta and Uusiautti (2013) who define Indigenous people as people who are disadvantaged descendants of the people that inhabited a territory prior to colonization or the formation of the existing state. The San people of Zimbabwe like other San people in Southern Africa tend to fit most of the criterion for being indigenous to their territories because of the existence of archaeological and historical linkages with the pre-colonial state. These point to the fact that they were the original inhabitants of such territories. More importantly, the San people of Southern Africa's survival depend on access and rights to their traditional or ancestral lands and the natural resources in those territories. This further qualifies them as indigenous people.

McCormack (2012) notes that the term 'indigenous people' is political and can be variously appropriated by different groups in different kinds of contexts. The consequences of the use of 'Indigenous people' as a political tool is that it is more likely to create new divisions and less likely to promote the common good than policies based on individual citizenship rights in liberal-democratic states as noted by McCormack (2012). Although countries like Zimbabwe and Namibia have embarked on indigenisation, often promulgating Indigenisation Acts, McCormack (2012) problematises the term 'Indigenous people' – he states that it reintroduces 'obsolete notions of the native and primitivism and essentialises cultural others'. Despite the controversies emanating from the use of the term in different countries, globally, the term is acceptable as supported by the United Nations Declaration on the Rights of Indigenous people. The phrase indigenous people does not necessarily refer to primitivism, as McCormack (2012) argues, but to people that were dispossessed, robbed of their land and resources during the colonial era – the challenge for some writers is that this term exposes and essentalises the colonial plunder that some Eurocentric scholars would want to sweep under the carpet. This chapter acknowledges and sympathises with the historical background of the San people of Southern Africa as the first inhabitants of the region and the forceful displacement from their ancestral lands and resources during the pre-colonial era up to present day. Therefore, in line with the United Nations Declaration on the Rights of Indigenous Peoples and the definition put forward by African Commission on Human and Peoples' Rights (2005), this chapter recognises the San as the Indigenous people of Southern Africa. This recognition is not necessarily to call for special rights for indigenous people but to acknowledge that these are people and communities which have been dispossessed for centuries and hence are impoverished. The recognition of painful histories of San people from pre-colonial times to the present day is important in understanding their privation in Southern Africa.

Dispossession of Land for the San People of Southern Africa

Even though there are discourses to the effect that Africans could move freely within their borderless continent (Mtapuri, Nhemachena & Benyera 2018), the San people are believed by Eurocentric scholars to have inhabited the entire South of the African continent way before the migration of the Bantu. They were allegedly "displaced" by the Southward movement of the Zulu, Nguni, Sotho, Khoi Khoi, Nama and other African groups. San people were easily "displaced" because they did not keep livestock and hence other groups interpreted this to mean that the San had no need for land. The San retreated southwards and permanently occupied the drier regions in the Kalahari. Even though they retreated and settled in drier areas, they looked settled in areas which were rich in natural resources namely fauna and flora. Since the 1950s the San have been under great pressure to abandon their hunting and

173

gathering lifestyle even as colonialists, through their transnational corporations, engaged in "modern" day hunting and gathering of African resources including land and minerals (Nhemachena & Dhakwa 2017). Despite sometimes active resistance, by the mid-1970s close to nine tenths of the region's San population had been dispossessed of their traditional territories and their source of economic and political autonomy as noted by Suzman (2001a).

The struggle for ancestral lands by the San people of Southern Africa came to the lime light through the San people of Botswana who are also known as the Basarwa. Ndahinda (2011) is of the opinion that the Basarwa acquired international fame since the mid 1990s due to events surrounding their forceful removal from the Central Kgalagadi (Kalahari) Game Reserve (CKGR), which they claim are their ancestral lands. The history of the Basarwa as traditionally hunter-gatherers and their presence in Botswana is believed to date back to at least 40 000 years, much longer before the other Bantu-speaking people inhabited the region. The struggle of the Basarwa for ancestral lands has its roots in the creation of the CKGR in 1961. Ndahinda (2011) in agreement with Sapignoli (2016) suggests that the CKGR was created by the departing colonial administration and the idea behind its creation was to protect wildlife resources and to reserve sufficient land for traditional use by hunter gatherer communities of the central Kalahari. This shows that from the early years of the creation of the CKGR, the needs of the traditional lifestyle of the Basarwa hunter gatherer was evident. A 1963 regulation on the control of entry into the reserve provided that no other person other than the Basarwa Indigenous to the CKGR shall enter the reserve without first having obtained a permit in writing from the Ghanzi District Commissioner as noted by Ndahinda (2011). This regulation has been very important in the Indigenous rights discourse in Botswana because it embodies recognition of the historical right of the Basarwa as an Indigenous people with a right to access the ancestral lands they had occupied for more than 2000 years.

From 1985, the government of the Republic of Botswana adopted policies aimed at encouraging communities living within the

CKGR to move outside the reserve as noted by Sapignoli (2016). Botswana's relocation of the Basarwa out of the reserve drew a lot of controversy and criticism from Indigenous organisations. According to Sapignoli and Hitchcock (2013), the most controversial of which was the relocation of over 2 000 people out of the Central Kalahari Game Reserve (CKGR) between 1997 and 2002. The San people challenged the government's decision to relocate them from the reserve in the courts of law. The High Court of Botswana ruled in favour of the Basarwa as the lawful occupants of the CKGR lands and settlements and this gave the Basarwa the right to return to the CKGR in 2006 as noted by Ndahinda (2011). Mikalsen (2008:302) notes that the San Bushmen of Botswana have argued that they do not want to live in lands which are not theirs, if the government want the Basarwa to access basic services it should bring the services in their ancestral lands . In the same line of argument Andersson (2002) cites one Basarwa who notes ' —*if they really want us to modernise why don't they bring the schools and development to us in our ancestral lands*'? However, the government of Botswana has been intolerant of the Basarwa's unique culture and they have not supported their return to CKGR with the necessary basic services as highlighted by Sapignoli (2016).

Similarly, the San people of Namibia have been faced with the same fate as the Basarwa people of Botswana. Before independence, the colonial government reserved a specific area which they called Bushmanland (present day Tsumkwe East in Otjozondjupa region) for the San community. The town of Tsumkwe was created as its administrative centre. This area comprised more or less the traditional hunting area of the Ju'/hoansi San and it was occupied almost entirely by this group. Hays (2016) alleges that the colonial South African Government had planned to relocate other San groups into that area as their homeland. However, this plan did not materialise as power shifted from the South African government to the first independent government in 1990. The result was that the San people are now scattered all over Namibia in areas where they are minorities and lack any land rights.

In 2001, eleven years after Namibia's' independence, a comprehensive study was undertaken to assess the general standards of living and status of the San people of Namibia. The study was led by James Suzman who compiled a report entitled **An Assessment of the Status of the San in Namibia**. The study concluded that:

> A decade after independence, San stand out due to their dependency, extreme poverty, political alienation and a variety of social, educational and health problems. Of course, these problems are not unique to San, and many other Namibians are just as poor and marginalised as they are. However, what makes San conspicuous among Namibia's poor is the fact that while only a proportion of the members of each other language group are extremely poor, San are almost universally extremely poor (Suzman 2001:143b).

The publication of this report led to increased efforts by the government and other development partners to improve the living conditions of San communities through various initiatives. It was during these efforts that led to the establishment of the Division of the San Development in the Office of the Prime Minister (OPM). The main objective of the Division of the San Development Program was to ensure San integration into the mainstream Namibian economy, in line with Vision 2030 (the country's long-term development policy) and specific national development programmes as highlighted by the Office of the Prime Minister (2008). Though it might have appeared a noble objective, it is important to note that the aim of assimilation of the San people was not in line with the Indigenous people's rights movement which stresses the right to self-determination as articulated in the Article 7(1) of the ILO Convention 169 and later in the UNDRIP (2007). Assimilation of indigenous people into the mainstream will directly translate to permanent loss of ancestral lands and livelihoods.

Non-governmental organisations also increased their efforts and activities in San communities as a way of improving the existing conditions in San communities. It is important to note that most of such efforts were aimed at halting the displacement of the San communities and attempting to bring them into the mainstream and making San communities have easier access to land. According to

176

Dieckmann *et al.* (2014), between 2001 and 2010, a few San communities' had improved access to land and land rights. For example the N‡a Jaqna Conservancy in Otjozondjupa Region was gazetted in 2003 for the benefit of mostly San communities in the area. This was followed by the granting of user rights to San communities staying in the Bwabwata National Park (BNP) in 2006 on a Community Based Natural Resources Management (CBNRM) program. Although the contribution of CBNRM to indigenous people livelihoods remains contested, the granting of user rights to the San people in Bwabwata National Park has allowed them to benefit from their ancestral lands through the proceeds of meat from trophy hunting. They also benefit from gathering of fruits and herbs.

Other efforts by the government of Namibia to uplift the standards of living for the San people have been the purchasing of a number of farms for resettling San communities in Kunene, Oshikoto and Otjozondjupa. In cases where San communities are resettled away from their ancestral lands and are required to engage in mainstream livelihoods like subsistence farming, it results in permanent loss of ancestral lands and the total loss of their hunter-gatherer lifestyle as they are no longer allowed to hunt. Of all the San tribal groupings in Namibia, the Ju/'hoansi San of Tsumkwe East managed to hold on to a remnant of their ancestral lands where they can still partially practice their hunter-gatherer livelihoods. Their ancestral lands are under present day Nyae Nyae Conservancy (former Bushmanland). Hays (2016 citing Douglas 2000) suggest that Bushmanland, was created by the South African Administration because the land was considered to be unsuitable for cattle farming and agriculture, but appropriate for Bushmen hunting and gathering. Like other communities, the post-independent era brought much hope to the Ju/'hoansi people of Nyae Nyae as they hoped to recover their ancestral lands which they lost during the colonial era.

After Namibia's independence in 1990, to the disappointment of the Ju/'hoansi, the new government proposed to dispossess the Ju/'hoansi people of Nyae Nyae of their remaining ancestral lands. When, the then President of Namibia, Sam Nujoma visited Nyae Nyae in 1991, he felt the area was fertile to sustain large herds of cattle, a view that was not shared by all Ju/'hoansi who felt other people should not be rewarded for poorly managing their environment including the Herero who were eager to exploit Nyae Nyae for grazing resources as noted by Biesele and Hitchcock (2011). In the early years of Namibia's independence, Nyae Nyae Development Fund Namibia in collaboration with Ju/'hoansi people of Nyae Nyae, firmly opposed attempts by the government to turn their ancestral lands into a game reserve as noted by Gargallo (2015). They actually lobbied the government in support of a model of community conservation under which the Ju/hoansi secured control of land and natural resources. The government was more receptive to this model; this led to the proclamation of Nyae Nyae Conservancy which became the first conservancy registered by the Ministry of Environment and Tourism. It is important to note that the Ju/'hoansi people of Nyae Nyae managed to fight for retention of their ancestral land through their collaboration with external stakeholders more specifically the Nyae Nyae Development Foundation Namibia. Nyae Nyae Development Fund Namibia's history and involvement with the Ju/'hoansi dates back to the early 80s when the Marshal family donated funds for the establishment of the cattle fund. Over the years, the cattle fund has revolved into the present day NNDFN which is a non-governmental organisation working to support and empower San communities in Namibia. A study by Dieckman, Thiem, Dirkx and Hays (2014) concluded that of all the San "tribal" groupings in Namibia, the Ju/'hoansi people of Nyae Nyae's welfare was much better. This can be attributed to the fact that they have managed to hold on to ancestral lands.

The importance of ancestral lands to indigenous communities cannot be over emphasised. To indigenous people, it is their main source of livelihood. Contrary to that, current development models, traditional economies and ways of life, such as nomadic hunter-gathering or subsistence farming, are regarded as outdated and primitive forms of survival and they are obstacles to development. Ethno-historic literature and oral history tend to suggest that territoriality among the Tshwa of Zimbabwe has been important. The Tshwa had vast areas of land that they saw as their own and they were reportedly well aware of the identities of the people who had rights to specific places (Hitchcock, Murwira and Clench (2016). As Hodson (1912:227 cited by Hitchcock, Murwira and Clench 2016) notes:

> Bushmen in this country generally have their own well defined districts in which they hunt, and it would be bad for a Metsibotlhoko Bushman to hunt in the Sebanene District. They do not like leaving their districts at all, and nothing at all will tempt them to do so. If a native wishes to form a cattle post, he sends the cattle to the Bushmen, not the Bushmen to the cattle.

This confirms the fact that the Tshwa have strong connections with their ancestral territories which is characteristic of indigenous people. Their territories in Western Zimbabwe and northern Botswana tended to be either close to pans or along fossil or contemporary river valleys. Pans that contained water for extended periods were important locations as they provided water as well as serving as focal points for wildlife. Tshwa territories contained all the resources necessary to sustain a group including water, wild plants and animals, shade, materials for home construction, tool manufacture, medicines and body decoration (Hitchcock, Murwira and Clench (2016). One can deduce that prior to their forceful alienation from ancestral lands; they used to live vibrant lives.

The San people of Southern Africa share a similar history of violent dispossession of ancestral territories. Like the San people of Botswana (Basarwa) and Namibia, the Tshwa people of Zimbabwe underwent the same situation back in the 1920s. When the then Rhodesian government passed the Game and Fish Preservation Act prior to 1929, the San were evicted from the area to be designated as the Hwange Game Reserve and relocated to Tsholotsho (Madzudzo, 2001: 82; Davison, 1977). As a consequence, several hundred Tshwas were relocated out of the reserve, mainly to areas south of the reserve, in what are now the Tsholotsho Communal Lands, part of Tsholotsho District. There were also Tshwa who were moved north to the Robins Camp area and to the town of Hwange and other areas to the west of Hwange. The creation of national parks in San territories was viewed by the colonial and postcolonial administration as a way of bringing about development. The pervasiveness and profoundness of impacts that result from these large scale development projects impact heavily on Indigenous peoples and thereby threatening their culture and even existence. Doyle and Gilbert's (2010) concur with Barras (2004) who describes civilization which can be equated to development to mean the dispossession of lands; the demise of culture and the attempt to make *white* people out of Indigenous people. The same sentiments are shared by Bamba's (2010) observation that Indigenous peoples have been experiencing, witnessing and becoming victims of this so-called 'devil's gift' out from this developmentalism'. For Bamba (2010), Indigenous people's lands have been taken over and their homes have been destroyed in the name of "development". Bamba (2010) laments the killing of Indigenous people – including helpless women and children who were tortured, kidnapped and brainwashed. Thus, one can conclude that the current state of the Tshwa's continued marginalisation and impoverishment was mainly caused by their forced detachment from their ancestral lands which are their source of livelihood. The implementation of development projects has robbed Indigenous peoples of their lands and natural resources. For the Tshwa people of Zimbabwe and other San communities; the land and the environment support and sustain life as the base of fishing, pastoralism, hunting and gathering.

Today in Zimbabwe, the Tshwa are among the poorest and most powerless ethnic groups in the country, inhabiting desert-like areas in North and South Matabeleland (Davison, 1977; Madzudzo, 2001; Panos Southern Africa, 2005). This can be traced back to their forceful removal from the present day Hwange National Park. They were relegated to unproductive areas which can hardly support their hunting and gathering lifestyle. Their current state of affairs confirms Tegegn (2014:52)'s argument that 'there is nothing more sacrilegious to Indigenous communities than threats to their land and environment'. They are part of what, within the discourse of

Zimbabwean nationalism, has been termed the minority ethnic groups.

Relatively few studies have been made of the Tshwa as compared to other San "tribal" groupings across Southern Africa. This may be attributed to their small population of approximately 2000. Compared to other ethnic groups in Zimbabwe, and in comparison to the San found in Botswana, Namibia and South Africa, the San of Zimbabwe have the lowest socio-economic status of all groups both in the country and across the region (Suzman 2001; De Wet 2010; International Labour Organisation 2010; Dieckmann *et al.* 2014).

Global Marginalisation of Indigenous Communities

As indicated earlier, the issues of the San people of Southern Africa may be equated to the discourses and struggles of indigenous people. Indigenous peoples can be found in practically every region of the world, and living on ancestral homelands in major cities, rainforests, mountain regions, and desert plains, the arctic and small Pacific Islands (Watene and Yap 2015). Clarke (2001) notes that Indigenous people are generally concentrated in remote and inaccessible areas such as remote and mountainous areas which are usually rich in valuable and unexploited natural resources such as forests, wild animals and minerals. Wherever they live and whoever they are, all share painful histories of marginalisation, exploitation and discrimination. Their past continues to haunt them, sometimes many generations or even centuries later. This is heavily reflected in their situation today. They continue to be the most marginalized and vulnerable people in the world. Indigenous people continue to be over represented amongst the poorest people around the globe. A study done by Carino (2009: 21) revealed that:

> While they constitute approximately 5 per cent of the world's population; Indigenous peoples make up 15 per cent of the worlds' poor. They also make up about one-third of the world's 900 million extremely poor rural people.

Despite being a considerable population of the world's poor, the main development agendas are silent about the poverty and marginalised situation of the Indigenous peoples. Despite their marginalisation and vulnerability, Indigenous peoples are the custodians of some of the most biologically diverse areas on earth. Their territories cover approximately 24% of the land worldwide and host 80% of the world's biodiversity (Watene and Yap 2015). They speak a majority of the world's languages. They are estimated to speak 4000 out of the 7000 languages spoken on planet earth (UN-ECOSOC 2009). Moreover, Indigenous people's traditional knowledge, cultural diversity, values and sustainable ways of life make an invaluable contribution to the world's heritage and these are embedded in the landscapes and natural resources within their territorial homelands. Despite such importance, the situation of Indigenous peoples in many parts of the world continues to be critical. Indigenous peoples continue to suffer discrimination, marginalisation, extreme poverty and conflict. Giving an introduction on the State of Indigenous Peoples of the World, the Secretariat of the Permanent Forum on Indigenous Issues (2009:1), summed up the state of Indigenous peoples as follows:

> Indigenous peoples face systemic discrimination and exclusion from political and economic power, they continue to be over-represented among the poorest, the illiterate, the destitute, they are displaced by wars and environmental disasters, the weapon of rape and sexual humiliation is also turned against Indigenous women for the ethnic cleansing and demoralization of Indigenous communities. Indigenous peoples are dispossessed of their ancestral lands and deprived of their resources for survival, both physical and cultural; they are even robbed of their very right to life. In more modern versions of market exploitation, Indigenous peoples see their traditional knowledge and cultural expressions marketed and patented without their consent or participation.

The above remarks were supported by findings from different studies done by Hughes (2003), Doyle (2009), Carino (2009) and

182

Tauli-Corpuz (2010) on poverty and marginalisation of Indigenous peoples. The studies found that Indigenous people were disproportionately represented among the poorest of the world's population in both the developed and developing countries. A previous study done by Hall and Patrinos (2007) on Indigenous people, poverty and human development in Latin America concluded that poverty among Latin American Indigenous people was pervasive and severe. The case proved not to be any different in Africa's Indigenous people as highlighted in a study by Sapignoli and Hitchcock (2013). It, in fact, affirmed the popular view that Indigenous people in Southern Africa were poor and marginalised. Similarly, a study by Doyle (2009) came to the conclusion that being Indigenous has been described as synonymous with being poor.

Today Indigenous peoples are minorities within their ancestral homelands. Marginalisation, coupled with continued existence on often remote traditional lands, makes their lives, values and cultures vulnerable to development projects that require (and impact on) natural resources (Watene and Yap 2015). The foregoing analysis shows that the marginalisation of Indigenous peoples is a global challenge. It is often assumed that the marginalisation of Indigenous people is only a challenge in developing countries. However, several studies have found that even in developed countries, Indigenous peoples lag behind non-Indigenous people in terms of most indicators of well-being (Carino 2009). Where ever they are found, Indigenous people live shorter lives. They have the least access to proper health care and education facilities. In the labour market, Indigenous peoples suffer the highest unemployment rate and where they are employed; their salaries are generally lower than their non-Indigenous counter parts.

Considerable studies done in Australia over the past decade indicate that according to social and economic indicators of employment, education, occupation, income, housing and health, Indigenous people are worse off than other Australians as noted by Banerjee and Tedmanson (2010). In terms of life expectancy, native Aborigines live up to 20 years less than the non-Aboriginal Australian. Obesity, Type 2 diabetes and tuberculosis are some of the major health concerns amongst Indigenous peoples in the developed world. These health challenges are more evident in Indigenous populations who are detached from their traditional livelihoods and are living in urban areas where they find themselves struggling to cope. Such statistics may not be available for the Tshwa in Zimbabwe because there is no specific recognition of them as marginalised or indigenous people. This is coupled with the fact that among the different San "tribal" groupings of Southern Africa, the Tshwa are the least researched.

A study by Carino (2009) found that in Australia, the Indigenous unemployment rate was 15.6 per cent in 2006, or just over three times higher than the non-Indigenous rate. Furthermore, the study found that the marginalisation of Indigenous peoples in Australia was more serious in rural and remote communities where people frequently do not have access to affordable adequate food, water and housing and they have poor access to basic services and infrastructure. Similar evidence of marginalisation of Indigenous peoples was also found in Canada. A study by Assembly of First Nations (2009 cited in Carino 2009) found that fewer children from Canadian Indigenous communities graduated from high school, and far fewer reached colleges and universities. New Zealand is another country ranking high in global comparisons of human development, but where there exists persistent disparities between Maori and non-Maori peoples in areas such as paid work, economic standard of living, housing, health and justice. In New Zealand, many Indigenous communities were found to have poor access to schools. This is evidence of the poverty and marginalised situation of Indigenous people in the developed countries.

The situation of Indigenous communities is even worse in developing countries. Indigenous peoples are increasingly vulnerable to forced displacement as a result of mining, hydroelectric dams, agro-industrial enterprises, rising sea levels, conflict, conservation and tourism among other things (Watene and Yap 2014). A study done by Doyle and Gilbert (2010) revealed that in June 2009, Indigenous peoples in northern Peru in Bagua organised a peaceful protest against the granting of concessions for the exploration and exploitation of gas, oil and gold to transnational companies in the Amazon region. This was opposed by armed police and the encounter translated into a bloody conflict which resulted in the death of several people and with many more people injured. The conflict between the police and the Indigenous peoples of Bagua is a tip of the ice bag on how bad the conflicts are between Indigenous communities and governments and corporations over the exploitation of natural resources in their territories in countries throughout the world and more especially in developing countries. Such has been the treatment of the Kenyan government in relation to various communities such as the Ogiek and Sengwe, not to mention the Botswana government in dealing with the Basarwa or the San. It is in this context that Indigenous peoples share the common goal of having their survival, cultural values, and rights to ancestral lands and natural resources recognised. Indigenous peoples are concerned with creating space (both nationally and internationally) to articulate, pursue and reclaim the lives they value (Watene and Yap 2015). Hence Indigenous peoples are organising at the global, regional, national and local levels to resist these externally imposed threats to their ownership of their resources, the survival of their culture, ancestral lands and resources. Such resistance is difficult for the Tshwa people of Zimbabwe mainly because of their small overall population and their socio-economic status. Unlike in Namibia and Botswana where the San people have been supported by external stakeholders in their struggle for survival, the Tshwa have had no strong support from external stakeholders until recently.

Loss of Ancestral Lands by Indigenous People

The concept of private ownership of land, deriving from colonial robbery, is alien to most Indigenous peoples who live by the concept of a collective moral right to own and use the land. They have therefore never claimed Eurocentric legal titles of ownership to the land. That is why national governments and companies do not consider Indigenous peoples as the legal owners of the land. Although the international convention ILO 169 and UNDRIP recognise the collective right of Indigenous peoples to their ancestral territories, only very few countries respect this. A study by Hibbard, Lane and Rasmussen (2008) on Indigenous peoples, land use planning and resources management revealed that Indigenous peoples felt that state-directed land and resource planning have largely failed them and it has contributed in many instances to their marginalisation. This is because Indigenous people require a choice and ability to pursue objectives of their own that are usually totally different from those of the dominant groups. Indigenous peoples are often referred to as the original owners and stewards of the environment, as they are caring, protecting, and managing agricultural and forest lands in a sustainable manner (Hibbard, Lane and Rasmussen 2008; Sengupta 2014). Their traditional knowledge is essential in the sustainable use of resources and central to their inclusion in the development process.

Tegegn (2014) argues that for many African countries, there is clear evidence that Indigenous peoples have been robbed, defrauded and marginalised through dispossession and forced displacement that have not brought compensation or created favourable conditions for social development and consequential upliftment. This is because the neo-liberal policies of development and economic growth are advanced by dominant models of governance which are purely western. It has been observed that more often than not, the resultant projects of "Euro-modernity" have not benefited the Indigenous communities but this has in fact advanced their marginalisation. This is true of the San people of Southern Africa. In Namibia, the Hai||om people, an indigenous San community, were forced off their ancestral land in the 1950's to pave way for the creation of Etosha National Park. The Hai||om had to eke out a living as farm labourers, sadly they remain one of Namibia's most disadvantaged peoples today. The same applies to the Tshwa of Zimbabwe who were moved from the present day Hwange National Park by the colonial authorities to pave way for the establishment of the national park.

The issue of poverty in Indigenous communities is closely related to the state of environmental conservation because their livelihood depends on it. That is indeed why the discourse on alternative paradigms of development that place the environmental movement at the juncture of corporate globalisation should inevitably deal with the plight of Indigenous people as noted by Tegegn (2010). Another study by Popova (2014) assessed the degree to which conservation benefited Indigenous communities as a means to combat poverty and ecological degradation. The study focused on the conservation initiatives conducted during the period of 2002-2012 on the territories of groups classified by the international law as Indigenous peoples. Popova's (2014) study found that the creation of protected areas has been a continuously growing conservation strategy that since 1996 has expanded more than 50% worldwide, despite a history of disturbed livelihood and forced resettlement associated with it (West, Igoe and Brockington 2006). The study revealed that the most disturbing among the areas studied was on the African continent, where the creation of protected areas caused dispossession and poverty in local communities. In Africa, the proportion of the land given to protected areas remains one of the largest in the world. The study concluded that the role of Indigenous communities in conservation on their territories since the 1990s has been marginal. The majority of the projects examined in the study have been imposed upon Indigenous groups with varied degrees of success as tools of conservation and of creating social equality. Indigenous communities were found to benefit most in those states in North America, Arctic and the Pacific where Indigenous individuals enjoy a greater degree of legal and social protection as members of cultural minorities and citizens of specific states. The study found that Indigenous communities benefited from the conversation programmes which were implemented in their areas through the creation of economic opportunities, support for communities' cultural needs and enhancement of traditional practices and the development of constructive relations between Indigenous communities, the state and conservation specialists. In contrast, the study found that Indigenous peoples who live in the states with high degrees of poverty and corruption, specifically in African countries remained most vulnerable to conservation initiatives conducted on

187

their territories. Their vulnerability was evidenced through documented displacement and poverty, leading some researchers to question the significance of protecting nature at the cost of disturbed livelihood and destroyed cultural practices. This is true of the situation of the San people of Southern Africa more specifically in Botswana, Namibia and Zimbabwe where the San were forcibly relocated out of their ancestral lands to pave way for the establishment of national parks and game reserves. Hau and Wilde (2010) describes the conditions of Indigenous people as *rich poor* because their territories have most natural resources yet they cannot enjoy them in accordance with their world views because their sovereignty over the natural resources in their territories is not being respected. Barelli (2012) calls for respect for Indigenous people's land ownership rights, territories and resources because they are vital for their continued cultural survival and vitality.

Anaya (2013) argues that food insecurity among the San people of Namibia was closely linked to the social, economic and cultural disruption that resulted from their loss of land ownership rights and access to land and related resources. From the Tshwa's perspective, their removal from Wankie Game Reserve in the late 1920s and early 1930s is one of the most unfortunate events in their history (Hitchcock, Murwira and Clench 2016). According to Hitchcock, Murwira and Clench (2016), Tshwa believe their dispossession of ancestral land had major impacts on their economies, social systems, and overall well-being. Their original ancestral lands housed present day Hwange National Park. Hwange National Park is the largest national park in Zimbabwe which covers more than 14600square kilometres. Hwange National Park has more animals and a greater variety than any other park in the country. It is also home to more than 400 species of birds. One might be tempted to suggest the abundance of fauna and flora resources in present day Hwange national park would have sustained the Thswa for centuries had they not been dispossessed of their ancestral lands.

Loss of Bio-cultural Diversity, Traditional Knowledge and Culture

To Indigenous people, their culture is a very important and constitutive part of their well-being such that they regard it as part of their value for life. For them, any threat to their culture is also a threat to life itself. Some of the economic and corporate activities carried out by private companies with the support of the state government have posed serious threats to the survival of Indigenous people's culture, their traditional knowledge and the biocultural diversity found in their ancestral lands. Indigenous cultures are fundamentally connected to, and remain inseparable from, not just people but the ownership of the natural world, including land (Watene and Yap 2015). For Indigenous peoples, the mountains, rivers and lands form the basis of their social organisation, economic system and cultural identification such that any detachment and displacement from the natural environment threatens their survival. A few of the economic activities being carried out across the globe does consider Indigenous people's ownership and interconnectedness with the environment and hence most of the activities have been carried out to the detriment of the livelihoods of Indigenous peoples. The disconnection of Indigenous peoples from their natural environment has resulted in them being further marginalised because of the loss of biodiversity and traditional knowledge. This has threatened the survival of Indigenous people on planet earth. Their traditional languages are also facing extinction. It is expected that roughly 90 percent of all existing languages may become no more within the next 100 years; and the associated traditional ecological knowledge will also be lost (UN 2010). The protection of Indigenous knowledge and their ways of life is not just relevant to Indigenous peoples but to the planet and its inhabitants.

Tshwa Culture after Decades of Land Dispossession

The Tshwa hunting and gathering culture is deeply connected and intertwined to ownership of ancestral lands. Like other San "tribal" groupings in Southern Africa, the dispossession of ancestral lands has negatively affected their culture and language mainly because San communities end up living as minorities. This is the same situation faced by the Tshwa people of Zimbabwe. A study by Hitchcock, Murwira and Clench (2016) notes that a relatively small number of Tshwa households speak Tshwao, the Tshwa language (32 of 149 households interviewed). Many of the fluent Tshwao speakers in the study were elderly. The Tshwa expressed a desire for their children to learn this language and to gain a better understanding of Tshwa culture. The Tshwao language, despite recent recognition of San language in the Zimbabwean Constitution, is at risk of extinction in the coming years. Hitchcock, Murwira and Clench (2016) note that the Tshwao language is at a critical juncture where without formal support and development it is at risk of extinction, due to the low number of fluent Tshwao speakers. Most fluent Tshwao speakers are elderly and a number pass away each year. Hitchcock, Murwira and Clench (2016) note that community-based organisations in western Zimbabwe, along with local NGOs such as the Tsoro-o-tso San Development Trust, are seeking to promote San cultural heritage and identity.

Hitchcock, Murwira and Clench (2016) further note that efforts are being made to provide agricultural and development assistance to Tshwa and their neighbours in the Tsholotsho area by Community Technology Development Trust (CTDC), the Tsholotsho District Council as well as by several INGOs. This is contrary to their hunting and gathering culture as San people. This is a further display of evidence that the Tshwa hunting and gathering culture is on the verge of extinction as a result of land dispossession. This situation is not unique to the Tshwa but generally applies to most San tribal groupings in Southern Africa. Hitchcock, Murwira and Clench (2016) allude to the fact that many aspects of traditional hunting and gathering knowledge are in the process of, or have already been lost in most San communities. They further note that most San communities have a common usage of bush (veld) food, medicinal herbs and other natural resources. This varies from the marginal use to seasonal reliance and in a few areas where hunting is permitted;

traditional hunting and tracking skills endure. Other traditional practices, including healing ceremonies and dances and medicinal use of plants vary from group to group, but are still relatively common.

Natural resources are important sources of subsistence and income for indigenous communities including the Tshwa. For the Tshwa, access to some of the important trees and shrub species is restricted if they are in protected areas, including Hwange National Park and in the Forest Areas that are covered under Zimbabwe's Forest Act 19:05 (Hitchcock, Murwira and Clench (2016)). The availability of natural resources to the Tshwa and other indigenous communities in Southern Africa has been negatively affected by climate change. Zimbabwe, as other Southern African nations, is faced by unpredictable and extreme weather patterns related to global climate change. Areas such as Tsholotsho District are susceptible to both drought (as of late 2014, early 2015) and flooding (as seen in early 2014). Prolonged drought periods ultimately compromise the productiveness of natural resources thereby affecting the livelihoods of the Tshwa. Drought or floods curtails the capacity of Tshwa households to benefit from the natural resources.

Conclusion

This chapter looked at the effects of land dispossession on the livelihoods of the San people of Southern Africa and more specifically the Tshwa people of Zimbabwe. This chapter acknowledges the San people as the original inhabitants of Southern Africa. The dispossession of ancestral lands has negatively affected their livelihoods and put them in marginal positions economically, socially and politically. The dispossession of ancestral lands has put their hunting and gathering culture at the verge of extinction. This study concludes that there is dearth in research and documentation of the Tshwa indigenous people of Zimbabwe's culture and more importantly in the recognition of them as indigenous people. Hence, they are regarded like any other Zimbabwean, without recognition of the importance of their culture and how their painful history of land dispossession and cultural disregard has contributed to their present marginalised position. The assimilation policies pursued by the government of Zimbabwe have contributed to the demise of the Tshwa culture. This has also worsened the marginalisation of the Tshwa people.

References

AFRIZIM (2018), The San people, Africa's ultimate survivors https://www.afrizim.com/blog/san-people-bushmen/

Australian Council for International Development (ACFID). (2014) Effective developments practice with Aboriginal and Torres Strait Islander communities, https://acfid,asn,au/sites/site,acfid/files/resource_document/ Effective-Development-Practice-with-Aboriginal-and-Torres-Strait-Islander-Communities,pdf.

Bamba, J. (2010) Indigenous people self-determined development: Lessons from Kalimantan Credit Union Movement, International Expert Group Meeting: Indigenous people: *Development with culture and identity Articles 3 and 32 of the United Nations Declaration on the Rights of Indigenous People*, New York, 12 - 14 January 2010: Department of Social and Economic Affairs, United Nations.

Banerjee, S. & Tedmanson, D. (2010) Grass burning under our feet: Indigenous enterprise development in a political economy of whiteness, *Management Learning*, 41,147–165.

Barelli, M. (2012) Free, prior and informed consent in the aftermath of the UN Declaration on the Rights of Indigenous People: Developments and challenges ahead. *The International Journal of Human Rights*, 16(1), 1-24.

Carino, J. (2005) *Indigenous people human rights and poverty: Indigenous perspectives,* 7(1): TEBTEBBA Foundation, Madrid.

Carino. J. (2009) Poverty and Wellbeing, in *The State of the World's Indigenous People*. New York: United Nations.

Clarke, G. (2001) From Ethnocide to Ethno development? Ethnic Minorities and Indigenous People in Southeast Asia, in *Third World Quarterly*, 22(3), 413-436.

Corntassel, J. (2008) 'Towards sustainable self-determination: Rethinking the contemporary Indigenous rights discourse', *Alternatives: Global, local, political*, 33(1), 105-132.

De Wet, P. (2010) *South Africa's Unfinished Business: The First Nation Indigenous KhoeSan Peoples*. Saarbruchen: Lap Lambert Publishing.

Dosch, S. D. (2012) Understanding Latin America Indigenous Movements: From marginalisation to self-determination and autonomy? *3rd International Seminar & Workshop on Latin American and Asian Studies (LASA III) Institute* of Occidental Studies: Universiti Kebangsaan Malaysia.

Doyle, C. & Gilbert, J. (2010) Indigenous People and Globalization: From 'Development Aggression' to 'Self-Determined Development', *European Yearbook of Minority Issues*, Vol 7(1), 219-262.

Doyle, C. (2009) *Indigenous* people and the Millennium Development Goals – 'sacrificial lambs' or equal beneficiaries? *The International Journal of Human Rights, 13(1), 44-71.*

Hall, G. & Patrinos, H. (2012) *Indigenous People, Poverty and Development.* New York: Cambridge University Press.

Hau, V. M., & Wilde, G. (2010) 'We have always lived here': Indigenous movements, citizenship and poverty in Argentina, *in The Journal of Development Studies*, 46(7), 1283-1303.

Hibbard, M., Lane, M. B. & Rasmussen, K. (2008) The split personality of planning: Indigenous people and planning for land and resource management, *Journal of Planning Literature,* 23(1), 151-131.

Hitchcock. R. K, Murwira, A & Clench, B. B. (2016). The San in Zimbabwe: Livelihoods, Land and Human Rights. International Work Group for Indigenous Affairs, University of Zimbabwe.

Madzudzo, E. (2001) —Zimbabwe‖. In Robins, S., Madzudzo, E. And Brenzinger, M. (eds) *Assessment of the San in South Africa, Angola, Zambia and Zimbabwe.* Windhoek: Legal Assistance Centre, Pp 77 – 105

Mtapuri, O., Nhemachena, A. & Benyera, E. (2018) Towards a Jurisprudential Theory of Migration, Foot-looseness and Nimble-footedness: the New World Order or Pan-Africanism, in Nhemachena, A., Warikandwa, T. V. & Amoo, S. K. (eds) *Social and Legal Theory in the Age of Decoloniality: (Re-)Envisioning Pan-African Jurisprudence in the 21ˢᵗ Century.* Bamenda: Langaa RPCIG.

Ndahinda, F. (2014) Historical development of Indigenous identification and rights in Africa, In: Laher, R, & Sing Oei, K, (eds,) *Indigenous people in Africa: celebrations, empowerment and group rights.* Pretoria: Africa Institute of South Africa.

Nhemachena, A. & Dhakwa, E. (2017). When Did the Rain Start to Beat Us? Discursive Dispossession and the Political Economies of Misrecognition about African Mining, in Nhemachena, A. & Warikandwa, T. V. (eds) *Mining Africa: Law, Environment, Society & Politics in Historical and Multidisciplinary Perspectives.* Bamenda: Langaa RPCIG.

Nthomang, K. (2002) Exploring the Indigenous minefield: Social policy and the marginalisation of the Bushman in Southern Africa, in *Journal of Social Development in Africa 17(1)*, 99-121.

Popova, U. (2014) Conservation, traditional knowledge, and Indigenous people, *Indigenous Struggles to the 21st Century,* 58, 179-189.

Sarivaar, E., Maatta, K. & Uusiautti, S. (2013) Who Is Indigenous? Definitions of Indigeneity, *European Scientific Journal Special.* 1(1).

Simpson, L. (2002) Indigenous Environmental Education for Cultural Survival, *Canadian Journal of Environmental Education,* 7(1), 13-25.

Suzman, J. (2001b) *Regional Assessment of the Status of the San in Southern Africa: An Assessment of the Status of the San in Namibia,* Report Series Report No, 4 of 5, Windhoek, Namibia, Legal Assistance Centre.

Tegegn, M. (2014) The impact of Dominant Environment Policies on Indigenous People in Africa, *In:* Laher, R, & Singoei, K, (eds,) *Indigenous People in Africa: Contestations, Empowerment and Group Rights* Pretoria, South Africa: Africa Institute of South Africa.

Chapter Nine

Interrogation of the Nexus between Land Restitution and Poverty Alleviation in Contemporary Zimbabwe

Blessing Makunike

Introduction

The chapter discusses land redistribution as a way of alleviating poverty by redressing colonial dispossession and displacement. Colonialism in Zimbabwe contributed to the impoverishment of the Black majority because it resulted in their deprivation including the creation of social and economic distress. Zimbabwe gained independence in 1980, bringing to an end colonialism which started as administration by the British South African Company (BSAC, 1890 – 1923). Various pieces of legislation, such as the Southern Rhodesia Order in Council 1898, the Land Apportionment Act 1930, the Native Husbandry Act No. 52 of 1951 and the Land Tenure Act No. 55 of 1969, divided land and apportioned it according to racial categories. The pieces of legislation forced the Black peasants into marginal areas, while reserving the best agricultural land for Whites, such that at independence, almost 42% of the country was owned by 6,000 (White) commercial farmers. Land reclamation therefore becomes an integral part of restoration aimed at enabling a given society to move towards the achievement of what the people living in it consider as being the conditions of justice, their happiness and self-actualisation. The main argument is that lack of access to land and appropriate tenure systems among the poor are an obstacle to poverty alleviation. A widely acclaimed aim of land redistribution is to redress the theft of land - restoring ownership and rights of access over the land by to Black Zimbabweans, and in the process redressing past, legal, cultural, ethical, moral and political wrongs.

The question on the extent to which land redistribution can be assumed to be a means by which poverty in Zimbabwe could be alleviated has many answers: answers which address direct and indirect links between land distribution, land ownership, and poverty; and which have implications for both macro-scale systems, such as national export earnings, and micro-scale systems, such as providing enhanced opportunities for individual or household subsistence, wealth creation, and food security. The assertion is that if land redistribution can correct colonial distortions by delivering land to a broad base of Black beneficiaries and raise the productivity and incomes of smallholder agriculture in Zimbabwe, it will then be a direct route towards alleviating poverty, hunger, malnutrition and unemployment.

Rationale for Land Restitution and Relationship to Poverty Alleviation

Sobhan (1993) suggests that one of the most potent forces generating pressure for land redistribution lies in the lack of access to land for a high proportion of the agricultural population. Zimbabwe is one of the countries in Southern Africa with highest proportion of the agricultural population. Hence landlessness is still a major issue in Zimbabwe and in the case of the latter; the concept of "landlessness" includes those land-poor households without enough land to ensure their subsistence. In Zimbabwe, the persistence of landlessness in rural areas long after the land redistribution were initiated after independence, indicates not just the inadequacy of the programmes, but also that the manner of the redistribution was not such that pressure for land could be eased. Further, the persistence of poverty in the rural areas in Zimbabwe does indeed suggest the land-hunger of the rural population which, over the years, has been also increasing.

The failure of land redistribution, to release enough land to the growing numbers of the landless, is also indicative of demographic pressures (Sobhan,1993: 104) The pressure puts a limit on the capacity of the land and this in turn leads to growth of under-employment of the agricultural labour force. Under-employment arises when the available labour force cannot be absorbed to work full-time on land. In turn, the high levels of under-employment and landlessness is manifest in the stagnation of real wages in the rural economy. Moyo (2008; 25) concurs that access to land is fundamental in Africa, for the survival of the majority of households, in the absence of alternative productive industry and infrastructures for employment in the services sector.

Sobhan (1993) further observes that for some time, the development of new high yielding varieties of seeds associated with the green revolution was widely recognised as a necessary ingredient in development. It created hope that increased labour absorption in agriculture lay in the diffusion of new technology. It was believed that this could arrest the falling real wages and the growth in under-employment and rural poverty. However, despite the high rates of growth in agricultural production associated with the green revolution, its full benefits have not been able to cascade through to the rural poor, on a sufficient scale, to arrest the increase in the numbers of the rural poor. For example, the rapid spread of new technology in Asia only marginally reduced the rate of growth of rural poverty. It is argued here that increased productivity alone, when achieved within a tenure structure of great inequality cannot be a substitute for land redistribution.

The limited impact made in the alleviation of rural poverty, through the diffusion of new technology and inadequate labour absorption capacity of the non-agricultural sector, means that poverty and landlessness are likely to remain permanent features of developing countries. This has led to a number of policy initiatives and resource commitments targeted at delivering resources to the poor. In Zimbabwe, in the early 1990s, these programmes included "food for work" programmes and other nutritional improvement programmes and skills enhancing programmes and direct service delivery programmes targeted at the poorest sections of the rural population. Such programmes may be incorporated into wide integrated rural development programmes and are often underwritten by aid donors. However, the survey results from Mashonaland East showed that most of these programmes have been infiltrated and eventually captured by the rural elite. Very few programmes exist in the portfolios of rural development which have restricted benefits exclusively for the poor. The poor are still with us and the structural basis of poverty, which has been at the core of the debate on agrarian reforms, remains as intractable today as it was before.

Alternative sources of employment in the rural economy have failed to develop fast enough and market forces have worked to drain resources from the rural areas and have stifled the development of rural industry. Moyo (2008) notes that this lack of productivity and growth in Africa is underpinned by the agrarian technological backwardness and inappropriate land and agrarian policies which arise from perennially declining terms of agricultural commodity trade and the extractive role of monopoly capital. Moyo (2008) further notes that this suggests that inappropriate economic and land-use policies and diminished access to land ownership and negative external integration are critical factors in explaining Africa's looming agrarian crisis.

The above makes a case for radical agrarian redistribution programmes which are more likely to realise growth in the agricultural sector, while arresting the increase of rural poverty. Agrarian redistribution programmes should create the basis for a more equitable access to land, and through this access to land, to markets and other public resources. Thus, agrarian redistribution programmes are rationalised by the need for equity in access to productive resources, and the elimination of socio economic and political differentiation within the peasantry.

World Bank reports comparing countries over time suggest that equity in land distribution is good for growth. For instance, the initial phase of China's high and sustained growth and poverty reduction spurt clearly was linked to its 1979 change from collective, large-scale farms to small family farms. When collective production was abandoned and key agricultural markets were liberalised, China's peasant sector initiated rapid economic growth, which dramatically reduced poverty. At the other end of the equity spectrum, one finds the countries that have not been successful in reducing rural poverty. These countries include, for example, Brazil, Colombia, Guatemala, and South Africa. Not surprisingly, these countries are characterised by high unequal landownership, with substantial public investments in large-scale farming. Van den Brink (ed) (2009: 9) points out that although these large-scale farms usually have become technically sophisticated, they make little use of labour and their mechanisation leads to rapid out-migration of labour from the commercial agricultural sector, into rural areas or urban slums, thus creating more rural and urban poverty.

In Zimbabwe, a large body of literature also makes a case for land redistribution (Moyo 1995; Tshuma 1997; Kinsey 1999; Scoones 2010.). Settler colonial rule perpetuated the setting aside of most of the fertile land for Whites and the adoption of discriminatory agricultural policies, oppression, marginalisation and impoverishment of indigenous people. To a great extent, one of the grievances of the Zimbabwean liberation war fighters was the land issue. Not surprisingly, most commentators on Zimbabwe's socio-economic and political reforms see the resolution of the land issue as a benchmark for evaluating the performance, success and failures of the government (Tshuma 1997).

Overall, land redistribution should have three major objectives: the first is to achieve political stability. This will ultimately be reached through land redistribution and creating greater access to land ownership by all Zimbabweans. Secondly, sustainable rural livelihoods and rise in rural incomes, economic growth and development. Thirdly, land redistribution should lead to social integration and the realisation of a peaceful and progressive non-racial society. The latter is an ideal which will be very difficult to realise especially if government and White land owners don't close the gap and work closely together.

Contextual Background of Land Restitution in Zimbabwe

During the settlement negotiations held at Lancaster House (1979), concessions by the White administration, in Zimbabwe, were minimal. As noted by several authors (Moyo 1995; Cusworth 1992; Bertus de Villiers 2003; Scoones *et al* 2010), the Lancaster House

Agreement set the terms for all land redistribution policy in the first decade of Zimbabwe's independence. Given the restrictions imposed by the Lancaster House Constitution (1979), much of the land redistribution of the first decade after the attainment of independence was aimed at resettlement for Black families. The original, largely political objective of the programme placed great emphasis on welfare and poverty reduction (Kinsey 1999).

The programme resettled more than 70,000 individual families into clustered villages and allocated each family a 0.4 residential plot, a uniform 5 hectares of arable land and the right to use a variable amount of grazing land on a communal basis (Kinsey 1999:180). Scoones *et al* (2010) and Kinsey (1999) note that the criteria originally used to choose beneficiaries emphasised the selection of poor families, in the communal areas, returning war veterans and those displaced by the war.

Although Kinsey (1999) argues that the welfare of the families that moved into resettlement areas dramatically improved in relation to families that remained in the communal areas, Bertus de Villiers (2003) contends that very often beneficiaries, being individuals who had few assets of their own, found it difficult to get started in resettlement areas. Combined with the budgetary, administrative and logistical difficulties faced by the resettlement programme, a new narrative emerged, which suggested that the programme was merely a social welfare sideline only useful for political purposes. It is further argued that another aspect of the resettlement programme was that the acquired land was owned by the state and not by the farmers or community responsible for working on the land. In strictly legal terms, the state was, therefore, the main beneficiary of the land redistribution programme (Bertus de Villiers 2003: 10). Although an occupancy permit was issued, it fell short of secure tenure in the form of a lease or freehold.

Kinsey (1999) brings an interesting dimension to the debate on the resettlement programme. The argument is that the resettlement programme was planned in the atmosphere of the *growth with equity* paradigm, then prominent in development thinking of the late 1970s and early 1980s, and the declared objectives of the programme were couched in rhetoric matching this theme. This "growth with equity" debate, in development economics, at the time showed, however, that many economists question whether growth and equity are not antithetical, their premise being that a period of sharp inequity must be tolerated in order to allow accumulation of capital for investment (Kinsey 1999: 180). This makes the choice of measures of the welfare gains from resettlement difficult, because of the need to factor in not only indicators that quantify dimensions of economic performance, but also those that tell us something about the distribution of growth.

On the part of the government, by the end of the first decade, it was felt that land redistribution, by way of the resettlement programme, had created sufficient political stability to warrant a shift in emphasis away from the landless towards those who had demonstrated a capacity to accumulate (Tshuma 1997: 136; International Crisis Group 2000). The government felt the need to place emphasis on economic returns. It promised a land tax to discourage speculative holdings and a commission to examine land tenure issues. It also made statements about reducing foreign and absentee land ownership and limiting the number of farms that an individual or company could own.

The "New" Land Policy of the Second Phase

The second phase of land redistribution in Zimbabwe was ushered in, in 1990 with a new constitutional dispensation. On 18 April 1990, the ten year period of entrenchment of the Bill of Rights came to an end. Instead of the 100% majority required to amend the Bill of Rights in the first ten years, a two-thirds majority sufficed. As the ruling ZANU (PF) party commanded more than a two-thirds majority in Parliament, it now had the power to amend the constitutional provisions relating to land.

According to Madhuku (2004), on the political front, by the close of the first decade of independence, land had emerged as a key political issue. This was mainly due to growing peasant disillusionment with the feeble and almost negligible pace of land redistribution during the 1980 to 1990 period. The government blamed its failure, to deliver on land on the restrictive legal framework of the Lancaster House Constitution. It therefore promised a radical redistribution process.

The second phase also came into being at a time when the government was reeling under a number of negative developments. Among such developments was the introduction of the Economic Structural Adjustment Programme (ESAP), whose impact on the economy and the general populace was negative (Masiiwa and Chipungu 2004). The situation was compounded by the emergence, in 1989, of a new and vibrant opposition political party, the Zimbabwe Unity Movement (ZUM). ZUM contested the 1990 parliamentary and presidential elections and ZANU (PF) used the land issue as a rallying point for support (Madhuku 2004). The efforts by ZUM and other opposition parties were supported by the rise of the foreign media and civil society organisations that also helped to disseminate information to the general public. This forced government to seriously think about re-invigorating the resettlement programme, which had slowed down over the years.

Given the foregoing, it was inevitable that the Constitution had to be amended to accommodate the new direction of land redistribution. Section 16 of the Constitution was duly amended by the Constitution of Zimbabwe Amendment (Number 11) Act 1990. The Act came into force in 1991 and was called the "Land Acquisition Act". It demolished the Lancaster House framework through three main features. First, it subjected all land, and not just underutilised land, to the regime of compulsory acquisition. This meant that even productive farms were henceforth liable for acquisition if the state so wished. Secondly, it replaced the "prompt and adequate" measure of compensation with a "fair compensation" within a "reasonable time". In general, "fair compensation" is less than the market value determined from a willing buyer–willing seller standpoint and is a more flexible yardstick. Thirdly, it prohibited the courts from calling into question the fairness or otherwise of any compensation formula to be provided by law (Madhuku 2004:133). Moyo (1995) adds that the amendment also gave the government the right of "first refusal" on all Land Sales, and established a Derelict

Lands Board, which allowed government to acquire derelict lands without compensation.

Moyo (1995:245), further notes that the legal changes were backed by a land policy statement announced in 1990, in the form of specific non-connected actions to be undertaken over an unspecified time frame. The land policy focused on five issues:

- It set a target to acquire five million more hectares in land blocks, to resettle 110 000 more households.
- It intended to review the land tenure situation in Communal, Resettlement and Small Scale Commercial farming areas;
- The selection of settlers and land use models in resettlement areas were to be reviewed towards emphasizing economic rather than social or subsistence criteria;
- It intended to promote Blacks in capitalist farming through training and agricultural support services.
- It intended to introduce a land tax.

Ancillary aspects of the policy included the increased supervision and regulation of land use, the reduction of foreign and absentee land ownership in agriculture, the reduction of multiple and company farm ownerships, the deregulation of farm sub-division, the retention of capital gains taxes by farmers selling land but reinvesting into agriculture, and the selling of maximum and minimum sub-sectors in relation to agro-ecological potentials (Moyo 1995).

Moyo (1995: 245) correctly points out that the land policy statement attempted to provide a comprehensive or inclusive position on various land policy concerns and problems resulting from the first phase of land redistribution. It encompassed moral, normative, technical, economic, administrative, political and macro-economic objectives, through the various means, such as constitutional amendments, decentralisation of land allocation, creating Black, large-scale commercial farmers and financing resettlement. But the issues were not actually linked in terms of a coherent, rational and logical implementation sequence. The influences of land policy measures on various problems were only implied. Nor was there any national consultative process to determine public opinion on the policy.

This had to be followed by a new Act of Parliament implementing the principles set out in the Constitutional and policy framework. Thus, the Land Acquisition Act was enacted in 1992. It elaborately laid out the principles and procedures for acquiring land for redistribution (Moyo 1995). The Act brought into being a new approach of "designating" land as a prelude to acquisition. Designation involved a piece of rural land being identified and earmarked for acquisition, within a period not exceeding ten years from the date of notice. Thus, designation was merely an act of communicating to the owner and the public, the intention of the state to acquire, in the future, the specified piece of rural land. Its main legal effect was to prohibit the sale, lease or disposal of land in question, without the prior written permission of the government. The justification was that it facilitated the acquisition of land in large blocs suitable for the implementation of the resettlement programme, and that it would facilitate planning for both the government and the farmers, since the land that the government intended to acquire would be clearly identified and demarcated, such that prospective farmers would know where to invest (Madhuku 2004).

Within a year of the enactment of the Land Acquisition Act, 1992, a second constitutional amendment affecting land was enacted. This was contained in the Constitution of Zimbabwe Amendment (Number 12), Act 1993. The main effect of the amendment, in relation to land, was that it amended section 18 and made the right to the "protection of the law" and, the "entitlement" to be afforded a fair hearing within a reasonable time by an independent and impartial court" to be overridden by other provisions of the Constitution. This meant that provisions of the Land Acquisition Act, 1992 which were prohibiting the jurisdiction of the courts in matters of fair compensation for acquired land, could not be challenged on the basis of a breach of section 18 (Madhuku 2004).

A third constitutional amendment followed before the end of 1993. This was the Constitution of Zimbabwe (Number 13) Act,

1993. This amendment was meant to make it clear that it was only in respect of land that the courts would not question the compensation payable. The right to approach the courts on any question relating to compensation was still available in respect of the compulsory acquisition of any other property.

The legal framework created by the new constitutional provisions and the land Acquisition Act, 1992, became the basis for the land redistribution process in this period. However, owing to fierce opposition of this legal framework, the next few years witnessed unending legal battles. On the one hand, the government sought to close any loopholes in the law, which could have been used by White commercial farmers, to undermine the effectiveness of the new law. On the other hand, White commercial farmers resorted to challenging the constitutionality of the new laws in the courts.

In 1997, spurred by pressure from the powerful war veterans, the government employed the relevant section of the Land Acquisition Act, to designate 1,471 large-scale commercial farms for compulsory acquisition (Moyo and Matondi 2001). The top down approach of the government, and the failure to consult widely with interested stakeholders, compromised the success of this initiative. The government then launched a broad-based consultation process, with a wide variety of non-state actors, in order to develop a national land policy and phase 2 of land redistribution and resettlement programme, which embraced the principles of transparency, accountability and participation. In its bid to raise funds for phase 2, government went on to organise a donors' conference in Harare in September 1998. By this time, however, international donors had grown suspicious of government's moves, particularly its passing of the Land Acquisition Act of 1992, which allowed the government to compulsorily acquire land (Tshuma 1997). Despite such negative developments, the government introduced phase 2 of the land redistribution programme to the donors. During this phase, the government aimed to finalise a new policy which would introduce an agricultural land tax, streamline sub-division regulations, improve tenure arrangements and test a variety of approaches to land redistribution, with the key objective of learning by doing (Moyo and Matondi 2001).

Masiiwa and Chipungu (2004) observe that there was a climate of mistrust, and financial commitments from international donors was disappointing. A number of issues were not clear to the donor community:

(i) The European Union's stance was that it would not commit itself to the land redistribution and resettlement programme on the basis of a policy document. What they wanted were concrete proposals for projects on how the government was going to carry out the land redistribution in all areas it intended to resettle people;

(ii) The International Monetary Fund (IMF) wanted government to employ a market-oriented approach that would involve taxation of underutilised land to induce sub-division of farms. This would, in turn, release more land on the market;

(iii) Some donors also wanted the redistribution programme to be integrated within a broad macro-economic framework that had specific targets aimed at fostering economic growth.

Despite the financial dilemma which followed the donors' conference, the government went ahead to launch phase 2 of the land reform programme in 1999. In the absence of credit facilities, a land redistribution programme, wholly financed by the government, inevitably had negative effects, chief among them, inflation.

In the same year, 1999, a Constitutional Commission was formed by the government to consult on a draft Constitution. One of the aims of the draft Constitution was to insert provisions that would make it easier and cheaper for the government to acquire land for resettlement. In February 2000, a Constitutional referendum was held and the draft Constitution was rejected by the majority. The Africa All Party Parliamentary Group (2009: 35) observed that President Mugabe took the defeat as a personal rejection, and with his blessing, the party machine acted swiftly to put in place a radical land redistribution policy which formed the cornerstone of his re-election campaign.

Apparently angered and frustrated by the result of the referendum, war veterans and landless villagers started a wave of invasions of commercial farms, marking the complexification of a crisis that had started with the colonisation of Zimbabwe. The commercial farmers were alleged to have campaigned for a "no" vote against the draft Constitution. Thus, violence directed towards White farmers and Black farm workers became part of political campaigns for the June 2000 Parliamentary elections, and led to the freezing of whatever donor support had been half-heartedly offered.

Madhuku (2004) argues that these developments showed the ruling party's waning support base, which was in contrast to the rapidly expanding urban support base for the opposition parties. In this context, ZANU (PF) had to devise a survival strategy and picked on the land issue as its strategic agenda. The use of the land issues had one significant difference from the previous periods. This time, the opposition and civic society had to be portrayed as opponents of land redistribution and that they were being sponsored by Britain and the western allies. ZANU (PF) was portrayed as the only movement that had a genuine commitment to land redistribution. This entailed an approach which was as radical as to fit the description of "revolutionary" and well-couched, to depict any critic, however moderate the criticism, as "counter revolutionary". This is why this particular phase of land reform was described as the "Third Chimurenga".

Pursuant to this political strategy, the rejection of the Government's draft Constitution in the Referendum of February 2000, was characterised as a conspiracy against land redistribution and on 18th February 2000, the first forceful land occupation by war veterans took place. These occupations were to become the main feature of the post – 2000 land redistribution process.

After the rejection of the draft Constitution, Parliament went on to amend the Constitution in April 2000. This amendment came in the form of the Constitution of Zimbabwe Amendment (No. 16) Act, 2000. The amendment was taken verbatim, from a clause of the draft Constitution that had been rejected in the referendum (Madhuku 2004). The perceived political benefit accruing to ZANU

(PF) in enacting, as law, a provision which had been part of a rejected proposal, was that ZANU (PF) would be seen as a party that rescued the people from the conspiracy against land redistribution, by those who opposed the draft Constitution. The Act empowered the Government to acquire commercial farms without an obligation to pay compensation for the land, but only for the farm improvements.

The amendment did not stop farm acquisitions as was expected. Instead, the acquisitions became more violent, as the June 2000 Parliamentary elections approached. Despite the ruling ZANU (PF) party winning the majority of seats, the acquisitions continued.

The failure of the inception phase and the rising pressure from people for land led the government to legitimise the violent farm acquisitions through an accelerated resettlement programme named "Fast Track". At first there seemed to be some confusion regarding the exact definition and scope of the fast track resettlement programme, among the majority of Zimbabweans. On its part, the government sought to explain this issue at a summit held in New York in early September 2000. The impression given by the Government was that the fast track resettlement programme was an accelerated plan for land redistribution.

The fast track resettlement programme had two models, namely the A1 and A2 models. The A1 model was targeted at the rural landless, who would be resettled in villages or self-contained small farms of about 5 hectares, depending on the natural farming region. The A2 model was a commercial farming land-use model, meant to empower the Black indigenous farmers.

Madhuku (2004) observes that the new Constitutional position led to amendments to the Land Acquisition Act of 1992. A substantial portion of amendments to the Act did not arise from the need to make the Act conform to the Constitution, but were designed to remove what the government press termed "bottlenecks" in the acquisition process. Essentially, this meant removing all procedural safeguards against abuse of state authority in the acquisition process. This also included making amendments as a response to the reaction of White commercial farmers. Because many amendments were a response to what government perceived as a concerted effort, by

White commercial farmers, to frustrate land redistribution, the amendment process was ad hoc to the extent that the Act has been amended at least once every year since 2000.

The first amendments were enacted in 2000 under the Land Acquisition Amendment Act, 2000. These introduced several changes, the most significant of which were to incorporate the new position of "no obligation to pay compensation" and to facilitate the fast track resettlement programme by repealing all provisions relating to designation of rural land. Whilst in the 1992 Act, a preliminary notice of intention to acquire land automatically lapsed after one year if there was no acquisition, this was considered as one of the "bottlenecks" and the 2000 amendments repealed this position and made a preliminary notice valid for an indefinite period, and could only be terminated either by withdrawal or acquisition of the land in question.

In 2001, further amendments were made via the Land Acquisition Amendment Act, 2001. These amendments were designed to condone Government's failure to observe the time limits imposed by the Act. For example, it allowed government to re-issue preliminary notices in respect of the same land where they had lapsed. In response to a ruling by the Supreme Court, which at that time included some judges from the colonial establishment, that the indefinite period was unconstitutional, the 2001 amendments reduced the period of validity to two years.

In 2002, another set of amendments was enacted. The first was contained in the Land Acquisition Amendment (No.1) Act, 2002. The main provision of the first 2002 amendments, related to the eviction of owners of land, which had been compulsorily acquired. This was in response to landowners who were considered to be resisting the land redistribution process, by refusing to vacate their farms. In terms of the amendments, once an order of acquisition had been made, the making of the order itself was deemed to be a notice to the owner to cease to occupy, hold or use that land forty-five days after the date of service of the order. The owner was allowed to remain in occupation of their living quarters on that farm for a period of no more than ninety days.

The second were contained in the Land Acquisition Amendment (No.2) Act, 2002 and were meant to reverse certain unfavourable decisions from the courts. Some farmers had started challenging acquisitions on the basis that the land was not suitable for settlement for agricultural purposes. A new provision was inserted into the Act providing that as long as the acquiring authority has stated that the acquisition was for settlement for agricultural purposes, then it shall be presumed that the land was indeed suitable settlement for agricultural purposes. The High Court had also ruled that failure to serve notice on bondholders invalidated an acquisition order. A new provision was inserted, to render the judgment ineffective, by allowing Government to serve subsequent orders in substitution of the invalid orders and thus still proceed with the acquisition.

While the above shows a spirited resort to the enactments of legal instruments as part of a new approach to land redistribution, this was merely half the story. The other half was that the Government condoned breaches of the existing law in furtherance of the political objectives driving the land redistribution programme.

The immediate response of White commercial farmers to land occupants was to resort to the courts, it having been clear under the existing law that the occupations were illegal. In March 2000, a month after the first farm occupations, the High Court issued an order that declared farm acquisitions "unlawful". The state accepted that the occupations were "unlawful". However, the Commissioner of Police did not enforce the order and decided to go back to the court seeking to be excused from enforcing it. The application of the Commissioner of Police was the beginning of the arguments, which were to be used to disobey court orders. He cited lack of resources to enforce the order. More fundamentally, he raised a purely political argument that enforcing the order would lead to public disorder as the persons involved were prepared to resist the police in furtherance of their quest for land. In other words, the police were of the view that it was not politically correct to enforce the law.

The Commercial farmers, having won in the High Court, but continuing to lose out due to political pressures decided to approach the Supreme Court with an application based on the breach of the

Constitution. In its judgment, the Supreme Court also criticised the "Fast Track Land Reform Programme," saying it did not meet the Constitutional requirement of a "programme of land reform". When it came to the remedy, the Supreme Court backtracked. It ordered the government to comply with the orders issued by the previous courts, but refused to give an immediate order restraining the government from continuing with land acquisition, it was thus succumbing to the political pressures that had built up around the land question.

The Supreme Court judgment gave government a major reprieve. Purporting to be restoring the rule of law, it enacted the Rural Land Occupiers (Protection from Eviction) Act, 2001. The purpose of this Act was to legalise all land occupations, which took place from 6th February 2000 to 1st March 2001. Any persons occupying rural land as at 1st March 2000 was given the status of a "protected occupier" and could not be evicted. In this way, the Government responded in an astute manner, to the pleas by the judiciary not to disobey its own laws, but to change them if it did not like them. In issuing the pleas, the courts seem to have been naïve, because in the period after 2000, the Government showed preparedness to pass, as law, any instrument, however objectionable, as long as it was in the interest of the ongoing land restitution.

For a Government that had gone to great lengths in passing a Constitutional amendment in 2000 and enacting four Land Acquisition Amendment Acts within a space of three years, it was very aware of what it had to do if it wanted to legalise the land occupations. Defiance of its own laws, which it had power to change, was simply a political strategy. The Government of Zimbabwe wanted to buy favours with party members and supporters. It wanted to be given space to fight forces opposed to progress in Zimbabwe. These forces included the opposition party (MDC) and some civic groups.

Madhuku (2004) notes that, armed with the new Act, the government itself went back to Supreme Court, which it had now reconstituted with progressive pro-land redistribution judges, seeking an order that stated that the rule of law had been restored. The matter was heard in September 2000 and presided over by the new Chief Justice Godfrey Chidyausiku. In that case, The Minister of Lands, Agriculture and Rural Resettlement and others v the Commercial Farmers Union, by a majority of four judges against one, the Supreme Court ruled that the land acquisition programme was now lawful as government had restored the rule of law. It upheld the Rural Land Occupiers (Protection from Eviction) Act, 2001 as constitutional. It ruled that the Government now had a "land reform programme" in compliance with the Constitution.

This Supreme Court judgment brought to an end the numerous court applications challenging the land redistribution programme itself and gave Government unlimited scope in pursuing its land policies. However, the judgment did not silence critics who argued that the land redistribution process in the post 2000 period continued to be contrary to the rule of law.

In response to these critics, Government passed yet another Constitutional Amendment (No. 17) Act, 2002 on September 4. This piece of legislation changed the legal procedures in respect of the compulsory acquisition of agricultural land in that it effectively barred any legal challenges, which had become rampant among affected former White commercial farmers. The Constitutional amendment also provided for the nationalisation of the land that had been identified for acquisition under the Land Acquisition Act, thereby repealing the Rural Land Occupiers (Protection from Eviction) Act.

Therefore, that the land question in Zimbabwe shows that law can be a very effective instrument of political expediency. Both the colonial and postcolonial states have used law to fashion land ownership in a manner most suitable for the vested political and economic interests.

The Case Study of Mashonaland East Province, Zimbabwe

Mashonaland East province is one of the 8 rural provinces in Zimbabwe and is situated in the North-eastern part of the country.

It is elongated and runs North-easterly and South-westerly relative to Harare province. The province shares its North-eastern border with Mozambique. To the East lies Manicaland province and it shares its southern border with parts of Midlands and Masvingo provinces. Mashonaland Central is to the North and Harare and Mashonaland West provinces share its western boundary.

Mashonaland East Province

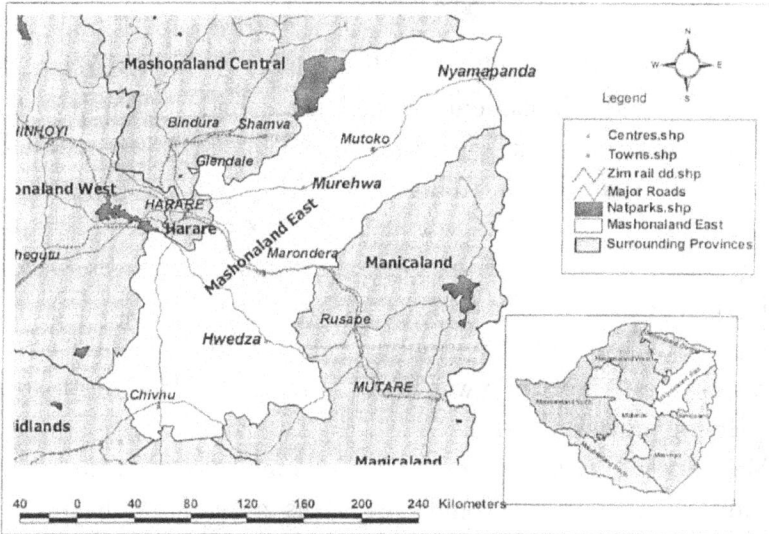

Source: Parliament of Zimbabwe, Informatics project, 2005

Administratively the province has 9 districts namely Marondera, Goromonzi, Murehwa, Mutoko, Seke, Mudzi, Hwedza, Chikomba and Uzumba Maramba-Pfungwe. It also has one major urban centre (Marondera Town), Ruwa Local Board, Acturus mining area and a smaller urban settlement of Chivhu town.

Impact of Land Redistribution in Mashonaland East Province, Zimbabwe

213

Interview results showed that people (general public and other stakeholders) were aware of and supported the programme for land redistribution, although with reservations about the mode of implementation.

Land reform, was characterised by cases of violence, which bred fear among the people. As a result, most respondents were not comfortable to freely discuss issues about land. However, the media was awash with information on the land redistribution exercise, popularly dubbed as *"hondo yeminda"* or *"chave chimurenga"*. The election manifesto for ZANU (PF) during the June 2002 Parliamentary and Presidential elections and the March 2008 Presidential and Parliamentary elections had a lot of land redistribution issues constantly phrased as "land is the economy and the economy is land". The ruling ZANU (PF) party used youth and women's leagues as well as war veterans for political mobilisation during and between elections. Their campaign messages were of "taking back our land" and "safe-guarding our sovereignty" The war veterans outfit had a military political culture and a paramilitary style of organisation. This group was heavily involved in land occupations and silencing opposing voices.

Mashonaland East province recorded high levels of awareness of the land redistribution programme. This applies to all the nine districts and to respondents of randomly selected age- groups. The province is also a stronghold of the ruling ZANU (PF) party.

Land allocations were done under the separate A1 and A2 models. The survey showed that most big farms (A2 model) were allocated to the elite and people with political connections to the ruling party. The elite refers to the urban beneficiaries who were already employed elsewhere. The appointment of the Presidential Land Review Committee in 2003 alleged anomalies in the allocation of land in the ruling party circles and the call for the ruling party members, most of whom were multiple farm owners; they were urged to surrender additional farms.

The A1 model of the land redistribution programme was meant to provide a solution to rural congestion. The survey, however, showed that some households, having been allocated new cropping and grazing land, did not surrender entitlement to their original settlements. Instead, they either commuted between the two sites or simply annexed the new plots to the old ones. It was also found that where old settlements were abandoned, some traditional authorities were re-allocating them to new settlers. Communal areas in Mashonaland East province remained fairly densely populated after land redistribution.

According to the Presidential Land Review Committee (August 2003: 91), there were 1135 farms in Mashonaland East province. As at the end of July 2003, 912 farms were gazetted for acquisition, 701 farms were allocated for resettlement under the Fast Track Resettlement Programme. 17 942 demarcations were made under the A1 model on 382 farms, while 3 683 A2 allocations were made on the remaining 319 farms.

Table 1: Allocation Patterns

District	No. of Farms			Total Hectarage			No. Of Subdivisions		
	A1	A2	Total	A1	A2	Total	A1	A2	Total
Chikomba	87	22	109	11558	27687	39245	3429	300	3729
Goromonzi	50	96	146	34933	46736	81699	1827	851	2678
Marondera	83	82	165	71213	65244	136457	3894	945	4839
Murehwa	75	25	100	81858	31557	113415	4145	424	4669
Mutoko	1		1	644		644	43		43
Wedza	34	20	54	44876	20545	65421	2360	345	2705
Seke	52	74	126	57429	59161	116590	2287	718	3005
Totals	382	319	701	302511	250930	553411	17987	3683	21668

(*Figures for Uzumba-Maramba Pfungwe and Mudzi were not available*)

Source: Adapted from the Report of the Presidential Land Review Commission, August 2003 p.92

In the districts of Chikomba, Goromonzi and Seke, more land was allocated under the A2 model, while in Marondera, the allocation between A1 and A2 was almost 50/50. The proximity of these districts, to urban centres was said to be one of the factors influencing such an allocation. The number of sub-divisions refers to the demarcations on the land by the Agricultural Research and Extension (AREX) teams.

Towards the end of the Presidential elections in March 2002, the state run newspaper, *The Herald*, published a series of adverts listing the names of those people who had been allocated land (6ᵗʰ March 2002–Supplement to the Herald). The authenticity of the lists was questionable, given that most people failed to get the land. It emerged later during the research, that the lists were for people who had qualified for land ownership. The Presidential Land Review Committee (August 2003) also noted that thousands of A2 model applicants were still to receive land. This was indicated one-and-half years after their names appeared in the press confirming that their applications had been successful.

One of the major criticisms of the land redistribution programme in Zimbabwe is its short-term effect on productivity. The assumption of this chapter is that an increase in production may lead to a decrease in poverty. It was evident from the interview that the resettled farmers were not producing to full capacity on the resettled farms. This could be because there was a low delivery of tillage services due to the breakdown of state funded tractors and the non-availability of fuel. Also, the supply of inputs was erratic; there was a shortage of seed and fertilizer. This resulted in some farmers not producing anything. The uncertain land rights, especially under the A2 model, could also have affected production, where most of the resettled farmers did not have sufficient and secure tenure to access credit. Production was also affected by a lack of farming skills amongst the resettled farmers. This was exacerbated by the absence of adequate extension staff to assist resettled farmers. There was little screening of beneficiaries, and production and technical considerations were of less significance. In the short-term, this destroyed the prospects of successful land redistribution, which could lead to poverty alleviation. However, it is necessary not to summarily judge the land redistribution as a failure – it needs to be given time to bear fruits.

From 2000, through to 2012, government support to agriculture services (research, extension, pest and animal disease control, etc.) remained at low levels, while support was provided for loss making parastatals (for example, Air Zimbabwe and National Railways of Zimbabwe) and short term drought relief measures to consumers

(ZIMSTAT, 2013: 16). Mashonaland East province was no exception. Droughts and decline of the national economy during the same period made the situation worse.

However, it is a fact that agricultural production in Mashonaland East and, in the rest of the country, is influenced by rainfall. Most crops are planted in November/December at the beginning of the rainy season and are harvested between January and April. Although, the massive irrigation infrastructure, subsidised in the 1970s to achieve wheat self-sufficiency, was vandalised and most pumps and pipes sold by villagers. However, supplementary irrigation of tobacco, maize, cotton, soya-beans, groundnuts and coffee remains important, from May to October, to offset mid-season recurrent droughts.

The survey also showed that an important dimension of poverty in Mashonaland East can be traced from the activities and sources of income that the poor and households are engaged in. Although agriculture plays a vital role in rural livelihoods, the contribution of non–farm income sources, remittances and activities based on environmental resources was apparent. From the interviews, it was evident that remittance capacity for most of the urban- based workers had declined and there was increasing significance of remittance income from the Diaspora. In all the 9 districts of Mashonaland East province, a distinctive characteristic of rural households is that families attempt to secure their livelihoods from a mixture of activities that range from crop and livestock production, natural resource based activities, casual labour, non–farm income generating activities and remittances from relatives working away from home. Rural households also generate income in cash, or in kind, which include food they produce for household consumption, and common natural property resources (such as fuel wood, wild fruits and edible insects, honey, tubers and roots).

By and large, much of rural agricultural production is highly labour intensive and often, labour demands are concentrated in specific periods of the year. The impact of the HIV/AIDS pandemic in Mashonaland East province was such that when an individual was sick, the household not only has to manage without his or her labour input but with loss of labour of the care-givers. Financial costs incurred during treatment also adversely affect disposable income that can be invested in farming. When they die, the household loses them together with their agricultural knowledge and experience and in some cases their remittances. Orphaned households of the younger age-groups faced the burden of poverty and lack of resources, which left them facing poor cropping seasons. However, although the impact of HIV/AIDS was noticeable during the survey, Government had not put in place a management plan to address the socio-economic effects among the resettled farmers. This is because health and agriculture, more often than not, receive separate research and policy attention in the land reform discourse in Zimbabwe.

Beneficiaries of the land redistribution programme were from a wide spectrum of socio-economic classes: civil servants, war veterans, business people, ruling party elites, urban dwellers, and to a lesser extent the rural landless. The heterogeneity of beneficiaries with different class status, gender and ages raises important questions with regard to some of the beneficiaries' commitment to long-term farming and productivity. The survey also revealed that other people who may not have been particularly passionate about farming joined the scramble to get a piece of land, seeing that there was nothing to lose, the land having been parcelled out for free as opposed to the "willing-seller willing-buyer" basis. Against this background, in Mashonaland East province, no significant development projects were implemented by some beneficiaries of the land redistribution programme on the farms allocated to them and most of the assets owned were either those which were left by the predominantly White owners or those received from the Government under the Central Bank sponsored farm mechanisation programme. There was no publicly known criterion of selection or list of beneficiaries of the farm mechanisation programme. In fact, most beneficiaries of the farm mechanisation programme were believed to be mostly senior ZANU-PF politicians and top civil servants. In all districts, new farmers also helped themselves to the produce abandoned by the "original" farmers at the inception of the "fast track" exercise.

The lack of developments and or investments on newly acquired farms can be linked to the question of access to finance. Historically, the large- scale commercial farmers were major beneficiaries of most of the formal agricultural credit facilities. Possession of "secure" tenure in the form of title deeds to land was the selection criteria. Newly resettled farmers on both A1 and A2 models did not have title deeds and so could not access formal credit facilities. A2 farmers were required to apply for 99-year leases from Government. These leases were, however, were not accepted as collateral by the banks.

To compound the financial problems of the resettled farmers, after 2000, Zimbabwe saw the emergence of a parallel market (informal economy) for most tradable goods. This was worse in the agricultural sector as farmers had to secure inputs from the parallel market. Consumers also had to procure agricultural produce from the parallel market, and even capital (cash) had to be sought on the parallel market. With Government maintaining an over-valued exchange rate, the agricultural sector faced potential collapse as the manufacturing sector, closely linked to it, could not process goods using parallel market finances and yet be forced by the Government to sell goods at controlled prices. However, marketing and price controls applied to maize, tobacco and wheat, due to their strategic importance to the national economy.

The Zimbabwe dollar was devalued in August 2006 by 60%. Three zeros were removed from the currency and the new official exchange rate to the United States dollar was set at 250: 1. The parallel market exchange rate was US$1 to Z$ 1 500, and by December 2006 the annual inflation rate was 1,281%. With the collapse of the exchange rate, multiple devaluation of the Zimbabwean dollar, and ever-increasing inflation, the formal economy came under stress. Price controls and regulations which were implemented by force, with the backing of the military and police, emptied shops of goods and drove agricultural markets further down. Many business people, who had earlier been eager to provide services in resettled areas (shops, bars, grinding mills, transport, and butcheries), closed as they could not run their businesses in the depressed economic conditions. In addition,

Operation Murambatsvina (clean up) in 2005 displaced many informal businesses, especially in urban areas and as much in small towns and service centres.

The year 2008 saw the peak of the economic crisis combined with highly contested parliamentary and presidential elections. As the popularity of ZANU (PF) declined, violence was unleashed by the latter and came to a climax before the second presidential run-off. Mashonaland East province had the highest number of cases of violence recorded by independent observers. Cases of assaults, theft/looting, discrimination and harassment were the common violations in the province. The continued presence of both serving and retired members of the Zimbabwe National Army, in some rural areas in Chikomba and Marondera West, was also recorded during the survey.

Conclusion

Land redistribution encompasses devolving land to the Black poor, who either possess little or no land. This is important because for the poor, land is the primary means of generating a livelihood and a main vehicle for investing, accumulating wealth, and transferring it between generations. While historical grievances over land dispossession are a given, these should be looked at together with the more generalised demand for the redistribution of land for productive uses. The key objective of the land redistribution policy in Zimbabwe should be to establish a more efficient and rational structure of land and natural resource utilisation. Such a structure should not protect the interests of minority elite groups at the expense of optimal land utilisation, increased productivity, employment growth, improved income distribution, and environmentally sustainable use of resources. This is what the research also tried to assess through an examination of land redistribution policies of the Government of Zimbabwe.

With regards to the case study, it appears that the level of awareness concerning the land redistribution programme was quite high in Mashonaland East province. However, it seems that not everyone was convinced by the reasons given for embarking on the land redistribution exercise. There were mixed feelings on whether it was a "vote winning strategy" or a "desire to revive the economy". While many people were aware of the programme and some benefited from it, government still has to convince people of the programme's good intentions.

The key issues, emerging from the discussion on the relationship between land redistribution and poverty alleviation in Mashonaland East province are the following:

- The survey of the Province revealed that the land redistribution programme corrected past colonial imbalances in land distribution. These imbalances were a source of poverty among the Black Africans in the rural areas.
- The impact of land redistribution on de-congestion in Mashonaland East, and especially the districts of Mudzi, Uzumba-Maramba-Pfungwe, Mutoko and Goromonzi was negligible. This was mainly because beneficiaries did not surrender their communal land.
- The land redistribution programme was implemented during a period of poor performance and decline in the national economy. Productivity was negatively affected because provision of inputs and support services was not satisfactory. Households, therefore, could not derive decent livelihoods from the newly-acquired pieces of land.
- The overall impact of land redistribution, in Mashonaland East province, was hindered by deficiencies in programme administration and management. Empirical evidence suggests that the land redistribution programme was not strictly for the rural poor, because it did not exclude those in wage employment in industry and from urban centres. The attainment of a truly transformed rural economy was elusive, because the elite urbanites (who maintained a firm foothold in the rural areas) and the politically connected benefited ahead of land hungry villagers. The lack of access to land remained a major cause of poverty among the majority of people in Mashonaland East province.

- Stakeholders, who were interviewed, welcomed the initiative to empower African people through land redistribution. They, however, pointed out that the policy thrust should have been to transform the lives of the rural folk, who constitute the majority of the poorest people in the country.

References

Bassett, T. J. and Crummey, D. E. (1993) *Land in African Agrarian Systems.* University of Wisconsin Press.

Binswanger-Mkize, H. P. Bourguignon, C. and van den Brink, R. (eds). (2009) *Agricultural Land Redistribution: Towards a Greater Consensus.* Washington DC: World Bank.

Cusworth, J. (1992) "Zimbabwe: Issues Arising from the Land Resettlement Programme" in Dudley, N. *et al* (eds.), *Land Reform and Sustainable Agriculture.* United Kingdom: Intermediate Technology Publications.

Hanlon, J. Manjengwa, J. Smart, T. (2013) *Zimbabwe Takes Back its Land.* South Africa, Stylus Publishing, LLC

Harold-Barry, D. (ed.), (2004) *Zimbabwe the Past is the Future.* Harare: Weaver Press.

Herbst, J. (1990) *State Politics in Zimbabwe.* Harare: University of Zimbabwe Press.

Hellum, A. and Derman, B. (2001) Land Reform and Human Rights in Contemporary Zimbabwe. *Balancing Individual and Social Justice Through and Integrated Human Rights Framework,* Working Paper

Helliker, K and Murisa, T. (2011) *Land Struggles and Civil Society in Southern Africa.* Trenton, New Jersey: Africa World Press

International Crisis Group, (2000) Blood and Soul: Land, Politics and Conflict Prevention in Zimbabwe and South Africa, USA, ICG/

Madhuku, L. (2004) "Law, Politics and the Land Reform Process in Zimbabwe" in Masiiwa, M. (ed), 2004, *Post-Independence Land Reform in Zimbabwe: Controversies and Impact on the Economy.* Harare, Friedrich Ebert Stiftung and Institute of Development Studies, University of Zimbabwe Press.

Masiiwa, M. (ed), (2004) *Post-Independence Land Reform in Zimbabwe: Controversies and Impact on the Economy.* Harare: Friedrich Ebert Stiftung and Institute of Development Studies & University of Zimbabwe Press.

Meredith, M. (2002) *Robert Mugabe. Power, Plunder and Tyranny in Zimbabwe.* Johannesburg and Cape Town: Jonathan Ball Publishers.

Moyo, S. (1990) *Agricultural Employment Expansion: Smallholder Land and Labour Capacity Growth.* Harare: Zimbabwe Institute of Development Studies.

- (1995) *The land Question in Zimbabwe.* Harare: SAPES Books.

- (1998) *The Acquisition Process in Zimbabwe (1997/98).* Harare: UNDP, Resource Centre.

- (1999) *Land and Democracy in Zimbabwe*, Monograph Series No. 7, Harare, SAPES Books.

- (2000)(a), "The Land Question and Land Reform in Southern Africa" in Tevera, D. and Moyo, S. (eds) *Environmental Security in Southern Africa.* Harare: SAPES Books.

- (2000)(b), "The Political Economy of Land Acquisition and Redistribution in Zimbabwe 1990 – 1999", *Journal of Southern African Studies* 26 (1): 5-8.

- (2000)(c), *Land Reform under Structural Adjustment in Zimbabwe: Land use Change in Mashonaland Provinces.* Uppsala: NordiskaAfrikainstitutet.

- (2002) "Peasant Organizations and Rural Civil Society in Africa: An Introduction" in Moyo, S. and Romdhane, B. (eds) (2002) *Peasant Organizations and Democratization in Africa.* Dakar: CODESRIA.

- And Matondi, P. (2003) *Land, Food Security and Sustainable Development in Africa.* Harare: African Institute for Agrarian Studies.

- (2004)(a) "The Land and Agrarian Question in Zimbabwe" Paper Presented at the Conference on Agrarian Constraints and Poverty Reduction: Macroeconomic Lessons for Africa, Addis Ababa, Ethiopia, December 17 – 18.

- (2004)(b). *The Land Question in Africa: Research Perspectives and Questions*. Dakar: CODESRIA.
- And Yeros, P (eds.) (2005) *Reclaiming the Land. The Resurgence of Rural Movements in Africa, Asia and Latin America*. London and New York: ZED Books.
- (2007) "Emerging Land Tenure Issues in Zimbabwe" African Institute for Agrarian Studies, Monographs Series, Issue No 2/7.
- And Helliker, K. and Murisa, T. (2008) *Contested Terrain: Land Reform and Civil Society in Contemporary Zimbabwe*. S and S Publications.
- (2008) African Land Questions, Agrarian Transitions and the State. *Contradictions of Neo-Liberal land Reforms*. CODESRIA.

Pazvakavambwa, S. and Hungwe, V. (2009) "Land Redistribution in Zimbabwe" in Binswanger-Mkize, H. P. (ed) *Agricultural Land Redistribution: Towards a Greater Consensus*. Washington D C: World Bank.

Roth, M. and Gonese, F. (eds), (2003) Delivering Land and Securing Rural Livelihoods: Post Independence Land Reform and Resettlement in Zimbabwe, Harare, The Land Tenure Centre of the University of Wisconsin- Madison and the Centre for Applied Social Sciences of the University of Zimbabwe.

Scoones, I. Marongwe, N., Mavedzenge, B., Mahenehene, J., Murimbarimba, F. and Sukume, C, (2010) *Zimbabwe's Land Reform, Myths and Realities*. Harare, Weaver Press.

Sobham, R. (1993) *Agrarian Reform and Social Transformation. Preconditions for Development*. London and New Jersey: ZED Books.

Tshuma, L. (1997) *A Matter of (in) Justice: Law, State and the Agrarian Question in Zimbabwe*. Harare: SAPES Books.

Government Sources – Reports

Government of Zimbabwe, (1995) "Zimbabwe Agricultural Policy Framework 1995-2020 (ZAPF)" Ministry of Lands and Agriculture, Harare
- (1992) *Land Acquisition Act*. Harare, Government Printers.
- (1992) Land Tenure Commission Report on the Appropriate Land Tenure Systems. 3 Volumes, Harare, Government Printer

- Poverty Assessment Study, September (1997) Ministry of Public Service, Labour and Social Welfare.
- (1998) Land Reform and Resettlement Programme, Phase 11: A Policy Framework
- (2001) "Land Reform and Resettlement Programme: Revised Phase ii." Ministry of Lands, Agriculture and Rural Resettlement, Harare
- (2002) "Fast Track Land Resettlement Programme: Progress Report, July 2000 to October 2002". Ministry of Lands, Agriculture and Rural Resettlement, Harare
- (2004) Census 2002, Provincial Profile, Mashonaland East, Central Statistics Office, Harare
- (2005) "*The National Budget Statement, 2006*", Ministry of Finance, Harare
- (2006) (a). "*National Development Priority Plan.*" Ministry of Economic Development, Harare
- (2006) (b). "Response to the Portfolio Committee on lands, Agriculture, Water Development, Rural Resources and Resettlement: 2006, Budget Performance Report." Ministry of Land, land Reform and Resettlement, Harare
- (2006) (c). "Agricultural production on Resettlement Schemes, Central Statistics Office, Harare

Utete, C. M. B. *et al,* (2003) *Report of the Presidential Land Review Committee*, 2 volumes, Harare, Government Printer.

Chapter Ten

The Gendered Dispossession of Land in Colonial Rhodesia: An Analysis of Thomson Kumbirai Tsodzo's *Pafunge* and Patrick Chakaipa's *Dzasukwa Mwana-Asina-Hembe*

Enna Sukutai Gudhlanga

Introduction

Land ownership and access remain critical in Zimbabwe whose economy primarily depends on agriculture. The importance of land-based livelihoods explains why colonialists had to put a number of repressive laws that enabled them to dispossess Blacks of their prime land and dump them to barren areas that were not suitable for human habitation. With the arrival of the "pioneer column" in Zimbabwe and the raising of the Union Jack flag on 12 September 1890, a new dawn in colonial Zimbabwe had begun. What is mind boggling is the fact that a White minority population stole the prime land while the Black majority population were dumped in barren areas some of which were infested by tsetse flies. However, while social science research has focused on dispossession of land, few scholarly works have looked at literary texts that bring out this dispossession by White colonialists. Since literature mirrors the environment from which it emerges, this chapter discusses the portrayal of the effects of land theft by White colonial settlers in Patrick Chakaipa's *Dzasukwa Mwana Asina Hembe* and Thomson Kumbirai Tsodzo's *Pafunge*. It critiques the authors' depiction of the massive dispossession that took place and the brutal pieces of colonial legislation that endeavoured to strip Black men and women of their land whose ownership and use they formerly and unreservedly enjoyed. The chapter argues that while Shona traditional culture accorded both genders the requisite space in terms of land ownership in the pre-colonial period, colonialists dispossessed both genders of this prime land which they formerly collectively owned. The chapter also maintains that the colonial dispossession of the African people's land also fragmented their life styles because land is considered sacred, it is a site of supplication and provides for the totality of a people's existence. It further contends that the idea of repossessing the land was noble since it had been colonially stolen from indigenous people without recompense, leaving them destitute. It also scrutinises Zimbabwean fiction's ability to portray the effects of the historical processes that took place in the gendered land dispossession of Blacks. Understanding these historical processes can act as an eye opener to critics of the Zimbabwean land repossession who quickly condemn it without considering how the land was initially stolen from Black people. The methodology for this chapter is critical textual analysis of the two selected fictional works. The study is informed by the Afro-centred theories of Africana Womanism and Afrocentricity.

Contextualising the Gendered Dispossession of Land in Colonial Rhodesia

The raising of the Union Jack flag in Salisbury signified a new dispensation in land ownership. Cecil John Rhodes and his British South Africa Company (BSAC) had intended to find another gold reef in Mashonaland as they had done in South Africa. After failing to get gold they then turned to land (Mafa, Gudhlanga, Manyeruke, Matavire & Mpofu, 2015). This resulted in the colonialists plundering the fertile lands that the indigenous men and women had previously occupied and collectively owned. In order to facilitate the rampant land dispossession the colonialists enacted some pieces of legislation that they used to steal land from Blacks. Chief among the pieces of legislation were the Rudd Concession of 1888, The Lippert Concession of 1889, The Matabeleland Order of Council of 1894, The Land Apportionment Act of 1930, The Maize Act of 1934, The Native Land Husbandry Act of 1951 and the Land Tenure Act of 1969. All these pieces of legislation legitimised the theft of land from the indigenous people, both men and women.

Of importance is the Matabeleland Order of Council which created infamous reserves for indigenous people only. This was a systematic mass land theft by White colonialists. The result was the formation of native reserves, barren areas which later became communal areas that housed dispossessed Black men and women. The Matabeleland Order of Council Act set the tone for the dispossession of indigenous people's land by the colonialists (Mtetwa 2015: 142). It also, according to Magaisa (2012: 198) "signalled the commencement of segregation and forced removals of Africans from their ancestral lands." Muchemwa (2015: 33) concurs that these colonial legislations made sure "that from the very outset of settler occupation, African land rights were completely written off and Zimbabwean land became the property and land asset of the BSAC." Accordingly, through these colonial legislations Blacks were condemned to what Phimister (1988: 325) rightly called 'cemeteries' referring to the Gwai and Shangani native reserves. The analogy of cemetery amply demonstrates that nothing grew there and Africans had been destined to die since nothing thrived in the barren areas that the colonialists had relocated them to.

The other colonial legislation that further entrenched what had been instituted by the Matabeleland Order of Council in the theft of fertile lands was the Land Apportionment Act of 1930. The Land Apportionment Act partitioned land into European and African reserves (Mafa *et. al.* 2015; Tshuma 1997). Furthermore, it forcibly removed Africans from fertile land which was their birth right and resettled them in areas that were far away from all forms of transport and communication (Tshuma 1997; Mafa *et. al.* 2015). About 51 per cent of the land was set aside for European colonialists (Tshuma 1997; Rukuni 2006; Vengeyi 2015; Mafa *et. al.* 2015). Under the Land Apportionment Act of 1930 the right of Africans to land ownership was abrogated. Very few Africans would only be allowed to purchase land in equally barren Native Purchase Areas (Tshuma 1997; Chitiyo 2000; Mafa *et. al.* 2015). There was overcrowding in reserves which resulted in population pressure on the land resulting in soil erosion. The colonial government quickly reacted to these problems by passing the Native Land Husbandry Act of 1951. This Act further imposed and enforced conservation measures on land occupied by indigenous people and to make matters even worse this Act mainly policed female agricultural activities (Vudzijena 1998; Moyo 1995a, 1995b; Mafa *et. al.* 2015).

After the Native Land Husbandry Act, the colonial government introduced the Land Tenure Act of 1969. The main aim of this Act was to entrench the division of land between the Whites and Africans. With Blacks being pushed to barren areas it meant that both men and women no longer enjoyed access to fertile lands as before. Men now had small pieces of barren land. Since there was not enough land for indigenous people, men no longer had enough land to share with women they only used the land as family land and could not allocate women small plots in which they used to grow what came to be referred to as female crops. Furthermore, chiefs could not equitably allocate land to married men since the size of the land had greatly diminished and it was barren as well. This means since the inception of colonialism, land ownership did not take into cognisance the female counterpart hence leaving behind a gendered ownership of land that left women out of the equation.

The implementation of the 1930 Land Apportionment Act and the 1969 Land Tenure Act saw the indigenous people being forcibly moved from their productive lands to create farms and estates for White people/farmers. A case in point is how the Whites forcibly moved the Gobo, Huchu and Ruya people from the Senderi area between Lalapanzi and Mvuma and created what was then called Central Estates (Shona people called it Senderi because they could not pronounce the new English name of their place correctly). People and their belongings were forcibly transported from ancestral lands in lorries to Silobela, Nembudziya and Gokwe (Marowa 2015). The Tangwena people were also forcibly moved from Gaeresi Ranch to Bende reserve area. They fought the eviction on the premise that they had occupied the land well before 1905 and it was handed down to them by their fore-fathers (Mugari 2015). Furthermore, the Chisa of Gotosa, Ngwenyeni of Marhumbini and the Xilotlela of Vila Sazaar were also violently removed from their ancestral lands to pave way for the formation of the Gonarezhou Game Park (Tavuyanago 2017).

The White colonialists used the new colonial legislations as a weapon to evict indigenous people from their ancestral land. Those who resisted the eviction like the Tangwena people had their huts pulled down and burnt, men, women and children were ruthlessly beaten (Mafa *et al* 2015). This marked the inception of the struggle to get back lost land which sadly has been gendered as it appeared that men were the ones who took the lead and hence were the affected parties in the displacements and loss.

When the Black people were uprooted from their ancestral lands they left behind their whole ethos of social existence. All these Black people who were moved left behind their fertile lands, ancestral graves and most importantly their worldview which informed their various institutions. This displacement caused untold suffering and had traumatic effects on a people whose strong ties to the land had been severed. The displacement meant that the black people also lost their indigenous knowledge systems behind such as rain petitioning shrines (see Nhemachena 2017), herbal medicines; utensils, vegetation cover, foodstuffs, wild fruits, crops and above all their traditions that had been handed down for generations and an identity that had been engraved in their land which they had left behind. The Black people in their new area of abode had lost a sense of place, had become aliens, outsider observers of their own culture and lost their roots. Faced with the paradox of being marooned in one place, but with a psyche that is haunted by the placelessness of not having their original home. They still continued to be foreigners or intruders in their so-called new home and would pine for the home they have been displaced from.

Also created as a result of the Land Apportionment Act were Native Purchase areas literally called *matenganyika* in Shona. These were scattered areas of freehold farms that were meant to compensate Africans for loss of their right to purchase land anywhere in the country. Cheater (cited in Magirosa 2015: 1) observes that "the Native Purchase areas would act as pinnacle of modernity, otherwise only available to whites; and something allowing independence and autonomy, not feasible in the reserves or even in most urban settings." These were therefore used to pacify Blacks who had been

231

dispossessed of their fertile land. Examples of Native Purchase areas include Manyene and Wilshire in Mash East; Jobolinko and Tokwe in Midlands and Musengezi and Sanyati in Mashonaland West among others. These areas were initially farmed by white people before the land was racially designated into European and African land (Magirosa 2015; Shutt 1997). Well to do Africans were given the option of buying these newly demarcated properties which no longer fitted into European realm. Of note is the fact that this land was often in remote areas and of poor quality and this explains why it could not fit into the newly designated European land. Thus the colonial government was implementing its policy of divide and rule since the middle class Africans who would have acquired land under the Native Purchase Area Scheme would feel contented that they owned land and would never consider fighting to regain their land since they had been pacified to believe that they owned land. The Native Purchase Area scheme also further marginalised the female gender, for it were only male Africans that had the right to purchase that land.

Not only did the Black people lose their material possession but spiritual connection to the land. This included the people's identity, their sense of being and thus their spiritual anchorage. With the loss of their land, the Black people's ancestral graves were desecrated and hence their spiritual roots dismantled. Zhuwarara (2001: 12-13) aptly captures this when he says,

"Apart from undermining the economic independence of the African…the loss of land severely disrupted the smooth functioning of the African belief systems….African societies regarded the land as home of the ancestral spirits….the land functions as a geographical and metaphysical world….[t]hus removing the African from his land was tantamount to severe disruption of meaning and coherence which the ancestral lands had always provided him."

Shoko (2007) concurs when he says that the land is regarded as a special gift from the ancestors, with all the products of the land such as crops, trees and animals emanating from the spirits who own the land. The land therefore provided sustenance for the people.

232

Displacement therefore meant a fragmentation of the cultural essence of the people and resulted in there not being a sense of history —as nearly all displaced inhabitants were settled in foreign lands. The Black people's physical and emotional attachment that was based on their land, cultural and economic activities was fragmented. The ruthless actions of the White men who disregarded the values and beliefs of the Black people and their attachment to their land and relocating them in new areas meant that their whole ethos of existence had been broken, and to put it in Achebe's words things had fallen apart. This was true dehumanisation of the African people. The selected fictional works for this chapter vividly demonstrate the effects of the dispossession of Africans' prime land by colonialists. It is against this historical background that colonial penetration and its effects on the gendered dispossession of land in the two novels is analysed. The loss of land did not discriminate against gender but women like their male counterparts lost out on the most priced economic possession of their time. Women also lost their important stake as spiritual leaders epitomised by the renowned spirit medium Nehanda. Thus, land distribution under the colonial banner did not consider the previously gender equity regarding space for farming and spiritual activities. Women were silenced and land distribution to the Black people highly gendered.

The chapter uses the qualitative research method. Qualitative research is grounded in subjective interpretation of selected fictional works' depiction of the gendered dispossession of land in colonial Rhodesia. It relies heavily on critical textual analysis of Thomson Kumbirai Tsodzo's *Pafunge* and Patrick Chakaipa's *Dzasukwa-Mwana-Asina-Hembe*. The chapter critiques how the colonial and Eurocentric religious systems worked in cahoots in dispossessing Black men and women of their prime land and relegating them to barren areas. In this analysis the questions therefore to ask are: To what extent does Shona fiction portray the historical processes that took place in land dispossession of Blacks? Is Shona fiction able to present the effects of the colonial dispossession of land? Is there any significance in understanding the historical processes of land dispossession in redressing land ownership in modern day Zimbabwe?

Theoretical Framework

The chapter is guided by Africana Womanism and Afrocentricity. Africana Womanism was propounded by Cleonora Hudson-Weems (1993). The Africana Womanist theoretical paradigm advocates that African women and men are compatible and work together to liberate themselves from the evils of colonialism. She further affirms that the theory includes all men and women of African descent in fighting against the challenges that the African community faces (Hudson 2007). Hence this theory which understands that African women are under the three cards that militate against them namely race, gender and class helps in the understanding of Shona fiction's portrayal of the gendered dispossession of land in colonial Rhodesia. Africana Womanism was chosen to re-look at the male -female relations that had been negatively affected by the colonial incursions. Women like their male counterparts have had to grapple with land loss, an issue that appears to have escaped the attention of many researchers. The chapter is also informed by the theory of Afrocentricity which was coined by Molefe Kete Asante (1980). Afrocentricity is a theory "which calls for all African phenomena, activities and way of life to be looked at and be given meaning from the standpoint and worldview of Africans" (Gray 2001: 3, Asante cited in Hudson-Weems (2007: 29). Using Afrocentricity allows for an understanding of the male female relations and how they physically and metaphysically relate to land. Therefore, it is prudent that the understanding of male-female relations as they relate to the physical and spiritual dispossession of land be appreciated using Afrocentricity and Africana Womanism. Both theories guide the chapter in the understanding of the cultural and historical processes that have dispossessed and marginalised Zimbabwean men and women from their land as envisaged in Shona Fiction.

The Colonial Farm as a Form of Gendered Dispossession of Land in *Dzasukwa-Mwana-Asina-Hembe*

Patrick Chakaipa's novel *Dzasukwa-Mwana-Asina-Hembe* (1967) is an epitome of dispossession of land of the African people. The novel depicts how colonialism and its concomitant agents of Christianity, urbanisation and presumed modernity have availed new methods of accessing land in the colony (Biri 2015). *Dzasukwa-Mwana-Asina-Hembe* which when literally translated means that the beer has been sold out and the beer pots washed clean, but the children have no clothes signifies how the dispossessed men and women now spent all their merger resources on alcohol at the expense of their families during the colonial period. Chakaipa depicts the farm as a microcosm of the larger Rhodesian colony in his novel *Dzasukwa-Mwana-Asina-Hembe*. He uses it as a metaphor for the colonisation and domination of the whole country. The colonial theft of African fertile land by White colonialists is neatly captured where Kufahakurambwe cycles from his new home area in the reserves to Vhuka's farm where he now works and has to cover large tracks of fertile land that have been fenced off as Vhuka's farm. The farm has very good vegetation, tall grass and rich dark soils (p. 3). These attributes typify fertile soils that have been stolen away by White people through a methodical exclusion of indigenous men and women from fruitful areas to those unsuitable for human habitation. Mugari (2015: 65) has also noted this methodical displacement of Blacks from fertile areas and concurs that Whites lived in "fenced-off European farms and towns while indigenous people were herded into areas of least agricultural potential called native reserves." The fact that Vhuka's farm is fenced off denotes the physical demarcation that outlaws indigenous men and women who are deemed trespassers on the White man's privately-owned land. With this new dispensation of stolen and privatised property ownership, "the white man has expropriated public space and inheritance for the individual, altering the communal custodianship to land practiced before and in the process, he robbed the majority of an identity and self-definition which came with belonging to land" (Chidora & Mandizvidza 2015: 344).

Similarly fictional writers like Chenjerai Hove in his novel *Bones* (1988) depict that the colonial male farmers owned large tracts of land in the form of farms. Manyepo the White farmer in Hove's *Bones* possesses such "fields that stretch forever as if they were the sky" (Hove 1988: 35). The stolen and privatised property and individual ownership of land presented by Chakaipa and Hove in their novels set on a colonial farm depict the effects of the colonial dispossession of Black people's prime land.

Chakaipa in *Dzasukwa-Mwana-Asina-Hembe* also neatly captures how land dispossession by colonialists has also resulted in deprivation of the Black men and women's cattle. The colonialists ended up with a large herd of cattle which they stole from the indigenous herd. On Vhuka's farm there are a lot of cattle which Kufahakurambwe observes grazing on the farm (p. 3). Colonialists grew their herd yet Black people were not allowed to have not more than 5 beasts. Ironically, Blacks were forced to sell their cattle in some cases to the White man at paltry prices (Mtetwa 2015). Paurosi brings out the issue of cattle dispossession when he reveals to Mavis that Black people are not allowed to have many beasts since they are deemed to overgraze the limited pastureland (pp. 108-109). Ironically Vhuka has many cattle which have enough grazing land compared to the few more Paurosi would have bought for his parents (Gudhlanga 2016), highlighting the lack of parity regarding land ownership amongst Blacks and Whites.

Dispossession of Black people has resulted in Blacks living on the farms at the mercy of the White man; they are subjected to physical violence. Vhuka does mete out punishment on the foremen for lying (why he had not turned up for duty) but it appears it was the White man's habit of brutalising the people on the farm. Farmers normally used the *sjambok* to exert physical torture on their labourers (Gudhlanga 2016). This is reflected where one of the women who work on the farm says to the foreman "*Rambai muchitireverera kumurungu kuti dzimwe nguva arege kupota achirova vanhu*" (p. 14). (Continue to plead on our behalf to the white man so that he stops beating people). To which Kufahakurambwe responds, "*Handiti vanhu vanorohwa pamusana poumambara?*" (p. 14). (Is it not true that

236

people are beaten because of their misconduct?). The woman's message that Vhuka subjects people to physical violence typifies the lack of freedom on the farm. Kufahaurambwe's response justifies Vhuka's use of physical punishment for the workers on the farm. Chakaipa had to give this justification to make his novel pass through the censorship board. Literature that portrayed the White man in bad light was not published by the Rhodesia Literature Bureau (Chiwome 1996, 2002).

Chakaipa through the image of violence also demonstrates that if people are exposed to excessive violence they usually retaliate; this explains why Kufahakurambwe had to fight back the White man. Even the women on Vhuka's farm such as Mrs Chikomba confront Kufahakurambwe to tell the White man not to beat them up. This demonstrates that they too had had enough of the violence that was being perpetrated against them. This is a clear demonstration of how the Black people in colonial Rhodesia eventually took up arms to fight for their land because of the mistreatment they had experienced (Gudhlanga 2016). This is what Afrocentricity and Africana Womanism theories encourage, that Africans should chart their own destiny and not to be passive recipients when wrongs are being exerted on them.

Dzasukwa-Mwana-Asina-Hembe also explores how the farm translates itself into a frontier that alienates Black and White races. The physical location of the White man's house on the farm points to this- it stands alone in a spacious area while the compound for Black people is overcrowded (p. 4). Through the contrasting images of the big and affluent farm house on one hand and the overcrowded and poorly built round dagga and pole thatched huts on the other, Chakaipa vividly paints a picture of the impoverishment of the dispossessed Black men and women on the farm. The nature of compound signifies the transient nature of Blacks on the farm; their stay is temporary so their homes are hurriedly put up structures with no sense of permanence. Conversely, the farm house is a solid edifice and occupies a permanent space on the White farmer's land. Even the road that leads to the White man's house is wide and well serviced juxtaposed to the narrow, beaten footpath to the labourers' compound (p. 4). Through these contrasting pictures, Chakaipa brilliantly exhibits the rootlessness nature of the Black men and women who live in abject poverty against the comfort and opulence of the White man. Despite moving on the farm, the Black person still does not belong there because s/he has been spiritually and physically uprooted from his ancestral land. The inculturation of the Black indigenous man and woman on the farm meant they were now alienated from their culture having adopted that of the White man and that of migrant workers. Chikowero has revealed the stigma and denigration of migrant people revealing the fact that farm workers were looked down upon. Additionally, the general suffering of dispossessed men and women is aptly captured in Thomas Mapfumo's song "Pfumvu paruzevha" which when literally translated means strife in the reserves. Magosvongwe (2013: 165), and Chambati and Magaramombe (2008) have also observed this gap that divides the White luxurious residence and the overcrowded Black compound on the farm in *Dzasukwa-Mwana-Asina-Hembe*.

The novel reveals how through Mavis and Paurosi's mother, women were equally affected by land loss. The two eke out a living from the barren reserves, Chakaipa vividly captures the strong relationship between women and the land. Women in Shona cosmology contribute a lot to the well-being of the family hence the adage "*musha mukadzi*" (In order for a home to thrive very well it is because of a woman who works very hard). Through Mavis and Paurosi' mother, Chakaipa paints a brilliant picture of women who continue to engender a powerful relationship with the land, through their farming activities to feed the family despite being dumped in barren areas. Through Paurosi's mother and Mavis, Chakaipa demonstrates women's propensity to work on the land, they are the ones who till the land for the benefit of the family. This is in line with what most scholars who have researched on the African continent have established that the farmer in Africa is a woman (Schmidt 1990, 1992; Mvududu 2000; Paradza-Makura 2011). Men just oversee but do not do the actual tilling of the land with women being the primary agricultural producers on the continent (Schmidt 1992). This logic also applies on White farmer's land where the Black people (men and women) are the actual farmers tilling the land and the White people just oversee the process – in other words, the Black men are logically the White people's women in these instances. This explains why Kufahakurambwe's family suffers because the real farmer in the family, *mai* Mavis, abandons her duties and jointly pursues beer drinking with her husband. However, Kufahakurambwe's family is bailed out by Mavis, their daughter who has teamed up with Paurosi's mother and tills the land to produce food for the family despite the colonial land dispossession. Chakaipa demonstrates that women in African traditional culture were not confined to the kitchen, they tilled the land. African women are also reduced to selling beer to earn a living. While women used to buy men's labour through beer, *nhimbe* (work party), in traditional Shona society they are now using the same beer as a source of livelihood. In the traditional set up women used beer to lure men to come and join them to work in the fields. After the land has been colonially stolen from them, the women are very creative, enterprising and very quick to adapt and embrace change as it comes. Women are very chameleonic in character; they now either brew beer for sale or provide cheap labour on the farm to fulfil their obligation of being the primary food producers for the family in African cosmology (Gudhlanga 2016).

Chakaipa's *Dzasukwa-Mwana-Asina-Hembe* has managed to present the effects of the dispossession of land in a colonial context. Through the social critique of alcoholism he has managed to portray the effects of dispossession of land on indigenous men and women in a colonial context. However it is important to critique Chakaipa's social vision in the novel. Even though Chakaipa has managed to evade the censorship laws of the Literature Bureau by presenting white people in good light he sometimes overdid it in his novel *Dzasukwa-Mwana-Asina-Hembe*. He presents dispossessed men and women as being contented with living on the farm despite the violence that colonial farmers perpetrate in these establishments. The Blacks who have been dispossessed of their fertile land make no effort to regain it. According to Africana Womanism and Afrocentricity, people of African descent, both men and women are at the centre of charting out their history but Chakaipa's characters seem to be satisfied with the new colonial set up. There is ample evidence on the history of Zimbabwe which testifies to the brutal nature and harsh environment on which Black men and women suffered on colonial farms (Zhuwarara 1994; Magosvongwe 2013; Chidora & Mandizvidza 2015; Mafa *et. al.* 2015). These men and women were not docile but were actively involved in the process of regaining back the stolen lands as amply demonstrated in Irene Staunton's *Mothers of the Revolution* (1990).

Religious Hypocrisy and Gendered Land Dispossession in *Pafunge*

Thomson Kumbirai Tsodzo's *Pafunge* (1972) satirises the church/colonialism partnership in the dispossession of people of African descent. The title of the novel *Pafunge* ("think about it") is an invocation to the reader(s) to perceive beyond the root cause and effects of land dispossession, not just to the rural folk but to the city dwellers as well. The author utilises that invocation to evade the Literature Bureau's draconian censorship laws that prohibited any work that was assumed subversive from being published. Similarly, a quick reading of the novel might not present adequate discernment of the gendered dimension of land dispossession. However, a careful analysis of the novel further divulges alienation of indigenous men and women as an effect of dispossession. The gendered perspective is expounded by the fact that in an African worldview, men could only access land once they got married, under customary law. Bachelors or single men were not allocated land but could only acquire it through marriage when they were allocated that land by the chief. The analysis of the novel adopts Afrocentric and Africana Womanist approaches which do not discriminate between men and women in matters pertaining to land. This implies that the alienation of the African people from their land through the colonial establishment of the mission station also had effects on gender and land ownership in African cosmology.

From another angle the portrayal of the Christian church could reflect the deep founded hatred amongst the African people for the new religion. Since they had lost their traditional ways of worship, their sites and their gods, the Black people do not take the new religion seriously hence the derision by Masango and his compatriots. The new religion is regarded an intruder religion which is complicit with the thieving of land and livelihoods. Its hypocrisy is evidently exposed and this does not auger well with the Black people. The preaching of the 'gospel' in the beer hall could well underline the lack of space even for worship for the Black people. Additionally, the beer hall and the church also act as the opium of the people providing solace against the harsh realities that the people face away from these homes. They also act as apparatus that kept the people subjugated without interrogating the status quo.

Pafunge depicts the church through the establishment of mission stations which inculcate Christian values amongst Africans and eventually stripped Africans of their traditional beliefs. Despite its principles of egalitarianism, the church rarely questioned the land theft but was complicit with the colonial system that was stealing land from Africans. The church was known to be a silent partner in all this and did not take a public stance against the constricting legislations imposed by the colonial regime and the attendant malpractices (Vengeyi 2015).

Moreover, most of the missionaries who attempted speaking against the colonial enterprise from the 1960s onwards did so in their individual capacities. Even though these individual missionaries spoke against colonialism, the church as the generic establishment of mission stations nor through a unified voice did not castigate it. The church not only participated in taking away fertile land for farming purposes but also stripped Blacks even of the infertile land for the establishment of mission stations. Tsodzo accurately captures this through his portrayal of Mharapara Mission (p.1).Of significance is the fact that missionaries, like their colonial settler counterparts, did not occupy vacant land but displaced Africans who were originally settled in these areas before the established mission stations (Mtetwa 2015). Vengeyi argues that the Jesuit Missionary group of the Roman Catholic Church was part of the pioneer column that invaded and stole land in Zimbabwe (Vengeyi 2015). Tsodzo, like Chakaipa, masks the story of Black dispossession of land "in an elaborate satire of colonial Christianity" (Chiwome 1996: 112).

Quite a number of historians and literary critics concur that the church collaborated with colonialism in stealing African people's land. Chitando (2005: 142) argues that "most of the farms in the church's possession were gifts from Cecil John Rhodes for successfully serving the colonialists in stealing the Black people's land." The Ndau hymn composed by the colonial missionaries aptly captures the words *"Tora nyika, ndipe Jesu ndodakara ndiye"* (Take all the land, simply give me Jesus and I am happy) (Vengeyi 2015: 133). African land which had been taken away by the missionaries was designated and governed as 'Christian villages' (Zvobgo 1996). In these Christian villages Christian values were propagated. These values endeavoured to denigrate African traditional religion and in the process confirm and legitimate colonialism since the congregants were taught not to be preoccupied with earthly life for they were going to find eternal joy in heaven. The inculcation of such values by the church made Black men and women docile- believing that owning land or any material possession would hinder their reception of Jesus Christ as their personal Lord and saviour. In the process, the church sanctioned colonialism through its teachings that made indigenous men and women not to question the colonial enterprise. Mugambi (1995) also observed the hypocrisy of the church in pretending to be preaching the word of God but simultaneously brainwashing Africans into disregarding their prevailing estrangement from the land.

In *Pafunge,* through Reverend Lovedale's house, Tsodzo manages to capture the rift between White missionaries and the Black Africans who have been dispossessed of their land. Reverend Lovedale's house is the most beautiful house at the mission station as compared to the houses of the Black teachers, nurses and other groups of workers manning the activities of the mission (p. 45). Tsodzo presents the hypocritical nature of the missionary enterprise which despite preaching equality, demarcates people along racial lines. Like in the colonial farming system, Blacks at the mission station also do not have permanent residence. Anna, a nurse at the mission station, lives in a small room even though she belongs to a group highly revered at the mission station. As an African her stay at the mission station is temporary for this is now privately owned land which belongs to White missionaries and the church. People of African descent who are on the mission station are only there to man the mission and assist in the propagation of Christian values among their fellow Africans through inculcation of Christian values to enhance docility and the permanent establishment of the colonial set up.

Anna, like her daughter Rudo (who eventually becomes an orphan), has no roots, identity, a home or even a relative that we hear of in the novel. The mission station therefore houses the dispossessed men and women who no longer have a place to call home. Anna is buried at the mission and she requests through a letter that her daughter be looked after by the White reverend at Mharapara mission (p. 27). The paradox is complete; while the mission station is the prototype philanthropic institution, it is largely to blame for severing of familial African ties leading to the destruction of the African society. Even though the church has spiritual comfort it cannot do much to uphold the African family. Anna and Rudo's lack of place they can call home symbolises dispossession of the African people at the highest level (Gudhlanga 2016). In Shona worldview people will always have a rural home but Anna and her daughter do not have one, neither do they have any known relatives. This signifies the climax of the dispossession of the African people such that they became homeless as they saw the mission station as their adoptive home.

Colonialism, through the establishment of mission stations, has condemned Black men and women into reserves where they could not grow enough crops to sustain their families. The area that surrounds Mharapara mission where the rest of the villagers live is a desolate expanse which could not sustain the production of crops to feed the Black families that live in that reserve. Winnie Nhamo, an emaciated child and malnourished child residing in the reserves, reveals this (p. 28). Her parents had been impoverished to the point where they fail to grow the basic vegetables and cereals to feed their family.

The colonial establishment has not dispossessed Black men and women through mission stations alone but through the creation of urban centres where most Blacks do not own houses. Mr and Mrs Masango, Josiah Rugare and Phainos Kamunda all live in rented accommodation. The urban set up establishes a new form of ownership of land; in order for one to own a house they should have title deeds which symbolised private ownership of land and not the untitled communal prevalent in Shona society. In contrast, Whites in urban areas have very big houses and live in low density suburbs. When Josiah Rugare first comes to the city he works as a gardener at a White person's house which is an epitome of opulence and security. Josiah lives in the servant's quarters (pp. 37-39). This gives a glimpse of the lavish lifestyle of Josiah's employer's house when juxtaposed to Masango's house where Josiah now lives with Rudo. It can also be contrasted with the single room which accommodates so many people that Rudo observes on her first day on her way to the beerhall in search of her husband (p. 4). Black families live in abject poverty in urban areas because the urban area just like the farm and the mission station are colonial establishments that drive on the capitalist economy. Blacks in urban areas are only there to provide cheap labour for the capitalist economy. To demonstrate that Blacks do not own the houses in urban areas Mrs Masango tells Rudo that money determines one's tenure in the urban areas yet it is difficult to come by in urban areas. Once one fails to raise the money to pay for the houses they leave for the reserves (p. 5). Through Mrs Masango's short lecture to Rudo, Tsodzo depicts the picture of homelessness among Black men and women in urban areas.

Coupled with poor accommodation for Blacks in urban centres, is the inadequacy of such. The new area of abode for Black men and women dehumanises them and strips them of the dignity and human identity they formerly enjoyed. Tsodzo clearly captures this new place of abode for dispossessed Black men and women in colonial urban establishments through Rudo who observes a whole family sharing a room (p. 4). Through the image of an overcrowded room, whose relationships are considered taboo to be sharing a room in the traditional African culture, Tsodzo demonstrates the lives of Blacks in urban areas having been stripped of their dignity. This explains why parents sleep in the same room with their sons, daughters and even strangers because they could not afford decent accommodation. The colonial set up has reduced the African family to such very dehumanising conditions. In traditional Shona culture boys and girls had their own different huts where they could sleep and be free to discuss issues that concerned them; they would never sleep in the same room with their parents. This adequately exhibits how land theft has deprived indigenous men and women of their dignity.

Furthermore, through Phainos Kamunda, Tsodzo depicts how the colonial government used western education as a disempowerment tool. Western education was meant to divert indigenous men and women's attention away from more important things like fighting to repossess their land. Althusser (2001) has underlined the pivotal role of the ideological state apparatus in keeping people subjugated and not question the status quo. The education system meant that the Blacks looked up to the culture of the White man while denigrating his own. The result was an alienated generation of youths preoccupied with nonentities or trivialities of life. Phainos Kamunda is one such example who is preoccupied with memorising English jaw breakers that do not contribute anything meaningful to his life nor that of fellow Blacks. To add to this Black men and women aspired to work in white collar jobs, leaving out the land which was the economy. In other words, they ended up joining the colonial establishment thereby becoming part of the system. Consequently, indigenous people were made to look down upon Agriculture as a subject and yet it is the backbone of the economy in agro-based communities like Zimbabwe. Relegating Agriculture and making it a seemingly useless and dirty preoccupation was meant to dissuade indigenous men and women from recognising the importance of the land that had been forcibly taken away from them. They focus on trivial issues such as mastering the coloniser's language and useless high sounding English jargon at the expense of regaining back their land which had been stolen from them.

Tsodzo's *Pafunge*, like Chakaipa's *Dzasukwa-Mwana-Asina-Hembe*, has managed to depict the consequences of the theft of the indigenous people's land in a colonial context. However, even though he has managed to present the dispossession of land in his novel, Tsodzo fails to give the African people agency to take charge of their destiny. The dispossessed Black people in his novel wallow hopelessly in poverty in the reserves, urban areas and also on the farms. The urban space, just like the farm is presented as a place of escape for the landless Zimbabweans. The Black men and women in Tsodzo's *Pafunge* have no means of extricating themselves from the theft of land that the colonial establishments have condemned them to. This, however, is a misrepresentation of history of the Black people and their reaction to land dispossessions. Blacks consistently showed some disgruntlement with such a set up and eventually took up arms to fight the oppressors and regain their land. According to Africana Womanism and Afrocentricity, people of African descent, both men and women are at the centre of charting out their history but Tsodzo's characters seem to show weak forms of discontent that are simmering through the political church sermons in the beer hall. Through such satirising sermons, Tsodzo presents the church which purports to champion human rights as having failed to provide guidance to Rudo in the first place as the solution to her problems.

Despite the stated shortcomings of Tsodzo's social vision, he should be applauded like Chakaipa for effectively obscuring the theft of the Black people's land through colonial establishments of a mission station, an urban centre and a farm in his religious satire. If he had gallantly presented the novel as one of the theft of the indigenous people's land by White colonialists his novel would not have passed through the strict censorship of the Rhodesia Literature Bureau. The novel, though not giving the indigenous people the agency to chart their own destiny, amply presents the mission stations, urban areas and farms that have restructured the Rhodesian landscape into native reserves and in the process re-defined the indigenous people's new relationship with the land (Magosvongwe 2013). Thus the African has consequently become a foreigner in his/her land of birth. S/he no longer enjoys the benefits of his/her ancestral land which is now being enjoyed by the colonial settler criminals in the guise of missionaries and urban dwellers.

Conclusion

The chapter has amply demonstrated how Chakaipa and Tsodzo portray the gendered dispossession of land in colonial Rhodesia. *Dzasukwa-Mwana-Asina-Hembe* and *Pafunge* were published during the colonial period and could not confidently discuss land dispossession in colonial Rhodesia. Taking such a stance would have resulted in the novels being regarded as subversive literature and would have never been published. Discussing land issues was considered political by the then colonial government. Thus the authors had to use their literary prowess to conceal land issues in excessive beer drinking and religious satire to capture land theft from Black men and women, and to present the different gender roles in relationship to land in a colonial set up. Through the use of metaphors, symbols and literary images the selected authors were able to expose the colonial pieces of legislation which resulted in the dispossession of land from Black people.

References

Althusser, L. (2001). *Lenin and Philosophy and Other Essays*. New York: New York University Press.

Asante, M. K. (1980). *Afrocentricity: The Theory of Social Change*. New York: FAS Printing.

Biri, K. (2015). "Zimbabwe Hauparari" (Zimbabwe Shall Not Perish): Pentecostal Discourses on Land, Nation-Building and Transformation in Zimbabwe. In Makwavarara, Z., Magosvongwe, R. & Mlambo, O.B. (eds.) *Dialoguing Land and Indigenisation in Zimbabwe and Other Developing Countries: emerging Perspectives*. Harare: University of Zimbabwe Publications, pp. 155-167.

Chakaipa, P. (1967). *Dzasukwa-Mwana-Asina-Hembe*. Salisbury: Longman.

Chambati, W. & Magaramombe, G. (2008). An Abandoned Question: Farm Workers. In S. Moyo, K. Helliker & T. Murisa (eds.) *Contested Terrain: Civil Society and Land Reform in Contemporary Zimbabwe*. Pietmaritzburg, Johannesburg: SS Publishing, Nutrend, pp. 207-238.

Chidora, T. & Mandizvidza, S. (2015). From Labourer to Farm-Owner: An Evaluation of the Legitimacy of the Black Farm Labourer as an Owner of Land in Chenjerai Hove's Bones. In Makwavarara, Z., Magosvongwe, R. & Mlambo, O.B. (eds.) *Dialoguing Land and Indigenisation in Zimbabwe and Other Developing Countries: Emerging Perspectives*. Harare: University of Zimbabwe Publications, pp. 340-355.

Chikowero, J. (n.d) "I Too Sing Zimbabwe": The Conflict of Ethnicity in Popular Zimbabwean Music. Journal of African Poetry. https://www.africaresearch.org/Papers/Np02Cwr.pdf. Accessed on 15 November 2018.

Chitando, E. (2005). The Sacred Remnant? Church Land in Zimbabwe's Fast Track Resettlement Programme. *Studies in World Christianity*, 2(11): 182-199.

Chitiyo, T. K. (2000). Land Violence and Compensation: Reconceptualising Zimbabwe's Land and War Veteran's Debate. *Journal of African Conflict and Development*, pp. 1-20.

Chiwome, E. M. (1996). *A Social History of the Shona Novel*. Eiffel Flats: Juta Zimbabwe Pvt Ltd.

Chiwome, E. M. (2002). *A Social History of the Shona Novel* (2nd ed). Eiffel Flats: Juta Zimbabwe Pvt Ltd.

Gray, C.C. (2001). *Afrocentric Thought and Praxis: An Intellectual History*. Asmara: Africa World Press.

Gudhlanga, E. S. (2016). Gender and Land Ownership in Zimbabwean Literature: A Critical Appraisal in Selected Shona Fiction. Unpublished D Phil Thesis, University of South Africa, Department of African Languages.

Hove, C. (1988). *Bones*. Harare: Baobab Books.

Hudson-Weems, C. (1993). *Africana Womanism: Reclaiming Ourselves*. Asmara: Africa World Press.

Hudson-Weems, C. (2007). Nommo/Self-Naming, Self-Defining, and the History of Africana Womanism. In C. Hudson-Weems (ed) *Contemporary Africana Theory, Thought and Action: A Guide to Africana Studies*. Asmara: Africa World Press, pp. 289-308.

Mafa, O., Gudhlanga, E. S., Manyeruke, N., Matavire, E. H. M. & Mpofu, J. (2015). *Gender, Politics and Land Use in Zimbabwe, 1980-2012*. Dakar: CODESRIA.

Magaisa, A. T. (2012). The Land Question in Zimbabwe: The Judiciary as an Instrument of Recovery? In Chigara, B. (ed.) *Southern African Development Community Land Issues: Towards a New Sustainable Land Relations Policy*. London & New York: Routledge, pp.195-221.

Magosvongwe, R. (2013). Land and Identity in Zimbabwean Fiction Writings in English from 2000-2010: A Critical Analysis. Unpublished D. Phil Thesis, University of Cape Town: Department of African Languages and Literature.

Magirosa, M. (2015). Matenganyika: The loss of Land in Colonial. *The Patriot*. 17 December.

Marowa, I. (2015). Forced Removal and Social Memories in North Western Zimbabwe, c1900-2000. D Phil Thesis in African History, University of Bayreuth and BIGSAS.

Moyo, S. (1995a). A Gendered Perspective of the Land Question. *Southern African Feminist Review*, 1(1): 13-31.

Moyo, S. (1995b). *The Land Question in Zimbabwe*. Harare: Southern African Political Economic Series.

Mtetwa, A. K. (2015). "Fishers of Land!" Missionary Church and Land in Zimbabwe: An Afrocentric Biblical Philosophy of Justice in Zimbabwe. In Makwavarara, Z., Magosvongwe, R. & Mlambo, O.B. (eds.) *Dialoguing Land and Indigenisation in Zimbabwe and Other Developing Countries: Emerging Perspectives*. Harare: University of Zimbabwe Publications, pp. 140-154.

Muchemwa, F. N. (2015). *The Struggle for Land in Zimbabwe, 1890-2010*. Harare: Heritage Publishing House.

Mugambi, J. N. R. (1995). *From Liberation to Reconstruction: African Christian Theology after the Cold War*. Nairobi: East African Educational Publishers.

Mugari, Z. E. (2015). Colonial Designs, Landscapes and the Mediation of Forced Removals in Post-Independence

Zimbabwe. In Makwavarara, Z., Magosvongwe, R. & Mlambo, O. B. (eds.) *Dialoguing Land and Indigenisation in Zimbabwe and Other Developing Countries: Emerging Perspectives.* Harare: University of Zimbabwe Publications, pp. 64-90.

Mvududu, S. (2000). Levelling the Playing Field: Social Policy and Development Issues. *Southern African Feminist Review*, 4(2): 43-60.

Nhemachena, A. (2017) *Relationality and Resilience in a Not So Relational World? Knowledge, Chivanhu and (De-)coloniality in 21st Century Conflict-Torn Zimbabwe.* Bamenda: Langaa RPCIG.

Paradza-Makura, G. (2011). *Innovations for Securing Women's Access to Land in East Africa Working* Paper. Rome: International Land Coalition.

Phimister, I. (1988). *An Economic and Social History of Zimbabwe, 1890-1948: Capital Accumulation and Class Struggle.* New York: Longman.

Rukuni. M. (2006). The Evolution of Agricultural Policy: 1890-1990. In M. Rukuni, Tawonezvi, P., Eicher, C., Munyuki-Hungwe, M. &Matondi, P. (eds). *Zimbabwe's Agricultural Revolution Revisited.* Harare: University of Zimbabwe Publications, pp. 29-61.

Schmidt, E. (1990). Negotiated Spaces and Contested Terrain: Men, Women and the Law in Colonial Zimbabwe, 1890-1939. *Journal of Southern African Studies*, 16(4): 622-648.

Schmidt, E. (1992). *Peasants Traders and Wives: Shona Women in the History of Zimbabwe, 1870-1939.* Portsmouth: Heinemann.

Shoko, T. (2007). *Karanga Indigenous Religion in Zimbabwe: Health and Well Being.* Hampshire & Burlington: Ashgate.

Shutt, A. K. (1997). Purchase Area Farmers and the Middle Class Farmers of Southern Rhodesia, 1931-1952. *The International Journal of African Historical Studies*, 30 (3): 555-579.

Staunton, I. (1990). *Mothers of the Revolution: The War Experience of Thirty Zimbabwean Women.* London: James Currey.

Tavuyanago, B. (2017). "Our Fathers and Grandfathers were born here." Shangaan Eviction Experiences from the Gonarezhou National Park, 1957-1968. *Historia*, 62 (2): 46-67.

Tshuma, L. A. (1997). *Matter of Injustice: Law. State and Agrarian Injustice in Zimbabwe.* Harare Southern African Political Economic Series.

Tsodzo, T. K. (1972). *Pafunge.* Salisbury: Longman.

Vengeyi, O. (2015). A Look at Zimbabwe's Land Reform Programme from the Perspective of Prophet Amos of the 8th Century BCE Israel. In Makwavarara, Z., Magosvongwe, R. & Mlambo, O.B. (Ed.) *Dialoguing Land and Indigenisation in Zimbabwe and Other Developing Countries: Emerging Perspectives.* Harare: University of Zimbabwe Publications, pp. 116-139.

Vudzijena, V. (1998). Land Reform and Community Based Natural Resource Management in Zimbabwe. In E. Mutepfa et al, Eds. *Enhancing Land Reforms in Southern Africa: Reviews on Land Reform Strategies and Community Based Natural Resources Management.* Harare: Zimbabwe Regional Environment Organisation, pp. 76-103.

Zhuwarara, R. (1994). Men and Women in a Colonial Context: A Discourse on Gender and Liberation in Chenjerai Hove's 1989 NOMA Award-Winning Novel- Bones. *Zambezia*, XX(1): 1-22.

Zhuwarara, R. (2015). *An Introduction to Zimbabwean Literature in English.* Harare: College Press

Zvobgo, C. J. M. (1996). A *History of Christian Missions in Zimbabwe, 1890-1939.* Gweru: Mambo Press.

Chapter Eleven

Fictionalising Resistance to Land Repossession: Political Economies of Displacement and the Imagination of a Better Zimbabwe

Nelson Mlambo & Jairos Kangira

Introduction

This chapter is about the literary representation of resistance to land repossession in Zimbabwe. It also focuses on the political economy of displacement and ways in which to build a better Zimbabwe. As a form of rhetoric of hope and a way of imagining a peaceful future, the chapter assumes an ideologically progressive strand that questions the status quo and yet invites the reader through exposure to short stories, to consider alternatives to the existing order as a means of coping. The chapter explores how short, imaginative narratives mirror the desirability of peace, the innovative ways to prevent violence –whether structural or direct physical violence - and the democratisation processes people often hope for in everyday life. The axiom which states that the pen is mightier than the sword finds home in the form of literary analyses like the one attempted in this chapter. This remark is particularly insightful in the wake of the Arab spring uprisings that rocked North Africa, the Kenyan postelection violence and the incessant wars in the Democratic Republic of Congo and Sudan, to mention but a few. More so, land in Zimbabwe has historically been a site of violence, blood, tears and emotional-psychological trauma. The present analysis can be understood to be falling into the realm of progressive literature, which is a way of interrogating life and its attendant contradictions in a hopeful manner. This form of literary analysis is ultimately valorising peaceful and peace-oriented coping mechanisms, though at the same time without silencing activism, as the following short stories demonstrate.

In the words of a renowned critic of Zimbabwean and African literature, Ngara (n.d.), creativity and responsibility are Siamese twins in art. Taking the thread of argument from Ngara, therefore, the submission being made here is also that in the literature explored in this chapter, what we see is a commitment by the writers to boldly and critically examine the political - economic ground in Zimbabwe, with the land issue serving as the backdrop, and to do so with plausibility, passion and responsibility. The underlying principle is couched on how the oppressed, downtrodden and vilified people devise mechanisms to survive, which can be summed up by the popular expression of the day *tofira mutrial*. This is a popular colloquialism which, when literally translated, means "we will die trying". This has become the *defacto modus operandi* for a people whose central means of production, the land, has been violently taken away from them, together with the attendant resources that emanate from the land. In other words, the greatest democracy that has been stolen from African people is the freedom or liberty to own materialities that are theirs – democracy need not only be electoral and political but it has to be also material (Nhemachena 2015; Nhemachena, Kangira & Mlambo 2018). In this chapter, the central concern is on illustrating the significance of fiction in imaginatively capturing the haunting and ever-present land issue in Zimbabwe, which is characterised by dispossession and repossessions of various forms, and how the people cope with and survive the political onslaught they face.

The chapter looks at three short stories, namely, "The ugly reflection in the mirror" by A. Kanengoni (2003), "Notes from Mai Mujuru's breast" by T.R. Mwanaka (2012) and "The chances and challenges of Chiadzwa" by E. Chinhanhu (2007). First the chapter forecasts a future-bound society with amiable interracial relations and also how the process can be represented in words as a precursor to real transitions. The chapter further takes a critical look at the potentialities the country portends in solving the land issue and how this is imaginatively represented. The aim is to explore how the artists imagine a better Zimbabwe and how the stories attempt to shape the consciousness of the reader towards peaceful reconciliation as the surest means to survive the injustices meted in the realms of everyday life. There is also an attempt to point out the critical questions on natural resources distribution as one sure way of ending the various crises in Zimbabwe in particular, and Africa, in general.

However, to fully explore and appreciate what these short stories are communicating in the context of land dispossession and repossession, resource politics, and the political survival and coping mechanisms in everyday life, there is a need to make a cursory glance at the theory of the chronotope by Bakhtin as a guiding theoretical framework to discuss the selected short stories. The chronotope, which emphasises the interpretation of texts as determined, shaped and informed by the time and space interplay in the story, is of great relevance here. In its original form, Bakhtin's concept of the chronotope refers to the intrinsic connectedness of temporal and spatial relationships that are artistically expressed in literature (Bakhtin 1981). The chronotope functions as the centre for concretising representation whereby the short stories' abstract elements find meaning, permitting the imaging/representational power of fiction to do its work. Explaining the concept of the chronotope and the generation of meaning in novels, thus of necessity, has to hinge on the idea that spatial and temporal dimensions are inseparable, where "... time, as it were, thickens, takes on flesh, becomes artistically visible; likewise, space becomes charged and responsive to movements of time, plot and history" (Bakhtin 1981: 85).

The most succinct explanation that Bakhtin gives needs to be presented in its original form here because it is the bedrock upon which the application of this theory in this chapter is constructed. For Bakhtin (1981: 250):

> Thus the chronotope, functioning as the primary means for materialising time in space, emerges as a centre for concretising representation, as a force giving body to the entire novel. All the novel's abstract elements - philosophical and social generalisations, ideas, analysis of cause and effect – gravitate toward the chronotope and through it take on flesh and blood, permitting the imaging power of art

to do its work. Such is the representational significance of the chronotope.

To take the thread of argument from the above, what is of critical significance is the introduction of history into the understanding of how life is presented and interpreted within different narrative frames; it is thus important to possibly think of parallels between the literary chronotopes and their real life equivalents. The chronotope becomes a very important concept to inform literary criticism in that it moves narrative away from the heights and depths of abstraction into more concrete levels, at times intimating towards verisimilitude. Thus there are, in this theory, provisions for interrogating and investigating the space where something happens and examining what comes in and what goes out, and to thinking of how new identities are ultimately formed. This line of thought is explored and amplified so that the *temporal* (post-independence Zimbabwe crisis of 1999 to 2009), the *spatial* (the geographical and emotive land issue in Zimbabwe as the setting of the short stories), and the fictional formation can be made manifest – thus it can be argued that fiction is a product of its time and place, capturing as it does the pressures and pleasures, fears and hopes of a particular people with a guarded propensity to create and recreate imaginative possibilities.

Literary Evocations of the Land Problematique in Three Short Stories

In Alexander Kanengoni's short story entitled "The ugly reflection in the mirror" (2003), we are faced with anecdotal and suggestive writing that expresses the aspirations of the people, with a particular emphasis on the critical resources of the country. The story "The ugly reflection in the mirror" is not so much about a narrative with a lot of action and a chain of events, but about a few minutes of encounter between two characters, yet positioning the centrality of land as a defining factor for the prejudices, stereotypes and barbarism that colour human relations. One is the narrator, a Black war veteran who has newly acquired a farm, and the other a White commercial

256

farmer. The brief encounter which they have is highly suggestive of how the author firstly positions the complex and archetypical motif of land in Zimbabwe that is characterised by the myriad forms of criminality and empire that include violence, disruption, uprooting and disposition. Secondly, the encounter helps the reader to imagine the means of moving beyond the horrendous nuances that are evoked in the history of plunder along racial lines through the way possibilities for co-existence, survival and coping strategies are hatched, inasmuch as the story confronts this sensitive and contentious issue of resources and interracial relations.

The first point that needs to be raised from this story is how the author presents multiracial harmony as a critical ingredient in the making of a better Zimbabwe. However, this critical issue has to be understood as a phenomenon that is foregrounded in land politics and economics. Thus the backdrop of colonial violence and land dispossession, which by nature evokes sadness and disgust are central to the encounter and the fictional-historical viewpoint presented here is that of confronting the irreversible nature of land repossessions that have taken place in Zimbabwe (Vambe 2005). Through understatement, the literary technique that is typical of the short story genre, Kanengoni presents the land as the essence of life and prosperity and a means through which both White and Black build a sacred heritage for present and future generations. The perspective presented by Kanengoni therefore is that of land re-possession and redistribution as something both inevitable and irreversible – a fait accompli (Gonye, Moyo & Wasosa 2012) which has to be accepted, negotiated and legitimised.

The first illustration on interracial harmony as a coping tactic comes through the title itself - "the ugly reflection in the mirror". This is a metaphorical title which speaks volumes about how interconnected the human race is, and that for the country to move forward, there is a need for true reconciliation. This is particularly significant in the wake of the unrest which followed the land repossessions which took place in the country of Zimbabwe and how violent the process became. This violence was mainly along racial lines and this regrettable violence is the metaphorical reflection in the mirror as there was White violence in the dispossession of Black people and then later there was Black violence as the Black people sought to re-possess the land. Therefore, in this story, by presenting two men, one White commercial farmer and the other a Black war veteran, the author is explicitly drawing the reader to the idea that racial harmony is desirable for there to be progress - this is a survival and coping mechanism which needs to be put into practice in order to solve the land issue. The "war veteran" is the narrator of the story and as the story draws to a close, after an enchanting dialogue with Mr Flemming, the White commercial farmer realises to his utter amazement how they are both human beings who can relate in a civil manner. "And then I also noticed the stoop in his old frame and I thought, My God, how like my late father he looks" (Kanengoni 2003, p. 108). This is the ugly reflection in the mirror, the encounter with the truth of the cords that bind humanity together despite the racial differences; when one looks in the mirror the reflection that comes out is that of the neighbour who can be any colour. This reflection urges the Zimbabwean citizenry and the reader at large to embrace this reflection so that together they can swim across the tide with a united and stronger front. This is corroborated by the way the narrator uses positive and legitimising language. Where the outside world talks of "farm invasions" and land invasions", the narrator talks oh he was "resettled" (Kanengoni 2003: 105)", which is a way of justifying, humanising and sanitising the processes that took place as a way of repossessing land in Zimbabwe. In other words, Kanengoni through this story seems to suggest that the end justifies the means and thereby celebrates the process of land repossession in Zimbabwe, as seen by how he also creates a white liberal and mutually opposed character, Mr Flemming who despite the apparent prejudices seems to be progressive and forward-looking.

Furthermore, by examining the chronotope nature of the short story, that is, set in a crisis-hit Zimbabwe, the story also calls for the people to confront the critical resource of contention which has partly been blamed for having been one of the causes of the Zimbabwean crisis - the land issue. Kanengoni, through this story, is suggesting that for the country to move forward and for the people to cope with the land issue's attendant challenges, there is a need to face reality so that solutions can be found. Avoiding the issue does not seem to help at all and Mr Flemming has thought deeply about it and critiques how, "My friends don't talk to me anymore," he said, and laughed carelessly "... because I tell them that no matter who comes to power, if he doesn't resolve the land issue, the people will chase him out of office" (Kanengoni 2003: 106). For the sake of progressing towards a better Zimbabwe, the author through Mr Flemming, ingratiatingly urges that some historical issues which are always resurfacing need to be bravely faced and embraced so that lasting solutions can be found. This is the invaluable didacticism of the story and through the institutionally weak and crisis-hit Zimbabwean story, a lot can be learnt. The historical contentions of land therefore need to be ironed out and this cannot necessarily be done through the political way or the SADC tribunal which has already had challenges in this regard. Mr Flemming is quite analytical and perceptive when he reiterates, "How am I expected to avoid this confrontation when Tony Blair disowns his past?" (Kanengoni 2003: 107). In other words, for one to make informed decisions with regards to the land issue at hand, some historical connections have to be made so that, informed by the past, one can safely manoeuvre through the various landmines which have been exposed by the economic and political crises like those of Zimbabwe. However, it can also be argued that the land is thus not only for farming but a store of value, dignity, identity, provision and investment.

Moreover, to survive the resource politics and economics which compounded the crisis and thereby preserve his land, Mr Flemming decides to strategically make linkages with the community around him, which is a literary universal along the lines of the trickster mode in traditional African folklore and pragmatic morality on modern lingo. "But that day, as we stood in the middle of my twenty-acre field of beans that he had helped me to plant, the man looked away into the distance and said there was nothing in the country as close to the hearts of the people as the land" (Kanengoni 2003: 105). Significant is the fact that Mr Flemming realises that "... this is the war we will never win" (Kanengoni 2003: 107) and in order to survive and protect his interests, that is the land he has, he begins to extend a hand to his neighbour who has been resettled next to his farm. That way he manages to keep his farm from repossession and also forges some new acquaintances, especially considering that his own friends no longer want to talk with him. Moreover, he also ploughs back into the community around him as he speaks of "... how he helped communal farmers from Musana and Masembura to grow paprika; how as a result, he had been issued with an EPZ certificate to enable him to export paprika to Spain..." (Kanengoni 2003: 106). The EPZ (Export processing zone) certificate is a form of certification which authorises someone to export the produce from his/her farm whilst those without the export processing zone certificate are not allowed to export but have to sell the produce locally. Whereas many other farmers are being chased out of their farms, Mr Flemming survives the "land invasion". The point here is to underline the fact that in a dystopian state of affairs these are realities which cannot be ignored (Baccolini 2004). However, what is salutary in the story is a presentation of the survivor personality through the likes of Mr Flemming. He knows that it is when we have land that we can make our dreams tenable and instead of selfishly and blindly holding on to the land that he knows belong to the indigenous people, he decides to share the God-given resource with them. Furthermore, it has to be emphasised that, the EPZ certificate which he gets is a certification for his farm to be regarded as an export processing zone - an authorisation that sees him sell his products outside the country thereby making him get the much needed foreign currency. The foreign currency he gets is the life blood of the companies in crisis-hit Zimbabwe and Mr Flemming pulls off this deal through realising that to survive during such political unrests one has to engage the communities so that everyone becomes a winner. Thus instead of simply thinking of land repossession which might imply an equally disruptive and violent phenomenon just like colonial land dispossession, perhaps there is a need for an ideological shift towards resource sharing.

Furthermore, another outstanding coping mechanism to survive the complex matrix of land in Zimbabwe is presented through the characters' acceptance of change. This change comes through self-evaluation, a critical reflection on the transitions happening in the society around and a rethinking of preconceived ideas and prejudices. These prejudices cut across racial lines and Mr Flemming manages to surmount these – he embraces a Black war veteran, gives him advice and shares ideas about farming, politics and ways to survive. Similarly the narrator also re-evaluates his preconceived ideas and stereotypical views of the White race. The narrator talks of how:

> ... right from the outset, the farmers always assumed a domineering attitude. You saw it in the elevated look in their eyes; you saw it in the arrogant way they wanted to control the discussion, reducing you to a mere listener. The most exasperating thing was their indifference as they put you through the humiliation, as if this was the only way there was to deal with blacks. That was how I had known it to be with the white commercial farmers. Perhaps it was my imagination. Perhaps I was seeing things that were not there (Kanengoni, 2003: 105).

The above quotation marks a transition in perception by the narrator. The desirability of peace and harmony in solving highly emotional matters like the land issue is demonstrated to be the best way for fostering togetherness. The repetition of the word "perhaps" is a mark of change in attitude and this change in attitude is in both the narrator and Mr Flemming. The land issue calls for concerted efforts from all racial and "ethnic" groups as both races are linked to the land and they owe their existence to this sacred resource. Therefore for one to imagine a better tomorrow there is a need to discard centuries old prejudices, shed of pretentious airs initiate dialogue and join hands to solve the inevitable. Mr Flemming and the narrator begin to build a more positive relationship and they both seem to be utilising the land for the betterment of the country. The story also uses repetition of how the two characters looked into the far distance, as if to imply that lasting survival and coping mechanisms are couched in building lasting interracial relationships that have roots in the land. To reinforce this idea, the author ends the story with some symbolism which marks the furthering of a brighter future for the two characters. "And then heavy drops of rain began to hit the ground and I continued walking across the field. We had never come this far before" (Kanengoni 2003: 108). The confrontation marks the breaking of new ground in their quest for survival and the rains which are beginning to fall symbolise the cultivation and flourishing of their relationship and the country's new beginnings as well. Brutal dispossessions, violent repossessions and forceful evictions have thus been the marks of both the empire and the post-colony and the author dares to usher the reader into a possible future of harmony; pretentiousness and hypocrisy are presented as surmountable vices and "ugly reflections in the mirror" on the road to equitable sharing of man's special gift from mother earth.

Finally, looking at the last two stories analysed in this chapter, the reader further meets with an admonishing voice that seeks to give direction to what needs to be addressed in order for a country to solve socio-economic challenges. Whilst Kanengoni's preoccupation was on agricultural land, the two short stories under discussion here demonstrate that the land means more – it is actually the basic means of existence and well-being. It is in the land that mineral wealth is mined and the mineral wealth of the country has to be well taken care of and made to benefit the citizens. The short stories "Notes from Mai Mujuru's breast" (2012) by T.R. Mwanaka and "The chances and challenges of Chiadzwa" (2007) by E. Chinhanhu grapple with violence, dispossession and imaginative repossession of the mineral resources which the people get from the land. They are stories about how the ordinary people do all they can to also get the newly found diamonds in the Chiadzwa area of Zimbabwe. Looking at the titles themselves, one can see a lot of significance. In the later, what stands out clearly is the fact that indeed there are challenges which are associated with the hunt for the diamonds in the area of Chiadzwa but amidst all the challenges there are chances – the land provides the diamonds and the ordinary people's claim of the diamonds demonstrates that there is a need for justice on land matters. In the former story, it needs to be pointed out that Mai Mujuru was the Vice President of the country during the time the story was written and by talking of her breast, the author metaphorically brings to the fore the idea of life, sacredness, and a strong willed desire and also intimates to issues pertaining to the heart. The breast gives milk, which is life to a child and through this connection the author demonstrates how the land and by extension the diamond as a natural resource is akin to a breast. When talking about "notes" the idea can be that these are ideas, some advice or piece of information and to interpret it that way also means that the author seems to highlight core issues which need to be addressed in order for the people to be satisfied that indeed they are partakers of the country's independence and also mineral wealth. Paradoxically it may also mean some bank notes, which still emphasises the key concern with material wealth as a means for survival and that the ordinary people are pining to lay their hands on these notes.

A tone of dystopian hope pervades the whole story by Mwanaka ("Notes from Mai Mujuru's breast") as we see how even in the post-independence Nation State dispossession is violent and brutal. State agents use brutal force as the nation turns against its citizens and the forceful evictions from their ancestral lands is far from securing the wealth of the country but a self-serving ploy by the powerful who want to have the fruits of the land all the themselves. "It was at the height of the political problems in the country. People were still scuttling all over the country trying to eke an existence", the story begins (Mwanaka 2012: 195). The story is about Daniel and Chris who resolve to hunt for diamonds in the Chiadzwa/Marange area. The area is heavily guarded but the need to survive makes them throw all caution to the wind. The repetition of the word "survive" in the story is telling. Even when death is threatening him, "Some would have given up, but Chris had to survive to tell the story, for Daniel and the other people who had died at the hands of the police here in Marange" (Mwanaka 2012: 193). From this quotation, what becomes clear is that there is use of brute force and violence by the state machinery, and the most egregious feature of this violence being the brutal killing of unarmed citizens who should have been the rightful owners of the land and the minerals that are found in it. What is clear is also how Chris really wanted to "tell the story" of such horrendous

263

acts by a "democratic" government and these words therefore demonstrate the irrepressibility of speech in a country under dictatorship.

Moreover, the story also demonstrates the interconnectedness of the land and violence in Zimbabwe; violence over land between the Ndebeles and Shonas in precolonial Zimbabwe; then the heightened imperial violence by the settlers as they dispossessed the indigenous people of their land without any conscience; the violence of the liberation struggle as the indigenous people wanted to get back their land and finally the violence by a state against its citizens for daring to want to have a share of what their motherland produces – the diamonds. Yet the ordinary citizens' resolve for justice is unshakeable as illustrated by Chris in this story. Furthermore, to illustrate the resilience of the young man, the writer speaks of how "He had survived before in this place" (Mwanaka 2012: 193). The reason why Chris becomes such a daredevil, risking his life, is because of the need to survive. The natural resources of the country afford him a way out, especially if he were to manage to pan for diamonds at the lot nicknamed "Mai Mujuru's breast" because as he reminiscences, "A breast to a little kid or even to an old man represents life, living, loving" (Mwanaka 2012: 197). So Chris and his friend Daniel strong-headedly find their way to the volatile diamond mine with the conviction that, "If you were to lick a bit of that breast, you would go home smiling yourself out of the Mufakose township into the lush, leafy suburbs of Harare" (Mwanaka 2012: 198). Whilst the story ends on a rather sad note, with the tragedy of Daniel's death, the point has been made. The natural resources are a key to the survival of the country and the ordinary citizens also deserve them to cope with the crisis. By using a metaphorical title and linking it to the then vice president of the country, Amai Mujuru, the story is a direct indictment of the politicians; it is a protest form of writing that is highly suggestive. The story gives direction and searches for survival paths in a crisis hit country like Zimbabwe. In the final analysis, the story demonstrates further the value of dystopian hope and protest literature in that it powerfully and intimately exposes the shortcomings of society so that corrective measures can be thought of and thereby bring about a brighter future.

In addition, Chinhanhu's short story "The chances and challenges of Chiadzwa" (2007) further demonstrates the resilience of the ordinary people in their bid to survive a socio-economic crisis through the utilisation of the natural resources available to them. When the diamonds are discovered all over the area, the people think that their prayers have been heard and they will avert the crisis. Indeed the land of their fathers and fore-fathers had opened doors for them into the proverbial Canaan. However, the government swoops in, sealing the whole area, mounting roadblocks and thorough searches of everyone who leaves or enters the area of Chiadzwa in Marange district. However, this only curtails but does not extinguish the people's desire to harvest the fruits of the land and survive. The people, using the trickster method manage to outwit the hegemonic authorities. The elders of the village meet at night to plan:

> So everything is in your hands, to be brave and save your fellowmen, or be cowardly and watch them die one by one as before. A lot of my contemporaries died without witnessing these diamonds, and I consider myself privileged to have at least seen them. It is God-given wealth. God has heard our cries over the years, and gave these stones to us. But now look ... (Chinhanhu 2007: 20).

This is the honest truth they are confronted with and instead of sitting down and watching, the people decide on a plan to trick the authorities and smuggle the diamonds. This plan is hatched in connivance with the traditional authorities and it is a plan to feign the death of one of the villagers who has to be buried outside the district of Marange. When the "corpse" is being transported to the burial place, they hide lots of diamonds and later meet up with an arranged buyer. The buyer gives the village men accompanying the corpse an amount of US$500,000 and also Z$44,000,000. As the story comes to an end, we see how "The villagers took their money, to be shared equally among themselves later, before each thought of where to spend the next few nights. But first they had to bury the empty coffin, which they did with a pomp and glee rarely seen at a 'funeral'" (Chinhanhu 2007: 22). This is another representation of the fortitude ordinary people have, their inextinguishable desire for survival and the resilience of hope. Instead of being bystanders succumbing to the wills of a hegemonic regime, the ordinary people demand a piece of the national cake and they do this through careful planning, the use of their wits and cooperation. They "spook" the authorities to hell, to use Fugard's terms, and manage to lay their hand on the natural resources which according to them are a God given gift and rightfully belong to them instead of a few members of the regime. God is a God of hierarchy and order but representatives that act on behalf of the citizens would need to fairly distribute whatever they get from the country's resources. Therefore what is apparent is that the land in Zimbabwe is a complex matrix of repeated dispossessions and repossessions and all these cycles are marred by brutality, violence and bloodshed. Yet the people's resolve to lay a claim on the land is inextinguishable.

Conclusion

In conclusion, therefore, the aim of this chapter has been to demonstrate the literary representation of land resistance, political survival and natural resource utilisation, how the ordinary people resist repression, and also about the resilience of hope. The chapter's main concern has been to show how the writers imagine possible coping strategies which are peaceful, non-violent and futuristic. The short stories analysed have represented the Zimbabwean crisis under discussion as a form of dystopia; with authoritarianism, the dehumanisation of the ordinary people and the oppression of the weak. However, the ultimate idea that carries the day is that this is a form of dystopian hope; beyond the gloom, the outrageous and the horrific is a world full of possibilities and it is this potential that needs to be celebrated. The short stories analysed here are hopeful and suggestive; the act of writing is a form of protesting and sounding the alarm, which is an act of didacticism, directing the reader towards the realisation that survival is ubiquitous and a possibility, thereby spurring the reader onwards.

In the chapter, the short story "The ugly reflection in the mirror" by Alexander Kanengoni suggestively presents some of the issues that need to be confronted in order for the country to solve the land crisis. The story calls for multiracial harmony and a peaceful resolution of the contentious land issue as well as community engagement and upliftment. This is ably done through the presentation of Mr Flemming and his encounter with the narrator who is a war veteran and as the story comes to a close, the two characters are headed towards a better Zimbabwe and they have sailed past the crisis. Whilst in the stories "The chances and challenges of Chiadzwa" as well as "Notes from Mai Mujuru's breast", the writers grapple with resource politics. The cyclical nature of violence around land was clarified and the goal has been to show that for the nation to sail past the land crisis, this issue has to be addressed and if handled well enough the socio-economic crisis may be contained. In the former short story, the people's ingenuity and resilience is celebrated as the author presents how they outmanoeuvre the authorities and manage to survive off the proceeds of the God-given diamonds.

Although sharing the land and other resources would help resolve the challenges of violence, there would continue to be problems if it is only African resources, including land, that are shared in the world – resources, including land, in other places of the world are also God-given and would need to be also shared with Africans in the interest of fairness.

References

Baccolini, R. (2004) "The persistence of hope in dystopian science fiction", *Modern Language Association,* Vol. 119, No.3, 518-521.

Bakhtin, M. M. (1981) *The Dialogic Imagination: Four Essays by M.M. Bakhtin.* Austin: University of Texas.

Chinhanhu, E. (2007) "The chances and challenges of Chiadzwa", In Staunton, I. (ed.). *Laughing now: New stories from Zimbabwe* (pp 16-22). Harare: Weaver Press.

Gonye, J., Moyo, T. and Wasosa, W. (2012) "Representations of the land programme in selected Zimbabwean short stories and Mutasa's *Sekai minda tava nayo* (Sekai, We now have the land): A fait accompli", *Journal of African Studies and Development,* Vol. 4, No.9, 207-217.

Kanengoni, A. (2003) "The ugly reflection in the mirror", In Staunton, I. (ed.), *Writing still: New Stories from Zimbabwe* (pp 105 - 109). Harare: Weaver Press.

Mlambo, N. (2014) *Trauma, Resilience and Survival Strategies in Crisis Times: An Afrocentric Literary Approach.* Saarbucken: Scholars' Press.

Mwanaka, T. R. (2012) "Notes from Mai Mujuru's breast", In *The Caine Prize for African Writing: African Violet and Other Stories* (pp 193 -201). Johannesburg: Jacana Media.

Ngara, E. (n.d.). *Artists must be Responsible Beings.* Retrieved from www.mazwi.net/essays/artists-must-be-responsible-beings.

Nhemachena, A. (2015) Envisioning African democracy in the twenty-first century: *Mwana washe muranda kumwe* and the coloniality of contrived "democracy", in Mawere, M. *et al.* (eds) *Democracy, Good Governance and Development in Africa.* Bamenda: Langaa RPCIG.

Nhemachena, A., Mlambo, N. & Kangira, J. (2018) Materialities and the resilient global frontierisation of Africa: An introduction, in Nhemachena, A., Kangira, J. & Mlambo, N. (eds) *Decolonisation of Materialities or Materialisation of (Re-)Colonisation? Symbolisms, Languages, Ecocriticism and (Non)Representationalism in 21st Century Africa.* Bamenda: Langaa RPCIG.

Vambe, M.T. (2005). "Fictional depictions of land resistance in Southern Africa", *African Identities,* Vol. 3, No.1, 17 -36

www.ingramcontent.com/pod-product-compliance
Lightning Source LLC
Chambersburg PA
CBHW050634280326
41932CB00015B/2635